EDUCATIONAL THERAPY IN ACTION

This book provides an in-depth look at what a little-known clinician, the educational therapist, does and how they do it. It goes behind the clinician's door to illustrate the unusual and broad range of interventions—both academic/vocational and social/emotional—that an educational therapist employs. This particular case study involves a young woman called Nora who had a severe but undiagnosed auditory processing disorder. She could not give meaning to the spoken language that came at her too rapidly, leaving her in a constant *fog of words* that she could not comprehend.

    This case discloses the problems, their causes, and the emotional toll that had to be considered when developing an effective educational/therapeutic plan for Nora. It vividly illustrates the dynamic exchanges and mutual learning that goes on between client and therapist. Parts One and Two illustrate how the psycho-educational interventions that addressed Nora's academic and non-academic needs were gradually formulated over the first year. Part Three provides a series of vignettes from subsequent years that illustrate the ongoing applications of the therapist's work.

Distinguishing Features

Explanatory Commentaries—The rationale behind particular techniques and interventions is clarified through a system of explanatory commentaries that inform the reader without distracting from the story. This approach makes the book both an instructional tool and a compelling story.

Organic Curriculum—The rationale for and application of an "Organic (personalized) Curriculum" is explained and applied throughout the book as a model for others to use in working with this population.

A Longitudinal Perspective—The initial work with Nora began many years ago, so this book provides a long view of her life and tracks the influences that educational therapy exerted on her development into a fully functioning adult.

Cognitive/Emotional Integration—The core of educational therapy—the interdependence of cognitive skills and emotional response—is clearly documented throughout the book.

In addition to educational therapy students and practitioners, this book is appropriate for those working in related fields such as special education, school psychology, school counselling, and social work in educational settings.

Dorothy Fink Ungerleider, founding President, Advisory Board Chair, and Fellow of the Association of Educational Therapists, is an educational therapist in private practice in Encino, California.

EDUCATIONAL THERAPY IN ACTION

Behind and Beyond the Office Door

Dorothy Fink Ungerleider

Routledge
Taylor & Francis Group
NEW YORK AND LONDON

KH

First published 2011
by Routledge
711 Third Avenue, New York, NY 10017

Simultaneously published in the UK
by Routledge
2 Park Square, Milton Park, Abingdon, Oxon OX14 4RN

Routledge is an imprint of the Taylor & Francis Group, an informa business

Library of Congress Cataloging-in-Publication Data
Ungerleider, Dorothy Fink, author.
  Educational therapy in action : behind and beyond the office door /
  Dorothy Fink Ungerleider.
    p. ; cm.
  Includes bibliographical references and index.
  1. Word deafness—Case studies. I. Title.
  [DNLM: 1. Education, Special—methods—Case Reports. 2. Auditory
  Perceptual Disorders—therapy—Case Reports. 3. Disabled Persons—education
  —Case Reports. 4. Learning Disorders—therapy—Case Reports. 5. Professional-
  Patient Relations—Case Reports. LC 4818]
  RC394.W63U54 2011
  617.8'606—dc22   2010046620

ISBN13: 978–0–415–88884–4 (hbk)
ISBN13: 978–0–415–88885–1 (pbk)
ISBN13: 978–0–203–83154–0 (ebk)

Typeset in Bembo
by Keystroke, Station Road, Codsall, Wolverhampton

Printed and bound in the United States of America on acid-free paper
by Walsworth Publishing Company, Marceline, MO

SUSTAINABLE
FORESTRY
INITIATIVE

Certified Sourcing
www.sfiprogram.org
SFI-00555
The SFI label applies to the text stock.

9/2/11

For my sister Joan—
who was always there with answers

For Tom—
who waited, through
ALL the years for completion

For John and Peggy—
who believed and supported

For the real "NORA"—
who made it all possible

CONTENTS

Foreword   *ix*
Richard D. Lavoie

Acknowledgments   *xiii*

Introduction   1

Beginnings: A Mother's Recall   6

PART ONE
Behind the Office Door: Building the Organic Curriculum   **13**

1 December: Making the Connection   15
2 Early January: The Reciprocal Compromise Principle Leads to the Organic
   Curriculum   25
3 Late January: Seeds of Collaboration   34
4 An Atypical Family Meeting   40
5 February: Goal-setting, Present and Future, in a Safe Haven   48
6 March: Alternate Routes to Word Mastery, Engaging the Teachers   54
7 April: A New Use for Soap Operas, Journal Writing, and Dreams of the
   Elephant Man   65

PART TWO
Employment and Continued Education: Living the Organic Curriculum **77**

 8 May: Job vs. Occupation vs. Career—and Lessons on Worry   79
 9 June: Traffic Tickets as Curriculum, and Other Misunderstandings   83
10 July: Lessons on the Job, Lessons in Literature, Headlines, and Fairness   89

11 August: College in Summer, Field Trip, and Videotape as a Learning Tool   97
12 September/October: College Texts and Morning Papers—A Whole New Path   103
13 November: An Interest in Autism Becomes a Saga   108
14 December: Social Challenges of the Holiday Season; Reviewing a Year's
    Growth   114

PART THREE
Continuing Change: Short Vignettes from Subsequent Years in Educational Therapy   **117**

Year 2   Working for Dad's Office: From Doubt to Confidence   119
Year 2   Role Modeling: The Pressure of Personal Appearance   122
Year 2   Knee Surgery, Pain, and Face-offs with Professionals   126
Year 2   Overcoming a Fear: Becoming a Flyer   129
Year 3   The Whole Dam Thing   133
Years 3 and 4   Job at COZY CLOZ: No Longer a Victim   135
Year 5 and On   Bumps and Potholes on the Road to Respect   141
Nora Now   Life Lessons and Uncommon Courage   145

EPILOGUE   **149**

Author's Reflections   151
Nora's Response to the Book   153

Appendix A   Rules for the Use of Commas   155
Appendix B   Place Value Cards   158
Appendix C   Barsch Learning Style Inventory   161
Appendix D   Test Scores and Excerpts from Psychoeducational Testing   162

Bibliography   166

FOREWORD

The limits of my language are the limits of my world.

Ludwig Wittgenstein

When my colleague and friend, Dorothy Ungerleider, asked me to write a Foreword for her new book, *Educational Therapy in Action: Behind and Beyond the Office Door,* I immediately and eagerly agreed . . . for somewhat selfish reasons.

I knew that writing this Foreword would provide me with the opportunity to be among the first to go on one of Dorothy's wonder-filled journeys. A copy of her first book, *Reading, Writing and Rage*, sits dog-eared on my office bookshelf. Twenty years ago, I was spellbound through its 200 pages while Dorothy wove the true and painful story of Tony and his struggles with learning, language . . . and life. Several times over the past two decades I find myself placing *Reading, Writing and Rage* in my briefcase when taking a long cross-country flight. Whenever I revisit Tony and Dorothy's voyage, I gain new information, inspiration, and insight.

As I read *Educational Therapy in Action*, I was, again, accompanying Dorothy and one of her clients (Nora) on a journey of discovery. We follow Nora through the pain, pride, victory, defeats and milestones that are experienced by all people who struggle with language. We also see the unique process of educational therapy up close, *"behind and beyond the office door."*

This dynamic technique is a combination of academic remediation, counseling, therapy and genuine friendship. Educational therapy, when applied by a pioneer like Dorothy, avoids the pitfalls of traditional remedial approaches (e.g., enabling, dependency, lack of generalization). In educational therapy, Dorothy and Nora frequently exchange the roles of "mentor" and "protégé" by learning from one another in a unique and unprecedented way.

Nora's learning and language is compromised by an auditory processing disorder. This complex disorder causes her to misperceive much of the language input that she receives every day. Lectures are confusing. Verbal directions are frustrating. Social conversations are exhausting. Movie dialogues are confounding.

If you are familiar with my work, you may know of the 1988 video that I produced entitled *F.A.T. City*. In this program, I use contrived activities that make language very confusing for the workshop participants in order to have them "walk a mile" in the shoes of students who struggle with learning. Although the video is over two decades old, it continues to be a staple in graduate programs and staff development projects.

The video was born of frustration. Very early in my career, I recognized the ironic fact that *most teachers did fairly well in school*. Further, *most teachers enjoyed going to school* (why else would they select a profession that places them back in the classroom?). Therefore, the student to whom teachers can best understand and relate is the bright, spontaneous, motivated learner. And the child that they can *least* relate to is the struggling, frustrated, disordered student . . . the student who *needs* their compassion and understanding. Ironic, huh?

I felt that if teachers and parents were given the opportunity to actually *experience* academic failure they would come to better understand the Frustration, Anxiety and Tension that the struggling student experiences daily.

So many times as I read *Educational Therapy in Action*, I reflected on this irony. Very few of us can *truly* understand the frustrations that Nora experienced every day. For us, language is a tool. This tool is at our ready disposal and we use it to convince, converse, cajole, complain, connect, create, coerce, confound, control, captivate, combat and confess. It is difficult to imagine what life would be like if—through no fault or choice of our own—this tool was taken from us.

When attempting to explain the impact of auditory processing disorders, I often use this analogy. Have you ever had a conversation with a person who has a very pronounced foreign accent? You have to listen very intently. You often fail to understand mispronounced words and must use closure to determine the word that you "missed." It is difficult to follow the conversation while, simultaneously, trying to figure out the words that you "misheard."

Welcome to Nora's World . . .

I was reminded of this analogy recently when I had a speaking engagement in Montreal. My wife and I took a wonderful guided bus tour through that historic city. The tour guide was extraordinarily knowledgable and wove fantastic tales of Montreal's rich history. But he spoke with a heavy French accent and I had great difficulty following his lecture . . . despite my best and most concentrated efforts.

At the end of the two-hour tour I was exhausted. This "language exercise" was frustrating and very tiring. It occurred to me that many of my students must experience similar feelings every day in school.

Welcome to Nora's World . . .

One of the F.A.T. City exercises enables (and forces!) the participants to experience a disorder known as "dysnomia." This is, basically, a word-finding problem wherein a person is unable to recall a specific word during conversations or discussions. We all experience the "word on the tip of my tongue" phenomenon on occasion, but people with APD experience it dozens of times daily.

To simulate dysnomia, I ask the participants to tell a Round Robin story where each person contributes a sentence. They are able to do this with ease and they weave a creative collective tale. Then I "give" them dysnomia by adding a new rule: they cannot use any words that contain the letter N.

Suddenly, these conversant, creative storytellers become stilted and dysfluent. They get "stuck" in sentences that they can't finish . . . they substitute their rich vocabularies ("fantastic") with baby words ("good"). The resulting story is disconnected, simplistic, and, frankly, boring.

Participants experience great frustration with this task. They sweat. They stammer. They break eye contact. They wring their hands. They pull at their hair. They complain. Some cry.

Welcome to Nora's World . . .

I am very verbal. Some might say *overly* verbal. My abilities to speak, converse and discuss are among my greatest strengths. In fact, I make my living by speaking. Language is my friend!

Last year, I developed a mysterious and severe case of laryngitis. The doctors were puzzled. I was frustrated. The treatment was simple: *No talking for five days*.

My "tool" was not working. My "friend" was missing. For five days—120 hours—my life changed.

I love talking on the phone . . . suddenly the telephone's ring was an unwelcome sound.

I would see friends in the supermarket . . . and I avoided them.

I was forced to cancel a speaking engagement . . . for the first time in thirty years.

I no longer enjoyed watching television programs or ballgames with my family . . . because I was unable to participate in the boisterous conversations that supplemented our TV watching.

Language—my trusted tool and friend—was no longer at my disposal. For five l-o-n-g and difficult days, my inability to effectively use language put significant and frustrating limitations on my world.

Welcome to Nora's World . . .

As with any good book, *Educational Therapy in Action* triggers memories for the reader. As I read Dorothy's manuscript, I was reminded of students, parents and teachers with whom I have shared my career. I was particularly intrigued by the way in which Nora's life changed while Dorothy endeavored to enhance Nora's vocabulary. As she mastered more words, her understanding and appreciation of her world was expanded and enriched. Dorothy's patient explanations and examples enabled Nora to see through the fog of words.

Welcome to Nora's World . . .

Dorothy's obvious delight at Nora's discoveries is inspiring. There is, perhaps, no better feeling than watching a student "get it" and knowing that your skill and tutelage allowed this to happen. Students who struggle need these explanations and clarifications. This book is filled with discoveries. It is a candid, crafted story of two women—a therapist and a client—on a journey that will change them both. The story has heroes . . . and a villain or two. It explores and demystifies the confusing and challenging world of a struggling adolescent as she approaches adulthood.

But it is also a story of great hope and optimism. There are victories and celebrations; progress and possibilities.

Mostly, it is proof that—when given a "safe harbor"—struggling students can conquer their dragons. Dorothy's office was that safe harbor for the remarkable Nora. A place of learning, growth, and discovery. That safe harbor made all the difference.

But Dorothy constantly reminds us of the need to challenge our students and gently but purposefully move them away from the tranquil bay and into the shoals and reefs of "real life."

Her message is clear:

A ship is safe in the harbor . . . but that's not what ships are for.

Welcome to Nora's World.

Richard D. Lavoie, M.A., M.Ed.

Bibliography

Lavoie, R.D. (1988). *How Difficult Can This Be? The F.A.T. City Workshop* (PBS Video).

Lavoie, R.D. (2005). *It's So Much Work to Be Your Friend: Helping the Child with Learning Disabilities Find Social Success*. New York: Simon & Schuster.

Lavoie, R.D. (2007). *The Motivation Breakthrough: 6 Secrets to Turning On the Tuned-out Child*. New York: Simon & Schuster.

ACKNOWLEDGMENTS

To the real "Nora" for your patience waiting for your story to be told—and even wishing to shed your anonymity so that people would finally believe you really did have a problem. Your involvement has given this book authenticity to unveil the process of educational therapy. Thanks to you and your parents for permitting me to write so personally about your years of struggle. Your story will benefit teachers, parents, and all kinds of professionals who work with individuals needing different approaches in order to learn. I hope this book has allowed you to recognize your extraordinary growth in understanding and problem-solving, as well as your courage through the painful times. My gratitude is boundless.

To Marianne Frostig, who gave life to the concept of educational therapy in America, and mentored my own development and that of the first professional association in this new field. Your voice will always be in our heads.

To my "chief advisers" Phyllis Maslow and Barbara Keogh, who always took the time for every question, told me the truth, and had the wisdom to help me make the book better. Your willingness to spend endless hours on rewrites and still believe in this project is deeply appreciated.

To my daughter Peggy, my "detail person," who, from the other side of the world, corrected each page with your skilled editor's eye and always, your loving encouragement of my efforts.

To my daughter-in-law Elizabeth, our family's most avid reader of serious literature, whose approval and cogent suggestions were catalysts for each improved version of the book.

To my son John, conflict-resolver, whose spirit cheered me on when my energy was waning and who believed that this book had to make it into print.

To my dear friends: Louise Silverberg, who read thoughtfully and advised from your head and from your heart; Ileene and Bert Dragin, who tolerated the years of discussion at dinner tables during the whole process.

To my many scholarly colleagues from educational therapy, speech therapy, and neuro-psychology, whose input was so important to this work. Here are just a few:

—Jane Adelizzi, whose specific suggestions on structure, organization of contents, and generous praise reassured me to go forward.

—Maxine Ficksman, whom I solicited to read with a critical mind and suggest corrections, but she liked it. She really liked it!

—Roberta Poster, who gave of her time to study Nora's symptoms and clear up my own fog about the specific nature of her auditory processing disorders.

—Farryl Dickter, who kept me honest about professional boundaries, definitions, and interpretations of tests and observations.

—Gail Werbach, Brandi Roth, and Lenore Terr for your generous counsel about navigating through the labyrinth of the publishing process.

Special thanks to the Routledge team. First, in New York, to Lane Akers—you've won my heart for being willing to hear me, respond to my vision, and make the requested technical adjustments! Thanks to Alexandra Sharp for reading with a critical eye to refine the text. In the UK, praises for Maggie Lindsey-Jones, who supported my plea, advocated for more readability and made those changes—even in the "eleventh hour." Special appreciation to Arnold Wolf for the cover image and to Hon To for refining the cover design to a new level. (Nora called it "intriguing.") For all of the copy editors and staff on both continents who helped to produce an error-free end product, I'm very grateful, and I hope you share my pride in the outcome.

And last on the list but first in my heart—to my husband Tom, who has put up with long hours of abandonment over long years, waiting for this manuscript to be completed. At last, dear, you have your wife back!

INTRODUCTION

The mysterious happenings behind the office doors of clinical therapists have always intrigued those on the outside. This book invites the reader in as a vicarious collaborator in the art and science of one client's educational therapy. It answers a specific question about a little-known clinician—the educational therapist. This question, which has plagued its practitioners since the beginning of our professional lives, is: "Just what does an educational therapist *do*?" *Educational Therapy in Action* seeks to answer *what* we do and *how* we do it, bringing to life in story form the core principles and the dynamic, interactive nature of this little-known clinical therapy.

What are the origins of this field? In the 1950s, the combined educational/therapeutic "heilpedagogie" created by August Aichorn in Vienna was imported from Europe by learning disability pioneers like Marianne Frostig, Katrina DeHirsch, and others who immigrated to our shores (Ficksman & Adelizzi, 2010; Ungerleider, 1986; Werbach, 1998). Individuals trained by such newcomers called themselves "educational therapists" before any specific university training programs were available. On their own, these trainees studied the combined coursework, core literature, and methodology from two disciplines: pedagogical/educational "teaching" and clinical/psychotherapeutic "treating."

In the 1980s, the Association of Educational Therapists (AET) was formed in the United States to *define* the field in its own right, *set standards of practice*, and *develop training programs and certification*. Over the years (Ficksman & Adelizzi, 2010), AET refined the definition of an educational therapist as one who "combines educational and therapeutic approaches for evaluation, remediation, case management, and communication/advocacy on behalf of children, adolescents and adults with learning disabilities or learning problems" (www.aetonline.org/about/defined.php#Definition).

But how does such grand combining actually work? More than 50 years after its introduction to our shores, *the help-seeking public and most other clinical professionals still have no clue what, why, and how educational therapists do our craft.* It is time to demystify the process.

First of all, our domain is education. "Teach" is what we do. But how we teach and what we teach is determined by the way we look at and listen to our clients, trying to see and hear more than is obvious to the layman. We work to analyze each individual client's *needs*—the deficits or areas of weakness, and personal strengths—innate capacities and learning styles. Then we utilize the procedures—the interventions, teaching techniques, strategies—that will allow learning to take place at all levels of education, in school or workplace. We meld together the academic science of education with the art of therapeutic listening and "investigative observation" during our clients' efforts at mastery of each task, whether it be in reading, writing, speaking, listening, reasoning, planning, organizing, and/or problem-solving. By blending together the processes of both teaching and treating, we determine *why* a client fails, *how* a client feels, and what interventions will be most relevant and effective.

Most crucial to the success of educational therapy, of course, is the *treatment alliance*—the working partnership between educational therapist and client—a reciprocal bond, the adhesives of which are trust, compassion, and honesty. We can never forget that each client also brings to the therapeutic table his or her singular blueprint of humanity—temperament, family genetics/ emotional climate, and contextual influences and expectations from the family, school, culture, and community—all of this impacting on attitude, motivation, and progress.

Educational therapists have other special roles. As *facilitators of understanding,* we strive to help clients comprehend their disorders and diagnoses, make peace with those "labels," and focus on their capabilities. We teach them how to explain their learning obstacles and accommodative needs to others in simple, positive ways that are easy for them to express and for others to understand. We mentor them to develop self-help learning strategies that work across all subject matter and in every situation. We act as *cheerleaders* for every effort they exert toward mastery of their goals, and we help them build self-confidence and autonomy. We are often the first ones in their life experience to acknowledge what they do *right* in a world focusing on what they do *wrong*. They must be cheered, even if they fail, to learn the purpose of each and every lesson. They are always surprised to learn that failure, too, has its own kind of reward.

But make no mistake: educational therapists are frequently challenged by issues that have no easy answers and require unrehearsed decisions. Consequently, we must consult and collaborate with colleagues from many disciplines for answers we may not have but must be willing to find, as well as refer clients to those whose expertise is more appropriate for their needs. In this way, we often become conduits of connection between all those people concerned with the client's well-being, thus serving as kinds of "educational case managers" and referral sources in an expanded role of *communication and advocacy.*

Educational Therapy in Action uses the story of one client, "Nora Tarlow," to bring to life the scope of the educational therapy process. Nora's story provided the perfect vehicle to expose the broad range of "psycho-educational interventions"—both academic/vocational and social/ emotional—that an educational therapist employs. Each educational therapy client offers a kind of laboratory for determining the most effective techniques and interpersonal attitudes that facilitate learning. Hopefully, the lessons learned from intensive work with *one client at a time* can provide insights for a theoretical framework applicable to the many in general education. When we understand the whole child in his whole world, we can share a model for planning differently. When we understand the characteristics needed in the teacher, perhaps we can train people differently.

When Nora and I first met, the cause of her anguish was unclear, but the range of her suffering was immediately evident. Nora was a 17-year-old, deeply wounded by years of failure and developmentally at the brink of two stages—youth and adulthood—and two worlds—school and employment. She longed for answers to understand herself—how she learns, why she couldn't for so many years, and what would eventually become her place in society.

Nora's disorder impacted upon every aspect of her life. She had been a profoundly confused child who evolved into an anxious, isolated teen unable to hold on to her teachers' instructions, her friends' conversations, or any flow of dialogue in any situation. Her impaired daily functioning deprived her of acquiring the vocabulary and language so crucial for successful performance in her surroundings. School was torture. Social gatherings brought terror. Movies were *all* mysteries (even the comedies). To be in a crowd was still to be isolated, a special kind of "social loneliness" (Margalit, 2010) caused by her bewilderment with the surround-sound of words that lacked meanings in her brain. Its profound impact on her emotions impaired feelings of accomplishment and connection to others in society. And for her first 17 years, she never knew why—or how to deal with it.

What was the cause? Based on her responses to psycho-educational tests and my observation over time of her responses to all paths of oral input, I became convinced that the core of her language deficits was an *auditory processing disorder.* She could not give meaning to spoken language that came at her too rapidly, leaving her in a constant fog of words that she couldn't comprehend. However, Nora was never professionally diagnosed by an audiologist. At that time, audiologists had no specific tests for such central types of auditory processing disorders, only for hearing loss and auditory discrimination difficulties. She had neither of those problems.

The emotional toll of her daily helplessness had to be addressed as part of an effective educational/therapeutic plan to lift the fog in which she lived each day. Too often, the link between emotions and learning goes unrecognized. This *therapeutic journey* brings you along experientially to clarify the role of an educational therapist in addressing these dual educational and socio-emotional needs.

Over the years and even now, the debate has persisted between those who diagnose *receptive language disorders* and those who prefer the label *auditory processing disorders* to describe the symptoms Nora exhibited. A professor of audiology, Teri James Bellis, in her comprehensive book *When The Brain Can't Hear* (2002), describes different types of disorders in auditory processing, with one particular type affecting the way the brain gives meaning to auditory input of language. Bellis dismissed the diagnostic debates as to whether these problems were either auditory processing or language disorders, reminding us (as if she were precisely describing Nora) that "auditory processing and language are interdependent, entwined in a complicated dance of sound and meaning that cannot be unraveled" (p. 54).

In her analysis of an exemplary case whose symptoms mirrored Nora's, she explained that a disorder of auditory processing disrupts the clarity of what is heard and can affect what is ultimately understood like "a short circuit somewhere between the hearing of the speech sound and the understanding of what the communication meant," and she pointed out a further diagnostic puzzle for such children: "(T)here did not appear to be any obvious reason why this child, who was easily able to pay attention to a task and appeared to be making a real effort, was having such comprehension difficulties" (p. 50). Nora's story shows just how much it was "not obvious," and how much even her own family could not comprehend the nature of this cloudy, misunderstood disorder.

* * *

This is a participatory story. You will become a participant in the dynamic exchange of mutual learning between client and teacher. The initial work with Nora, begun many years ago, has provided a long view of her life and shown the influence of the educational therapy on her outcomes as a fully functioning adult. On such a therapeutic journey you will encounter a new approach to remediation, what this author has named the "Organic Curriculum."

The Organic Curriculum is a therapeutic intervention personalized to the needs of each client during each session. It evolves "organically," that is, in a natural flow of lessons, growing one from the other, as gaps in knowledge appear and get clarified—in context and in the moment. Each client's own capacities, interests, motivations, and styles of learning are utilized in this approach to the constantly changing curriculum demands of school or the task demands on the job. Using the "roots" of the known and familiar (i.e., the client's prior knowledge) to grow the "trunk" (i.e., the foundational mastery of unknowns upon which to build), educational therapy techniques are customized to fit what works for each client in the context of each new unit of knowledge. Specific examples throughout this book help the reader to understand how this curriculum worked for Nora across all kinds of academic content. One thing is certain: this kind of teaching is never boring, always tapping the intuitive and creative skills along with the teaching techniques and knowledge base of the educational therapist.

Although this story is about only one client, and each client's learning and personal profile is unique, the universal characteristics of *the process of educational therapy* can come alive through such an intensive, longitudinal study of one. Hopefully, there will be many other stories to come, from other educational therapists with different trainings and intervention styles, to foster even further understanding of this therapeutic interaction.

You will be taken along to observe what Lenore Terr calls the "magical moments of change" (Terr, 2008), referring in her book with that title to particular moments in psychotherapy that reverse patterns and change lives. Terr acknowledged that her writing comes from a medical perspective but encouraged those in nonmedical therapeutic fields to "interpose your own words to our stories according to what you do in your own practice" (p.7). I accepted that invitation, even though educational therapy does not address the unconscious processes at the core of psychotherapy, but there are parallel phenomena of successful breakthroughs.

I experienced many of those magical moments with Nora. I couldn't always identify *how*, but I knew *when* it happened. The *why* is for you to decide as you read about Nora's educational therapy—the profound along with the imperfect moments, the successes along with the mistakes, my constant questions with their elusive answers, and the lessons to be learned by all of it.

Finally, I am grateful that the real "Nora" gave her approval to the content and word choice; she expressed great pleasure that her story is finally being told. If I wrote anything that she couldn't understand or did not recall as factual, it had to be modified or removed. In fact, her input is responsible for making this book more readable, especially for those with language comprehension issues. Nora has waited many years for its completion, and as a result of her patience we now have a "longitudinal study of outcomes," allowing you to see not only what she *was* but what she has *become* in her mid-adulthood.

Nora wished that her real identity could be revealed, but she accepted the fact that confidentiality would be violated for all the others described in the book, and that all people and places had to be given fictitious names. Her approval provided great satisfaction to me. Best of all, Nora Tarlow verified that I had done what I set out to do—to *clear the way for her by lifting the fog in which she had lived for too long.*

Style Notes

The narrative style of the book was selected to serve as a model of the kind of dialogue between client and educator in various teaching situations. Hopefully, others who work with or are parents of individuals with learning disorders will get ideas for strategies to actually try out.

Note that each chapter begins with a kind of verbal "road map" to guide the reader through the purpose of my interventions over each block of time, i.e., "Here's what I'm trying to do during this month, and here's why."

The book is divided into three parts. Part One brings the reader behind the office door, spelling out the process of forming and building the treatment alliance, determining the client's goals and academic/cognitive profile, and developing "psycho-educational" interventions through the Organic Curriculum to address the full range of Nora's needs during our first six months of work. Part Two continues the interactive process as we segue into the dual challenges of college and employment, "living the Organic Curriculum." You will be able to participate vicariously in Nora's process of growth: how language and listening issues were systematically addressed; how academic skills were mastered or adapted; how language-based fears were resolved or tempered; and how the behaviors necessary for more interpersonal confidence were developed.

Part Three comprises a series of particularly moving vignettes from subsequent years to illustrate later applications of our work together—beyond the office door—as her needs and capabilities changed with her developing maturation. The real-world outcomes during these years offer their own reality check on the efficacy of Nora's educational therapy.

[Throughout the chapters I have chosen to insert periodic commentaries in bracketed inserts such as this one, with a different text style, to help the reader better understand the reasons why particular methods, strategies, and non-academic interventions—the tools of educational therapy—were chosen to address Nora's individual needs. On reading the book herself, Nora remarked on the helpfulness of understanding WHY we did what we did. I hope the reader will feel the same way.]

BEGINNINGS

A Mother's Recall

The following narration was adapted from the first history-gathering conference with Nora's parents, Christine and Walter Tarlow. It was dramatized to synthesize the effects on the family with the facts of Nora's temperamental, developmental, and school histories during those years prior to our first meeting when they first sought my help.

Some people's beginnings foreshadow trouble. Nora's was such a beginning. She was ready to come, but the doctor wasn't.

Hold off, mother. Wait—don't push—the doctor hasn't come yet.

But Mother was screaming—screaming that the baby was coming out! Coming out screaming.

And she never stopped, this baby Nora. Six months of it is the way they remember her beginnings.

She was to be the gift, the compensation after Mother had lost the twins the year before, in her sixth month of pregnancy. "Hydramneus," the doctors called her condition—retaining water in the womb. Water pills were supposed to help, so she took lots of them. They helped with the water, but they didn't save the twins.

More hydramneus, more pills with Nora, but this fetus was a fighter, a survivor. Whether her parents would survive *her* was another matter.

"She screamed until she could walk . . . she never crawled, just stood up and walked at six-and-a-half months." The will to walk was ready; the legs weren't, so she had to wear braces—for a year and a half—to help the bones catch up with that relentless spirit. Mom revisits the memory: "*So* determined, that little girl! Almost frantic in her movements. Why, she actually threw herself out of the crib, braces and all. I remember trying to take her picture when she was three or four months old . . . Oh! There was no way. We couldn't calm her down. You couldn't hold onto her. She wouldn't stay in your arms—always wiggled to get away. And you couldn't hug or kiss her—it was like hugging a board. But the doctor was more polite. He called it 'very precocious motor development.' "

Christine Tarlow recalled isolated incidents from faded memories of Nora's early childhood, like her attempts to use the family playpen for some salvation. She'd counted on using it, having been spoiled by first-born Rob, who had been playpen-pleasured for two years. Nora lasted two days, two hours of each, just screaming. How old was she then—maybe six or seven months? Christine described the image of that little, intrepid child, pulling at the "cage," pulling herself up on the bars. In her quest for freedom, she actually began holding and walking, circling the pen. No "play" in that pen.

Christine shared her dilemma: "You couldn't hold her and you couldn't pen her. What was left?"

Once Nora began walking, the real fear for her safety began. The immediate concern was the swimming pool in the yard. The Tarlows put a wrought iron fence around the pool with a triple padlock system on a gate that had no crossbars so that Nora wouldn't be able to climb it. One day, by chance, they glanced outside and saw Nora's head fitting right through the vertical bars which had been constructed too far apart. That image brought the realization that bars weren't enough. Nora needed swimming lessons as early as possible.

Swimming was infant Nora's first triumph. At 18 months of age, she actually swam the width of an Olymic-sized pool. When she arrived at the pool, everyone would stop their lessons and watch the infant-star. Joe, her instructor, was so proud of her, but he would warn Christine that Nora's precocity was very dangerous because she was too young to learn to bring her head up and breathe. She swam under water just like a mini-dolphin, and she'd pop up only when he tapped her on the head.

Gradually, tiny Nora mastered the swimming and breathing, but their patience was running out with preschool-aged Nora-on-land. People were always closing doors to keep her out or keep her in—so many doors closing on little fingers that were quick-quick trying to keep them open. Then more screams of wounded fingers. Finally, a bone-weary Mom discovered that the stroller's mobile confinement offered her the only relief.

When she wasn't swimming or running, Nora was climbing—over everything. Her visit to brother's nursery school playground left all the teachers spellbound by Rob's little sister as she scaled the two- or three-foot spans between the monkey bars and somehow got to the top. All the teachers stopped watching the other children and just stared and pointed at this little one-and-a-half-year-old. Mom didn't think anything of it because that was normal stuff for Nora, but no one else could figure out how she got there.

Nora's first of many accidents started early, too, but the family had no way of anticipating which actions and which settings would lead to catastrophe. Only Mom recalled exactly how the magnum of champagne happened to fall on her forehead at that same age, 18 months, that Nora had learned to swim. Eighteen months, 18 stitches.

Mom relived the horror. "I must have seen it happen—I remember running to Nora and before I even picked her up, I remember looking at the bottle in horror, at the size of it— and picking it up, testing it to see how heavy it was—that was when I really got weak, 'cause it was *so* heavy. She was sitting on the floor and it cracked open her skull! Oh, I can still picture it—the corner cabinet and this magnum sitting up on top, and she on the floor and Rob and his friend, the Greek boy from up the street, came in and started to wrestle. They knocked into the cabinet and the bottle came down and hit her in the head. I remember running out of the house with her and up the street with Rob's friend, him running and screaming for his mother—and she took us to the hospital because I didn't have a car that day—and it was raining—and Walter wasn't due home for a half hour."

Walter Tarlow, Nora's father, came home that night to a note from Christine to call the emergency room. Hurrying to the site, he heard the champagne story from his wife and then the "assuring sounds" from the doctor on call that day that Nora would "be fine, no signs of concussion," but they would observe Nora for two days "just to be certain."

Could they trust this young doctor, still a resident in training, to really know what was happening inside Nora? Better not to think about it and just hope. This would be the first of many ER visits by Walter Tarlow on behalf of his daughter Nora.

Somehow, Mother, Father, and big brother Rob all survived Nora's first four tumultous years. Perhaps Christine's only child from a first marriage, Tracy, had given the Tarlows some prior experience with an unconventional child. Tracy's testy childhood evolved into a rebellious, out-of-control teen age.

Christine tried, alternately, to counsel defiant Tracy, nurture agreeable Rob, and contain whirlwind Nora. Then, making a radical decision of her own, she did something no one could have predicted. In defiance of the reasoned advice of her extended family, she became pregnant.

* * *

Christine was seven months pregnant when the middle-of-the-night phone call came from the desert police to "Come at once, Mrs. Tarlow." Foolhardy Tracy had been in a horrific auto accident. The 20-year-old rebel was killed instantly. There was no time for Christine or Walter to think. Just call a babysitter for Nora and Rob; then speed to the desert.

The next day, a bewildered Nora woke up and found her parents gone. To where? And why? And when her parents returned, what did they say? The confused 4-year-old saw her pregnant mother suffering, sobbing. Who knew how to explain the death, the loss, their grief? No one remembers what was actually said, if anything, to address the 4-year-old's confusion.

Two months later, Christine Tarlow left once again in the middle of the night. At this leaving, Mother gave birth to a baby girl. Nora had a new sister. Carrie. Serene Carrie, who just loved to be held. And Mom loved to hold her. And hold her. Mom was 39, and her family, she announced to all, was complete.

And while placid Carrie nestled at peace in their mother's arms that year, Nora chose to look more and more like a boy—roughhewn jeans, hair trimmed (by Nora's insistence, said Mom) in so masculine a cut that her kindergarten friends first mistook her for a boy.

For many youngsters, a family encounter with death often yields fear or cautionary behavior. But caution was not for Nora. She began to take increasing risks that resulted in a new string of accidents. At age 6, while pretending to drive the family car parked in the driveway, Nora released the brakes, destroying the car on impact with the tree across the street. She suffered a bloody gash, but her fear of the wound was overridden by her even greater fear of the hospital, so they ministered to her at home.

Christine's recounting of the car crisis triggered her recall of "the railing stories." Nora climbed railings. Any and every railing, encountered anywhere, like the one at the West End Mall:

"They had these nylon wires with the glycerin going down them to look like water coming down from this two-story balcony. Well, Nora must have been about 4-and-a-half or 5, and we were upstairs looking at the directory for something, and all of a sudden, I look up and Nora is dangling on the railing, half way over, just dangling there, two stories up! And I remember Grandma was there with me, and I don't know how we got her—we didn't know whether to go slowly or just leap and grab her. But she was always doing things like that, always on the tops of everything. Everyone's heart was always in their mouths over her when she was awake." No doubt the fear for her child's safety squelched any pride Christine might have felt at Nora's extraordinary physical dexterity and daring.

When asked about Nora's first words, Christine qualified her answer. "None of my kids spoke before 2, sentences maybe by 3. I can't recall exactly when Nora first talked or what she said. With all those kids, you know, I just get confused about who did what when, and I didn't have time to keep any of those baby books. I just don't remember about her language. She never had speech therapy or anything."

Walter Tarlow added his own concern with his observations while reading picture books with her: "She'd see a picture of a tree and say 'bush' and I was scared by that—those word substitutions. She could remember the names of tunes of every record she played, but she couldn't tell time, and about third grade, her mother and I felt something was not happening in school. I guess it troubled me because I hate to read myself, and I always had comprehension problems in school. I guess I was hoping Nora wouldn't have the same trouble."

Walter's comments led Christine to reminisce: "I did call her my Moon Child, because she always struck me as if she had come from the moon—different, you know? She had a way of looking at things or evaluating people that was so insightful but in an odd way. And then, of course, she'd mix things up—word meanings. Like the time my friends were over at the house and talking about playing bridge. Well, Nora thought they were talking about bridges that you drive over—she always looked at things a little bit different."

Untrained Christine Tarlow didn't realize, and not for years did anyone help her understand the reason why Nora's language seemed that of a "Moon Child." The expressions that seemed cute and different at that early age were the precursors of the language torments in store for Nora throughout her next 12 school years.

* * *

Seventeen years after that chaotic birth and the tumultuous beginnings, Nora Tarlow became my client in educational therapy that would span several years and cross over the bounds of school curriculum into the worlds of work, life challenges, and social interactions. Over Nora's first 17 years, the Tarlows had moved to different residences, and in the process had misplaced or lost the school records and few test reports that had been administered. Instead of such documents, the *school history* was provided to me through the anecdotes and fragmented memories of Christine and Nora. The following is an assemblage of those fragments that came to mother and daughter at various times during our work together.

No one remembered any special problems at Nora's first elementary school, from kindergarten through Grade 3, but the family moved to a new school in the middle of her 4th-grade year. Both Nora and her mother identified fourth grade as the beginning of the slide into trouble. By fifth grade, Christine noticed one behavior that somehow got her attention. Nora still couldn't tell the time. That observation, signaling to her that something was definitely wrong, became the catalyst for her to begin Nora in tutoring through 5th and 6th grades. Nora recalled having "at least seven tutors, all for very short times, and if they couldn't teach me, they did the schoolwork *for* me. All of them." So mother and daughter had a routine: Christine would ask Nora if she was learning anything from the current tutor. If Nora said "No," they would move on to another tutor.

Then came 7th grade in public middle school, a new horror particularly unforgettable to Nora. She became lost in the impersonal forest of departmentalization—multiple classrooms, multiple teachers, multiple textbooks, and minimal comprehension. For the first time, she was placed in some "special classes" [most likely resource rooms with small groups of students and more individual help], but she continued to struggle. One male teacher tried to help by giving her extra time after school, but even he was reportedly relieved by the Tarlows' eventual decision to put her into a private school for 8th grade.

Their school choice was Kingsley Hall, whose principal boasted "smaller classes where she could get more attention and individual help." Mom believed him. In actual fact, however, the teachers, with no special training, didn't have a clue how to help. Nora recalls that, by 8th grade she could read the words in her textbooks—she just couldn't understand what anything meant. Perhaps, for teachers untrained in special needs, her capacity to word-read concealed the more serious problem with comprehension, probably because of her testing tricks. She would revisualize the passages and then look for the right words in the questions. Often, the system worked well enough for her to pass the tests.

Without Nora realizing it, her teachers had learned to overlook any limited learning capacity for one major reason—Nora's superb athletic prowess. This very gifted capacity had made her welcome at Kingsley Hall. At last, Nora's exceptional preschool coordination skills that had given her mother such anxiety gained her real recognition and even praise. She was a star on both the softball and track teams. The coaches loved this driving competitor who helped them win the games. They looked the other way concerning her academic performance throughout the 8th grade.

Until the accident. In spring of the 8th grade, Nora was running from the team's softball field to get back to the school when she was hit by a car. The car hit her knee and dislodged the joint. It was such a serious leg injury that she required two surgeries that summer, but the school staff magically believed that her dysfunction would be temporary.

At the beginning of 9th grade, the Tarlows provided the real facts to the Kingsley Hall coaches: Nora would not be able to participate in sports that year. There would be no more softball. No more track. Suddenly, "like, overnight," recalled Nora, everything changed. When she couldn't participate, the painful truth was that Nora lost her value to the school. Her grades, which had always been average or borderline but never questioned, were suddenly made into an issue.

Nora recalled her feelings about that time:

> "I had entrusted the teachers to protect me and be honest with me. They told me I was doing fine. I used to speak up in class. I wasn't afraid to ask questions. Then one day, those same teachers who had told me I was doing fine were all on one side of the table telling me I wasn't good enough for Kingsley Hall! I had to leave!
>
> "How could I go home and tell my parents I'm being kicked out for being stupid?"

* * *

And that was how it ended. The Tarlows' outrage at the school's insensitive handling made no difference to the outcome. [**I had no idea at the time how profound an impact the Kingsley Hall expulsion had on Nora. I only learned, after this book was complete, how the emotional torment of this cruel act affected many of the interactions regarding trust and "being good enough" reported in the following pages.**]

The expulsion from Kingsley Hall led the family to another private school, Dunbrook. Nora remembers being told by someone that Dunbrook was "a more caring place, and at least they listen." Skeptical and deeply wounded, she entered another unknown environment on her own, without any preconceived plan for survival.

Three years later, I received the first call for help from Christine Tarlow. By then, Nora was a 12th-grade student at Dunbrook, having made it through 10th and 11th grades at this "more caring place" but still mystified as to why her learning struggles were mounting. Thus, at age 17, Nora and I began our partnership in educational therapy. This is where *our* story begins.

PART ONE

Behind the Office Door

Building the Organic Curriculum

1

DECEMBER

Making the Connection

In these early sessions, you begin to see what an educational therapist does to form a working partnership, plant seeds for trust, and see the client through her own eyes while also using various tools for evaluation. By sharing my insights with Nora during this first evaluation, I explain, in the moment, what the exercises and tests tell—and cannot tell—about the possible reasons behind her learning struggles. By listening to her descriptions of her study style and looking elsewhere for data from her early years, a "client profile" is being formed.

Notes and Impressions of Nora Tarlow

Age 17 years, 5 months, 12th Grade, Dunbrook Academy. Referred by her classmate Terry McCarthy, a former client of mine.

Finally arrived, shy, tentative, deeply apologetic for being a half-hour late. Tense. Explained she lost the address, then found it in the back seat of her car.

Lovely voice, innocent quality. A softness about her. Soft, honey-brown hair. Soft hazel eyes—avoiding direct glances. Soft porcelain Englishwoman's complexion, flawless. Pale rose, little-girl blush of cheeks from a Gainsborough painting. Healthy, athletic body, faded-beyond-blue jeans. Man-tailored shirt—disguising the softness, maybe? A slight limp in her walk. She saw me notice, explained her old knee injury, then admitted she'd played a weekend's worth of paddle tennis through the pain, denying the trouble. Club champion! Paradox—soft shyness and defiant determination. A competitor here.

She had no problem writing the personal stats I requested then: her name, address, zip code, phone number, age, birthday and year, school and grade. Any siblings? Two: Robert, age 20, and Carrie, age 13. All words correctly spelled and the numbers correctly sequenced according to the previous information from her mother.

Any "beasts" at home? Two dogs. She could spell "schnauzer" perfectly, and "lasa opso" almost perfectly. She printed instead of writing cursively. Preference, she responded when I probed, because "My handwriting is slow and sloppy."

[So much information is to be gained by these sometimes simple requests. Can she know the basic "numbers" and proper names of her personal statistics? Can she write, spell, and

correctly remember the facts of street, city, and siblings' names? Can she correctly sequence her zip code and phone number? Are there many phone numbers to retain, such as her own, her parents', her father's and mother's if parents are divorced? Is she right- or left-handed, which can lead to the inquiry about general "sidedness," such as which foot she kicks with, which eye she uses to look through a camera? Does she have any "beasts" in the home? I use beasts rather than pets because the word gets kids' attention, and over the years I've been stunned at the numbers of them who have snakes, tarantulas, and other exotic creatures that can only come under the broader heading of "beasts."]

Then, a few minutes of banter—ice-breaking conversation, setting a relaxed mood. Talk about Terry, the friend we have in common (my former student), how he saw her looking so confused in lectures. Looking frantically at everyone's papers, asking what the teacher said, having trouble keeping up. Terry advised, "You need Dorothy."

Terry had OK'd for my sharing his own incredible struggles and even more remarkable compensations that allowed him to function so well at Dunbrook. Nora is amazed—thought he was so smart. He is. Smart isn't the problem, I explain. She's confused by that. Definitely doesn't think she's smart.

We discuss jobs—the one (and only one) she'd had, and lost, at MacDonald's. Their instructions came at her too fast. She didn't understand. Too embarrassed to ask them to repeat, to slow down. Remembered lasting one day on the cash register, so terrified to even learn it, so she quit. One day and out. Drops hints of her doubt that she'll ever be employable.

[Every comment and explanation offers more clues to Nora's style and struggles, alerting me now to her trouble with oral directions.]

Next comes the Hard/Easy Interview. It helps her relax, helps me begin to know her through *her* eyes. I do the writing, and she describes her hards and easies.

[This particular interview gives exceptional insight into a client's self-perception of strengths and weaknesses. I divide the paper into two columns with a vertical line down the middle, labeling the left-hand column EASY and the right-hand one HARD. She is first asked what comes easy for her, in or out of school—what she knows she does well and/or really enjoys doing. As I expand my inquiry about each comment, the EASY list can grow to two or three pages in length, often making a positive psychological impression on students who have never thought they do anything well. The HARD column records those things, in or out of school, that are frustrating, that she wishes she could do better. More queries get her to expand on each bit of information offered.

The whole technique provides an opportunity to observe the client's facility with language and memory. Does she understand my questions? Do I have to repeat them or paraphrase them in order to be understood? How does she express herself in replying to them? Am I able to understand her answers, or do I have to probe further to get a clearer choice of words? Does she frequently claim that she can't remember? A further benefit of the Hard/ Easy Interview is that it allows me to write what she says, all the while generating a written record of the session—very useful throughout the educational therapy as a reference point for comparison of self-assessment at the beginning of the process and any changes by the end. It can also provide a documented starting point of initial goals for our work together.]

Nora knows what's easy for her. It's easy for her to do sports. Paddle tennis is her favorite. But I learn that Nora doesn't just "play" at it; she was club champion twice! She's able to explain how it differs from regular tennis, since I'm unfamiliar with the sport. [**I note that on familiar topics she is fluent in her descriptions and word choices.**] Softball is another strength, and she's on the school team. She loves swimming and adds that she used to race. When I probe about whether she won the races, she says with a shy smile, "I like to win in everything!" When I ask about her dreams for the future, she expresses interest in the recreation field for a possible career.

The EASY list expands as she relaxes and becomes more comfortable with the interview process. She's good at babysitting—loves kids. Pretty good at cooking—in fact, she can cook a whole dinner. Math is sort of easy, sometimes. She can read words without too much trouble and can comprehend most things she *chooses* to read—outside of school. When asked if it's easy for her to make friends, Nora shares that it was easy to make friends at her old school, but it's also easy to be shy, so making new ones at Dunbrook is more of a challenge. Her last item on the EASY list is "geography" and I register surprise, sharing that this is a first for me. Nora's face radiates to learn that no other client has ever listed geography in the EASY column.

[**Students love to hear about ways in which they are special, unique, unusual—and this is another advantage of the Hard/Easy interview because they are generating information that may never be mentioned in standardized or diagnostic testing. Her mention of geography is also a signal for me to think about the visual and spatial characteristics of geography—the very skills that I later learn are strengths for Nora and would put this subject on her EASY list.**]

We move on to Nora's list of what she wishes she could do better—the HARDS. Surprising me, she starts the list with "hand skills" like crafts and sewing, revealing her perceived discrepancy between her superb gross motor skills in sports and the fine motor skills of using her hands for intricate tasks. [**I think back to her earlier comment that her handwriting is "messy."**] She then acknowledges the major HARDS: reading comprehension at Dunbrook; making friends at Dunbrook; school itself at Dunbrook—especially literature and poetry. And drama—"they force you to do it."

The list goes on to more general topics rather than specifics about Dunbrook. Nora knows it's very hard to understand what she hears. And to take notes. She writes a lot but is never fast enough. Her final comment seemed more of a quest for answers: "It's hard to understand what's wrong with me—why I'm so dumb."

[**During the questioning of the HARD portion of this interview, students are asked to think about "what they wish they could do better," and this guideline often leads to non-academic wishes, such as wishing to know why school is so hard, or sometimes, comments like "I wish my parents would understand me better," or even "I wish I could be nicer to my brother when he's such a pest." The client is always asked for permission to share the HARD/EASY list with the parents during the parent conference, and particularly, if there is anything on that list that they do not want shared. Interestingly, after tens of hundreds of these interviews, I have only had two instances when clients asked that a few comments on the list be kept private from their parents. Most seem really eager that their parents know the client's own opinions about their strengths and weaknesses.**]

Nora opened up more freely now about why she thought so many things were hard for her at Dunbrook. "My first year there was in the 10th grade, and everyone else was used to the way they did things, but I never had a school where they didn't give me a book and where everything was lectures."

And so I learned that Nora was spending her high school years in a school whose teaching methods were completely different from anything she had experienced previously, a school where she had no established friends in the student body, and a school whose style of teaching was the polar opposite of her style of learning.

[Dunbrook, a private school, kindergarten through Grade 12, keeps its students with the same teacher, whenever possible, for all the elementary years, and teaches curriculum in blocks called "Blocks of Lessons," concentrating on only one subject for a set span of time, from one to four weeks. Students get the bulk of their information from the teachers' lectures and class discussions. There are some specific supplementary readings, often historic or scientific "primary sources," i.e., the original documents, distributed as photocopied hand-outs, but there are no textbooks. In short, Dunbrook is a perfect place for students who learn well through their ears. The students are expected to take detailed notes and copy material printed on the board, eventually to be assembled into Learning Block Books which they illustrate elaborately in their own individual styles. As for the social reality of Dunbrook, the bulk of the student body had bonded, many for 10 years, a reality that must have intensified the challenge to gain acceptance by a new arrival, our Nora, in the 10th grade.]

Late December

In the following sessions, I ask Nora's permission to do some testing to try to find out the particular strengths and weaknesses that would make up something I described as her "learning profile." Although Mrs. Tarlow had not found, spoken of, nor given me any previous evaluations, Nora reported that she had indeed been tested before, but no one had ever told her the results or included her as a partner in the understanding of herself as a learner. I assure her that I will share the implications of each individual test on the spot, as I understand it, but that the actual scoring, her "numbers," will take more time, and once that is completed, the meanings of the numbers, too, will be shared. I also tell Nora that as much as I learn from the testing, I learn even more about her from observing *how* she does things during our actual work together. The HOW is the key for both of us to understand why learning has broken down for her.

[This kind of demystification of testing and the inclusion of the client in understanding the purpose of each test makes a huge difference, I have found, in their level of cooperation and effort. As it turned out, Nora's numbers were discouragingly low in and of themselves, but I would never give such numbers any significance until I could justify the reason behind them (see Appendix D: Test Scores from Testing by Dorothy Ungerleider).

The particular diagnostic test most favored by educational therapists at the time of my early work with Nora was the Woodcock Johnson Psychoeducational Battery (WJPB), the precursor to the current Woodcock Johnson Revised editions (WJ-R and WJIII). We were thrilled when this was first published because it was such a comprehensive tool for providing an overview of the areas of achievement, processing, and cognitive skills, written for educators as well as psychologists to administer. The advantage for educational therapists to do at least some of the diagnostic testing on their clients is that it allows us to observe the behaviors and individual styles firsthand for clues at to the hows and whys of their responses. We can also question and probe when the opportunity arises to learn more than we ever could from just reading a score generated by another tester. Such a customized testing process takes more time, but it can be spread out over several sessions instead of having the one or two intense four- or five-hour days of testing that usually occur during more comprehensive psychodiagnostic test batteries by specialists in assessment.

The WJPB had two basic parts: Cognitive Tests and Achievement Tests. We could obtain a baseline of data from this tool and decide whether to supplement this with other achievement, reading, and perceptual tests to fine-tune our knowledge about the client's major areas of deficit and strength. If more specific or intensive assessment still seemed to be indicated, we could then refer our clients to specialists in speech/language, psychology, sensory integration, neuropsychology, vision therapy, or other areas of specialization.

The cognitive subtests of the WJPB examine fundamental skills of memory, sequencing, visual and auditory processing of information delivered variously to the eyes and the ears, and the broad range of language capacities, such as the ability to understand oral instructions, retrieve words from memory in order to give answers, demonstrate familiarity, comprehension, and application of vocabulary, as well as apply language-based and non-language-based strategies for various kinds of reasoning and problem-solving. The Achievement portions measure the range of aspects of reading, writing, and mathematics, as well as general knowledge acquired from school, family, and the culture.]

The signs of Nora's language struggles were clear right from the start of the cognitive testing, but there was another equally troubling pattern. Nora was *afraid to guess*—afraid to risk being wrong. I observed the fear taking form in the long silences, the puzzled facial expressions, the intense stare at my face for some clues to guide her. Her tendency was often to say, "I don't know" and then give up.

[These were the scoreless aspects of testing, the critical information-by-observation that fleshed out every clinician's toolbox for evaluation of difficulties, strengths, and intangibles that factored into each individual's performance.]

Nora struggled with every test that involved complex oral directions, even those that did not require a verbal response, such as the tests involving pattern and design analyses. If the spoken directions involved several complex sentences delivered at once, confusion and doubt ensued, not just from the wording and sentence structure but from some of the test formats themselves that were unfamiliar to her. However, there were breakthroughs. With encouragement and specific guidelines, Nora actually began to develop some new mental strategies for the problem-solving, learning from the "feedback," i.e., the standard test instructions that allow the examiner to tell students which items were answered correctly and which were wrong.

[These were very positive, hopeful signs for me to observe because Nora's effective use of test feedback hinted at her learning potential, her teachability. She also developed areas of trust because this testing experience would take place in a mode of encouragement, not one of pressure like the kind she experienced during school tests.] When portions of the test had time limits, however, all of her effort stopped. [This is a pattern too frequently true for individuals with compromised learning skills. Time is their nemesis—a time limit inhibits their thinking.]

Another pattern surfaced during the tests of non-verbal skills and reasoning, If the test items required a repeat of one kind of rule, much like math workbooks that had full pages of all subtraction problems or all multiplication problems, Nora could gradually master the strategies through trial and error and keep applying her newly learned rules. But when the items became a mixture of five or six types that all required different problem-solving procedures, she was once more defeated. [Here, then, was another clue: Nora cannot handle what is called "shift of set"—the ability to shift one's thinking from one kind of plan to another according to the demands of a problem.]

During the tests involving conceptual thinking and basic knowledge, once again *the individual answers rather than total scores* gave more meaningful insight about Nora. For her, one unfamiliar word would render the whole sentence or question misunderstood. Nora had never heard, for instance, that "kid" could mean a baby goat, so a question using that word seemed like nonsense to her. She confused the categorizing of Paris, rather than France, as the "country." She had no answer at all when asked, "What organ in the body takes in the air we breathe?," being stumped by the word "organ" used in that context. Word meanings became jumbled, interchanged—is it continent or country, infinite or infinitive? She was clearly embarrassed by her confusion. Unfamiliar wording, unconventional syntax of test instructions, like "Count backwards by 3s from 50" threw her. "You mean subtract 3 from 50?" She needed questions repeated, reworded, paraphrased so that she could understand them.

In the midst of that potentially torturous process, my job was to look for every sign of hope—to encourage hopefulness. I helped Nora to see that she *could* reveal which words she understood by their meanings even if she couldn't provide their exact opposites. She could explain, when encouraged to try, that "contaminate" meant "to give out germs," but finding the required synonyms and antonyms, those single words that meant the same or different, was out of her grasp. She surprised me with an occasional unconventional synonym, like the word "petite" for "small," and she was pleased with my positive feedback about it. It seemed that the reason she continued to try on every item was my persistent explanation of the importance of her helping me know *how her brain was working, what she was thinking, how she was reasoning for every task.* On tests involving vocabulary, I urged her to search her memory for explanations of what the words meant to her and where she might have heard them.

[This is not a conventional way to administer standardized tests, but I knew her low scores would not be compromised, since I was not coaching her with any answers. I was just probing to see how her brain worked—the strategies she used in solving problems and even how she arrived at the answers that would be scored "incorrect." The Hows of her thinking and the Whys of her responses would inform all of our work together.]

The tests of her ability to process sounds brought a different kind of torture for Nora. During the tests of sound blending (blending isolated sounds into words, like "buh-ay-bee" for baby) and auditory closure (the ability to supply missing pieces of messages by guessing, as one might do in hearing a lecture in a noisy room, like hearing "_ocket" and guessing it could be "pocket" or "rocket"), Nora was very intent, listening hard. During these tests, delivered by tape-recorder, Nora did something unique. When I asked how she was trying to get the answers, she explained that she was trying to *see* the sounds as letters, to *see* what was being said to her ears, and then put them, visually, into words. She couldn't succeed. It was coming too fast, and her wrinkled brow signaled defeat. But now I understood her efforts to visually compensate for "brain wiring" that didn't send the right signals for these orally delivered items.

[Regarding the need for auditory closure skills, normal listeners automatically fill in the missing segments while being completely unaware that anything is missing at all. Individuals with certain types of APD or language disorders may have a general idea of what the message means (as Nora does in the next test, below) unless they are completely unfamiliar with the vocabulary or context being discussed. In that case, they are frequently unable to fill in the missing segment and may miss the information completely (Bellis, 2002).]

The next test required Nora to repeat dictated sequences of sentences and numbers. Her performance verified again some classic signs of problems with memory for auditory sequences of words. "The school bells rang through the halls today." Now you say it, Nora. "The school bells rang and . . ." She lost it.

With encouragement to keep trying, she did reveal another important compensation: she could repeat the *general meaning* of the sentences dictated to her, even though she could never say them verbatim. This information was extremely useful because it helped explain how she could take in some kinds of knowledge from her environment, even if the intake was incomplete. Again, I shared with Nora my insight about this newly surfaced strength. It had never occurred to her that something good could be learned from a wrong answer!

Next we explored Nora's capacity for "active working memory," the ability to hold information in mind while you do something with it, such as taking notes during lectures or following a sequence of oral directions. [**Working memory is bound to be impacted by auditory processing disorders. Working memory difficulties are especially troublesome for doing complex math problems requiring a sequence of steps, procedures, and number facts that all have to be held in memory while the problem is being solved.**] For one particular test of working memory, Nora was given sequences of numbers and asked to repeat them in reverse order. She could only reverse three numbers correctly. Once again, she tried to *see* the numbers to mentally "read" them backwards rather than hold the oral sequence.

The impact of impaired working memory is so global that I couldn't bring myself to explain this yet to Nora until I could put the explanation in a context she would understand. We would have lots of time in our ongoing work to clarify what these diagnostic terms meant, once I could find the key to Nora's way of learning.

During the tests of Nora's visual system, I was now alert to speaking more slowly and keeping the oral instructions simple: "Find the little puzzle pieces that make up this design. Choose the right ones." Or, on another test, "Find two identical pairs out of a choice like this: 694 469 649 496 964 649. Find the two. Circle the two. Do it fast, Nora . . . Oh, they *do* all look alike, don't they?" She did pretty well, compared to the auditory tests. Too bad, once again, that these were timed tests.

Time issues surfaced everywhere; Nora needed *time* to take information in and *time* to respond to the best of her ability. A few of her performance errors also showed remnants of old torments—the letter reversals—knowing the b from the d and the 13 from the 31— that must have plagued her in the early years. They were still there—usually in hiding, but waiting to cause trouble when she least expected it.

The tests confirmed that Nora's trouble came from three different systems. Hers were not just language comprehension or auditory processing problems, which in themselves were formidable. Her brain was also scrambling visual symbols. A triple whammy!

[**As the test profile unfolded, I couldn't help wondering how this information was just being uncovered. Nora Tarlow was now 17 years old. Finishing 12th grade. At lecture-heavy Dunbrook. Are we just finding out that Nora can't hold on to what she hears? Was anybody aware of that when they counseled her to go to Dunbrook? What kind of testing had been done before? Even if it had been lost from all the moving over the years, did the Tarlows ever have these processing problems explained to them? The growing list of questions would provide my road map in the search for answers, but it also verified what I had learned from**

my years of practice: auditory processing disorders were the least visible and least likely to be suspected by teachers as a cause of weak school performance. Most teachers simply hadn't heard about them.]

* * *

At this break in the testing, it was time to help Nora understand, without alarm, the general meanings of each group of tests completed thus far. We would postpone the whole set of achievement tests for a different session.

"No wonder you have such struggles, Nora: you're in a school that does everything by lecture—to your *ears*—but you seem to learn best through your *eyes*! How do you manage to get along there at all?"

Her look, open and innocent, studying my face, was a look I'd seen scores of times from others whose struggles with learning had never been understood. It was that guarded, half-hopeful, half-fearful "does somebody really know what I feel?" look.

Softly, she took the risk and began confiding her survival strategy to this stranger who seemed to want to know.

Surprised when I asked her to go slowly, she asked, "Why?"

"So I can I write it down."

More surprise, and then open pleasure when I explain, "This kind of information from you is too important for me to lose. No one knows more about you than *you* do. I want to remember your exact words." **[Was she observing that even a teacher needs to ask for more time to make notes with exact accuracy? The modeling of behavior starts from the earliest encounters.]**

She went on then, but with a new importance to her delivery. "I take notes, real fast, but the words are coming in so fast, I have no idea what they mean, so I just write everything I can, like the titles of the topics. Then I go home and look up the people they were talking about in my encyclopedia to try to understand. I look up the words I don't understand in the dictionary, but then I don't understand the meanings. It takes me from 5 o'clock to about 11 every night, because I'm trying to understand it all, but it takes so long, and I get so frustrated that I usually just fall asleep."

No doubt about it, Nora gets a 10 for Effort. By her age, so many have just given up.

I share that fact with her.

She didn't know.

So much she doesn't know, but I feel confident now that she will learn, that she can learn. The stiff, often uncomfortable format of tests has given us a start. Every session will be revelation; her responses and questions will let us both learn where to go from here.

* * *

I would soon have a different source of insight about Nora. A few weeks later, Mrs. Tarlow located a nine-year-old report of a previous evaluation, done on Nora at age 8, by Dr. James Forest, a clinical social worker employed by a preschool psychiatric center in Los Angeles. The Tarlows had been in family therapy with him since the death of Tracey. They had sought the evaluation owing to Nora's school struggles and behavioral issues.

Based on Nora's scores on the Wechsler Intelligence Scale for Children (WISC), Dr. Forest described her overall scores in the lower range of normal with "a striking discrepancy" between her higher scores on performance subtests than on verbal subtests. In fact, he found that if she could actually handle test materials manually, the performance scores were even greater. She would skillfully manipulate a group of blocks according to size and color, but if asked to verbally explain various categories into which the blocks could be put, she was speechless.

Dr. Forest noted that she didn't seem to understand what was said to her very well and described her thinking as "concrete and unreflective" [referring to her better understanding of real objects or experiences that could be seen or touched rather than more abstract concepts]. When she was asked to arrange a set of pictures in order to tell a story about them, Nora arranged them at random and related what was happening in each picture without reference to the one before or after. [One has to wonder, looking back, if she really understood what was expected of her, of if she just heard the words "tell a story" so she told one for each picture.] Her especially low scores on subtests called "Information" and "Comprehension" suggested that Nora was not picking up general factual knowledge or the common-sense judgments to respond to life situations that most children get from daily exposure at home and in school.

Dr. Forest speculated, "She may see and hear things but she is not integrating them into a system of knowing and responding at the level expected for her age. Further, she is not formulating or asking the questions that another child might use to get information about something she doesn't understand." He noted her good motivation when test items were concrete or involved rote memory. During the test called Coding, where she was asked to fill in blanks to match the numbers to the symbols according to a certain code, he observed Nora's desire to fill in both sections of the test, even the one for younger children. His conclusion was that "blank spaces rather than wrong answers seem to make Nora anxious," and he guessed that, on a page of arithmetic that was too hard, she would probably need, similarly, to fill in every answer, right or wrong. [That was probably a very good guess by the doctor. This was a child who wanted to do the right thing but did not have a clue about how to find the right answers. Just fill in the page.]

Nora was equally enthusiastic about the Bender Visual Motor Gestalt Test, a measure of her visual perception (visual interpretation of the shapes and their relationships in space) and her visual motor, or hand–eye skills. She had to recognize and reproduce the designs in their correct relationship to each other on the page by following the model. Nora was enthusiastic about this test, commenting, "Oh, this is cinchy!" even when her drawings were distorted. She grasped the overall figures and integrated the parts into a proper whole, "but paid little attention to the correct nature of the parts regarding shape and number."

Dr. Forest speculated on the two possible explanations for her difficulty:

"(1) some malfunction in shifting her thinking when problem-solving, which might be caused by any number of factors, such as developmental lag, some weakness in her neural wiring, the nature of the task itself, etc.; (2) an emotional block based in fear of knowing, avoidance of reflection resulting in a superficial grasp of some situations and no grasp of others, leading to simplistic responses given impulsively as the first thing that comes to her mind."

He then hypothesized, "Her cheerful satisfaction with this task may have come from her belief that she did what was asked of her."

Dr. Forest's psychological profile of Nora indicated that she appeared "emotionally immature and insecure," avoiding threatening thoughts and feelings. Misunderstandings that frightened her led her to cling to those around her. At the same time, she detached herself from emotionally charged situations. Some tests indicated her attempt to be "strong in the face of fear and physically active enough to flee or beat off aggressors when necessary," perhaps explaining her preference for boys' clothing during that period of her life.

The doctor recommended continued family therapy, parent education about learning disabilities, educational therapy for Nora, and re-evaluation in one year. I never saw a report of a re-evaluation.

[I especially appreciated Dr. Forest's avoidance of any declarations about Nora's overall intelligence or future potential. I was not surprised at the lack of any tests for auditory processing, since those tests were rarely administered by psychologists at that time. There was such a lack of awareness then, even in the therapeutic community, of the role of auditory processing and the impact of faulty or incomplete input of information upon a child's performance. Although I was never able to contact him directly, I admired his clear reporting about her test behaviors and what they implied, along with his thoughtful speculation about possible causes for her struggles. Dr. Forest never placed Nora in a "diagnostic box" but rather described her behaviors and their possible implications. This information would prove even more useful to me after working with Nora for a period of time. Then I could go back and reconsider Dr. Forest's impressions in the context of my own.]

2

EARLY JANUARY

The Reciprocal Compromise Principle Leads to the Organic Curriculum

Norah's needs determine where we start. We begin our actual curriculum for our sessions by using my credo:

> **Reciprocal Compromise Principle:** *Begin with what your clients* **want** *to know, and soon they will let you teach them what they* **need** *to know. This chapter introduces the meaning and application of an "Organic Curriculum" which will be used throughout the year. Each school assignment becomes a curriculum of its own as it uncovers her limited knowledge base. Unique techniques evolve for making connections between words, concepts, and examples from life to begin lifting the fog of words that surround Nora daily.*

Since there was so much to be done, Nora and I planned the frequency of our meetings—for now, twice a week; more, if needed. With her classes at Dunbrook in full gear, we postponed the achievement tests that day in order to get right to her school demands. Remembering what I had told her about deciding what help she needed right now, she pulled her Learning Block notebooks out of her bulging backpack and spread out her target—the notes for an assignment to write an "ethnography." It was an unfamiliar word for both of us—a perfect beginning—to start with an unknown and figure out not only its meaning but her teacher's expectations for the lesson. Together, we tried the dictionary but remained uncertain as to how to proceed until we turned to the teacher's assignment sheet. It said, "Demonstrate your understanding of observer bias of anthropology researchers. Pick a particular social situation and observe it as if this were a new culture you had never seen before."

The teacher gave an example. "You might study the viewing habits of your family watching the 6:00 News in your house—and note each family member's pattern of viewing. Then interview them about why they did what they did."

That was helpful for me. Through this definition-and-example process, *I* was beginning to understand "ethnography." Not so for Nora. She was totally lost. And she lost no time in telling me so.

"I don't have any idea what to do. I don't even know what he's talking about! I finally figured out what 'anthropology' means, but what's 'observer bias'? And what's 'culture'? What does he mean, 'note each family member's pattern of viewing'? Do I run around and put notes on them while they're watching TV? They'll think I'm crazy! They don't even *watch* the 6:00 News—Nobody's even home at 6:00!" Her narration rose from a low complaint to a high-pitched wail.

No test could have confirmed my suspicions more. Nora's enemy is language. Words. Meanings, double meanings, abstract meanings of words. Like that word "note". A *note* is a piece of paper you write something on. Of course. Touchable, concrete thing-word. So how's she supposed to "note each family member"?

And Nora's almost zealous desire to please, to do it right, became as clear as her struggle with words. She felt compelled to conduct the task exactly as given in the teacher's example. But Nora was not aware that this was "just an example" to apply to some other activity the family might do together.

[How often do we provide an "example" without first checking to see if our students know the abstract meaning of that word itself? Giving an example requires the receiver to be able to generalize—to apply the principle used in the example to another life situation. My turn to "note"—note another area of need. Nora must learn to generalize. From that very first session, it was clear that language and its meaning was so fundamental to any sense of mastery of Nora's world that it had to take precedence over any other goal.]

And so we began a process that day which was to become our formula for Nora's acquisition of language meaning: We would talk about each meaning unit that she didn't understand, whether it was a word, phrase, expression, or a whole sentence, in the context that it was being used, and do whatever it took to make that language real to her.

When I shared this plan with her, she added the most valuable insight of all. "When I learn an idea from a book, I have to see it in real life. Once I've learned it in real life, then I go back to the book so I can recognize it in the book. This is real important for me, because if I just learn a concept in real life, I usually can't recognize that very same concept in a book, even if it's simple. That's why if I learn facts on a subject, and I sort of understand 'em on a test, I may not really understand the meanings of the words they used, or I just may not understand the way the question is asked. And if a question is asked a different way than I was taught, I would have no way of answering it."

Armed with my theory and her self-explanation, we began to tackle knowledge from theoretical to real, from abstract to concrete and back again, respecting the circular path she requested. We started with her latest assignment, "observer bias," "culture," and "noting behavior"—our first curriculum. Nothing else mattered but the *process* of gaining meaning about those few terms. Nora already knew what an observer was, having been one during countless paddle tennis tournaments. We compared the idea of being "observed" and being "the observer," our first entree into the mysteries of the same word with different jobs as noun and verb, although those grammatical terms were not yet mentioned.

"Bias" could be linked to her prior understanding of the word "prejudice," as when we judge people based on our already-formed attitudes. Again we linked the word to her world of paddle tennis. Did any of the crowd have a *bias* about who would win when they observed her match? Was she *biased* about who might be her toughest opponent in the tournament? Was there a *bias* about the ability of men vs. women at her club? Could she understand how people might observe things differently depending on their attitudes, their beliefs? She could. Could she understand that a scientist had to learn to observe as factually as possible and try not to be *biased* but just "note"; that is, to just observe and report exactly what he sees? She could.

From "observe and observer" Nora was now warmed up to accept the idea that she could use the same word with two different functions. It was an easy step to compare "the note" and "to note." Since a note was for writing on, then "noting" could be writing *about* something or taking notes or writing down what you have observed.

"So the teacher wanted me to write notes about how my family was watching the news?"

"That's it, Nora. Observe how they do it, and record the 'how.'"

"And she wanted me to tell it just the way it really happened, and not make up any of my own changes in what I saw?"

"You've got it!"

My first reward, of the multitudes to come in working with Nora Tarlow, was her glow of excitement that day when she left the office knowing how to write down notes about each of her parents' reactions and to remain an "unbiased observer." At the end of the hour, she owned those words—and thus armed, she was a force to be reckoned with.

* * *

Nora, like all my teen and young adult students, was told from the beginning that everything I learn about her, everything I observe, much of what I wonder about, speculate on, and question will be shared. She will be my partner in our joint diagnosis of her. And the best learning will come from our activities together. Feelings will not be left out. Her feelings, my feelings. I speculate about the degree of pain she must have suffered. And hidden, perhaps? Much secrecy, yes? Yes. She verifies it all.

And seeds of trust begin. I propose that she needs a "haven"—a safe place in which she can ask any question about any subject, and she will never be laughed at inside these four walls. We will work on her schoolwork, of course, but much more than that, we will work to demystify the world of words that she hears everywhere but doesn't understand. And that includes this office. She must stop me—question me—about anything I say that she doesn't comprehend. In this room, there is no such thing as a dumb or foolish question.

I instructed her to keep a tiny spiral notebook with her at all times, to jot down words she hears or situations she's exposed to that are confusing, and bring them here for us to learn, telling her a bit about what I call an *"Organic Curriculum"* because each thing that we talk about will sort of grow naturally—one thing from another, "like in nature." To me, organic meant living, and I wanted our studies to be alive, vital, relevant to her life and needs. I related the process to what we had done with the ethnography, and she could see how each word had grown from the one before it. She laughed when I confided that my husband thought "organic" was a foolish, unprofessional word for a curriculum, but it just felt right to me, and what did she think?

Nora took my side. Support, too, can be reciprocal. I expressed my appreciation for it.

* * *

Walter Tarlow, Nora's father, called to request a family meeting so that the family could have a better understanding of Nora's problem. Nora was opposed to the meeting and did her best to avoid or at least to postpone it. I was not yet sure about the reason for such strong opposition, but we scheduled the appointment nevertheless.

Before that family meeting and my initial meeting with the teachers at Dunbrook to hear their perspective, I wanted to finish the *achievement testing*. This would provide some standardized data about 17-year-old Nora's current levels in reading, math, writing skills, and general knowledge. Her overall reading scores on the WJPB, a compilation of three subtests, averaged at a mid-eighth-grade level, but the total never gives the full information. It is the *subtests* in each academic category that reveal specific areas of need. I learned that Nora could read lists of single words all the way up to the 11th grade level, missing just a few exotic words with foreign origins, like "silhouette." Her decoding of "nonsense words"—words that are not real but which use common letter patterns found in real words—was surprisingly high as well: at the 12th grade level. This was unexpected by me because this particular test usually reflects phonemic and other auditory processing problems. By age 17, Nora had obviously found a way to visually recognize and link word and morpheme patterns to the way they were pronounced.

Then came the passage comprehension tests, and there was no room for compensation here for all those years of unlearned vocabulary and basic information. This was Nora's reading "breakdown point." On the "cloze" test of the Woodcock, she was asked to silently read very short passages of increasing difficulty and provide a single word for the missing one, signified by a blank line. The word she supplied would have to fit the meaning of the passage and "cloze" up the missing part to make sense. The task was made more difficult for her, I learned, by the instructions to read it silently.

[Some students are terrified of reading aloud and do much better with the privacy offered by silent reading so that occasional word mispronunciations are not exposed, but some have been conditioned by years of special help to read aloud, and it gives them a kind of confidence that, if they mispronounce a word, the teacher may help. Of course, the rules of this standardized test did not allow for such help, but Nora seemed to need the option of reading aloud, perhaps to force her attention to the text. I offered her that modification. In that way, I could observe how the oral reading allowed her to adjust her reading time to process the overall meaning of the words more clearly.]

Even with the accommodation, Nora still scored at a painful 5th grade level, suggesting her difficulty was more than just attention. I needed more information, so I chose a second reading comprehension test, the Peabody Individual Achievement Test (PIAT), popular at that time, to see how Nora would perform with an entirely different approach to measuring reading comprehension. The PIAT used a picture format. On the PIAT, she had to read a sentence and select from a set of four pictures the one best described by the sentence. In this test, the printed sentence is shown first and then the page is turned to the pictures. I could observe Nora's double struggle not only to comprehend the sentence but to remember what it said on the previous page, out of view. She took extra time reading the sentences repeatedly, no doubt to compensate for the memory demand. There was the "active working memory" struggle again. Her score here was somewhat higher, at a 6.2 grade level, so that she was helped by the pictures but handicapped by the memory issues.

[The structure of a test often claims to be measuring one capability, but equally often

there is a second skill that may sabotage performance on the first. Once more, the lesson of testing is always to watch HOW the client arrives at answers and WHAT gets in the way.]

Nora's overall mathematics score was at the 8th grade level, putting her in the 15th percentile of students her age. Her calculation skills, scored generously at a 9th grade level, revealed her mastery of arithmetic fundamentals, including elementary levels of fractions and decimals, but no mastery at all of any pre-algebra or algebra problems, skills that should have been acquired at a 9th grade level. But the real breakdown in math skills surfaced in the language-intensive test of Applied Problems. These are administered from an easel-type book which calls for the examiner to read out the problems which the student is able to see simultaneously on her side of the easel. She is then asked to solve them either mentally or on paper. Nora had major difficulty doing any mental math computation and gratefully took the option of using paper and pencil, starting from the early elementary level problems forward until she reached her maximum ("ceiling") level. She had great difficulty understanding what was being expected of her when the problems were orally read to her, even though she was following along visually, and she required at least one repeat reading for all but the simplest of problems.

Watching her endure this demand, I could speculate immediately on her *integration* problems—that is, having to simultaneously blend the functions of auditory processing, visual input, with long-term and active working memory. Just on this one academic test, for instance, Nora was being asked to listen while reading, comprehend the question, focus on relevant parts of the problem, know which processes and strategies to use, and know how to *do* those processes correctly. There was only one merciful part of this torture—it was not a timed test. Consequently, Nora took the better part of an hour to complete just 16 problems, of which only six were solved correctly. The end result was an Applied Problems score at the mid-6th-grade level.

Why did Nora keep trying in this situation? I had told her at the start, and she really understood how important it was for me to learn *how* she thought and what parts of the process gave her difficulty. With that rationale she persisted with a kind of noble courage, ending the hour drained but proud.

* * *

The following session, we turned to the one remaining cluster of tests, this one to explore Nora's basic understanding of facts in three academic areas: science, social studies, and humanities. This knowledge cluster provided a window into the ways in which Nora may have acquired as much knowledge as she had. I would probe with each answer, seeking insight into where and how she learned these facts. Clearly, she had been exposed to some concepts, such as "hibernation," but in searching her memory for the word, it came out as "habitation."

[I make a note of that classic word-finding confusion—the words may be in there but she cannot retrieve the right ones when needed—another roadblock to add to her pile.]

Nora had an assortment of problems with this cluster. For some items, she simply could not understand the questions unless they were reworded. On one science question where, I learned afterward, she thought she knew the answer ("skeleton"), she was afraid to guess because she thought the answer would sound "stupid." On another, she revealed her confusion about the way gravity worked, believing it would pull you toward the sun rather than toward the earth. In social studies, she confused the famous people whose names she had learned with the acts for which they were famous. All those names and facts of fame just ran together. However, Nora's star shone through on the humanities portion, an area of definite strength, nearly at grade level. Nora had taken art classes and experienced working with different art media, which provided her with a familiarity with terms used on the higher levels of this subtest.

[Her performance here provided a key clue I was always seeking throughout the testing— the means by which Nora learns best and retains what she learns. Now I felt certain that Nora learned best—and more permanently—by experience. This was very important information for me to know about how best to proceed, and it verified what I had been doing intuitively up until now in our early sessions.]

* * *

There was nothing slothful about Nora as she attacked her new unit from Dunbrook, "The Physics of Light." On her own, she had turned to the encyclopedia that week for a definition of the word "physics" and concluded that it meant "nature." But today she shared her puzzlement: "How can 'physics' mean nature when you're talking about non-living things?"

I hadn't been ready for such a thoughtful question.

"Nora, listen to that question! Can you see that you are a *thinker*? If you can keep asking questions of everything you wonder about like that, you're on the way!"

Nora looked a little stunned by my reaction. She couldn't recall anyone ever praising her for asking a question. In fact, all she could remember was the reactions she got as a little child when she drove everyone crazy by constantly asking, "What does that mean?" or "I don't understand," testing their patience until they responded, "Oh Nora, you *never* understand . . . Stop asking so many questions."

So she did. She stopped asking—for 17 years. She stopped building, storing, and retrieving vocabulary that would be the foundation for all her future learning. Her right to grow had been aborted, not intentionally, but because nobody knew *why* she kept saying "I don't understand."

In the short time that we had begun to work, Nora had already shown that she *could* understand. She just needed to attack the process with a different kind of help. But, one day, when I mentioned that I wanted to "open a door" for her, her facial expression was so troubled that I asked what was wrong. She didn't like the sound of that. It was scary to her. Could I say it another way? So we discussed it, and she chose the word "guide".

"Let's just say that you're guiding me."

I respected the request (not knowing, until years later, why her reaction was so disproportionately strong).

Turning back to her assignment, she opened the photocopied pamphlet entitled "The Physics of Light, Preface to the First Edition of 1810." Of 1810? I knew Dunbrook embraced the philosophy of reading material copied from original sources. But a source from 1810 on the physics of light—for Nora? Stunning!

Impressively, she pronounced the words with perfect fluidity as she read the archaic prose: "It may naturally be asked whether, in proposing to treat of colors, light itself should not first engage our attention: to this we briefly and frankly answer that since so much has already been said on the subject of light, it can hardly be desirable to multiply repetitions by again going over the same ground."

She understood nothing.

That was the first paragraph of the first page. And there were 13 totally incomprehensible pages in the Preface with its 19th-century sentence structure and very strange word relationships. For Nora, we might as well have asked her to read the Bhagavad-Gita in Sanskrit.

She had penciled in her assignment on the cover page. "Sum up" it said as if this were an option, "and put into notebook."

I put the offensive document aside. "Talk to me, Nora. Does the rest of your class understand this stuff?"

"I ask them, but they don't know either. But I think they do, because they pass the tests."

"You certainly seem to read the words well," I focused on her strength.

"Yeah. The other tutors taught me how to read. But not to understand."

I paused to register the impact of that throwaway comment. She had said it so matter-of-factly, accepting that the failure was in the learner, not in the teacher.

[There's no going back, no point in making judgments, but I do note it and move on.]

"Do you have any notes from the lectures? Does the teacher explain it?"

"Yeah, I have notes but he goes so fast and I don't understand. When people talk, the words don't stay in the order they came in when they pass my ears. In elementary school, the scariest game for me was Telephone. I was always the one who blew the message. It always got back to me that I didn't say it in the right order."

She showed me her notes—pages of writings and sketches filled with isolated words, bursts of phrases, and unconnected clauses that testified to her sincere efforts.

We took two words from her notes—the first two: "luminous" and "illuminate"—and tried the traditional dictionary approach. The dictionary told us that "luminous" meant lots of things.

"1. Emitting light, especially self-generated light."

"2. Full of light; illuminated." Classic "dictionary-speak"—our second word being used to define the first.

"3. Intelligible; clear." What was that? Nothing about light there.

Nora had long ago learned to stop at Definition #1 in dictionaries—just get it done quickly. But what was "emitting" and "self-generated"? No help here.

We closed the dictionary and began the work of learning.

"Emitting, Nora, means *giving something out*—in this case, giving out light," I spoke slowly, deliberately, giving her lots of time to take it in, emphasizing the words that needed importance for meaning; "and self-generated means that somehow this thing that's giving out light is doing it *by itself*. Can you think of anything that gives off light by itself?"

She looked around. "The lamp?"

"What part of the lamp?"

"The bulb."

"Bravo. Now, does it give off that light by itself? Does it make its own light?" I began paraphrasing for Nora, saying expressions in different ways, so that at least one of them might have some meaning for her. These multiple versions of all phrases would become a part of all my conversations with Nora from that day forward.

"I think so."

"What lets it make light?"

"It's plugged in—the electricity."

"Exactly. Now try to think of something that gives off light but isn't plugged in; that completely generates its own light—gives off its own light—just like we give off sweat if we're playing too much paddle tennis." I connected the concept to her own life experience, crossing over to another context.

"I don't know."

"Sure you do. Think. What illuminates our whole world? What lights up our world?"

"The sun? Yeah, the sun!"

"You've got it. The big old luminous sun—that's about the most luminous thing I can think of. You see, the word 'luminous' *describes* the sun, and 'illuminate' is just a cousin of the other word. 'Illuminate' tells what the sun *does* to us. You know all that stuff in English that they try to teach you about nouns and verbs and adjectives. Well, all that means is the *job* each word has in the sentence. Like the word 'play'. When you play paddle tennis, the word 'play' tells what you're doing, but if I say, 'you're a playful girl' I've changed the word a little and given it a different job. Now it describes *the kind of girl you are* instead of *what you're doing*. Same thing with 'illuminate' and 'luminous'. If I want to illuminate this room, I want to light it up and that's an action, just like sitting or standing or playing is an action. Lighting up, illuminating, is an action I do to make this room have more light. And 'luminous' is the adjective that describes the thing giving me light, like the luminous lamp or the luminous fire."

"Or the luminous sun?" She made the connection.

"You've got it! Now what about that sun? Tell me everything you know about the sun."

Nora knew nothing about the sun. Or about the planets. Or the solar system or the moon or volcanoes or the origin of the earth. That day, the discussion of two words, *luminous* and *illuminate*, evolved into a discussion and full dramatization of the solar system with tennis balls, ping-pong balls, and whatever else we could improvise fast to make the abstract more concrete. We moved the balls around themselves, around each other, ourselves around each other and around the balls and around the "sun" (the lamp). We dropped objects while standing on stools and then on ladders. During that hour, we assumed whatever poses or actions it took for Nora to *feel* the movements of the solar system in space, the movements of the earth and its moon, gravity, day and night, the seasons and their changing hours of light. In passing, we even touched on the Big Bang theory of the earth's origins, the meaning of volcanoes (which are also luminous, thank you), astronomy as the science of the universe—one concept growing, flowing out of the other, in context, in conversation, explained, drawn, acted out until Nora's face showed that she understood each piece in context and was ready for more. Nora Tarlow was indeed the dream candidate for the "Organic Curriculum."

On that day, the physics of light helped us both realize that Nora could learn. Nora was not retarded, which she believed, which others suspected, which I doubted—but we both needed evidence to the contrary. Our very next session gave me even more evidence. Nora remembered *everything* we had discussed in this abstract-to-concrete—and-back-to-abstract, contextual way. For this next hour, I had found pictures from an old *National*

Geographic magazine that allowed her to see for the first time the incredible photographs of earth as seen from space. Her face became transformed, like that of a first grader experiencing the answer to a favorite wonder like why the sky is blue. Her excitement at learning such fundamental knowledge that most adults took for granted shone in a sudden flush of her fair cheeks. A new insight about Nora: she was a blusher whenever she was excited. And learning excited her. (Not to mention how much her learning excited me!)

At the next session, she brought new words from her teacher: *transparent, translucent,* and *opaque.* But instead of the fear and doubt she had shown during the previous week, Nora had a look of anticipation. She wondered what kind of fun we could have with these words, and after the formidable abstraction of "luminous" to deal with, this triplet was a piece of cake. Once we had defined the words operationally, we spent minutes in the room looking for examples and playing with things we could or couldn't see through, and things that just let light through. We disposed of the whole lesson in a fraction of time.

Something was happening to Nora. For the first time in her life, she believed she could learn.

Also for the first time, Nora had a safe place to ask anything and everything. Anything she didn't know, wanted to know, couldn't understand. And she seemed to know that she would never be laughed at inside this office.

3

LATE JANUARY

Seeds of Collaboration

First contact is made with Nora's teachers to build understanding and potential collaboration, including a visit to her most difficult class to empathize with the enormity of her task. We return to the Organic Curriculum, now applied to mathematics.

It was now time for me to make an initial contact with Dunbrook to seek the teachers' perceptions of Nora. Christine Tarlow had signed the necessary release forms that would give legal permission for us to communicate. First contact would be by phone, basically superficial, to establish some awareness by the teachers that Nora was receiving help and that the helper wanted *their* help, *their* input.

[The world of one-to-one remediation is personal, confidential, ideal—and unreal. Educational therapists must be aware that we work in isolation and are missing a whole vital piece in understanding our students in collective settings. We have much to learn from our colleagues in the classroom. Our challenge, of course, is to help them understand the nature and emotional consequences of our clients' learning disorders, as well as reasonable ways they might accommodate the schoolwork to their styles.]

Our team of two needed more "players." The teachers were key recruits with their access to observations of Nora in her world of groups, peers, interactions, responses to classroom activities and assignments—in other words, the real world of school. Their input, trust, and willingness to collaborate was vital. How did they perceive Nora's skills and struggles? From each one's point of view, what areas needed the most work? Was she able to ask questions, either in or out of class? How did she do socially?

John Coombs, the ethnography teacher with whom I now had some secondhand familiarity from Nora's assignments, was the first to return my call. He complained that "Nora doesn't participate" and described her classroom demeanor. "She's always very quiet, smiles and says she doesn't know the answers. Even though I urge her, she never asks for any help with the readings or in other classes. If she does, it's on someone else's coattails." He noted that she seems to pay very close attention but "never demonstrates any competence. She's a champ in sports, but never talks about that either. There's just no high opinion of herself about anything." Then he commented on her few friends, "quiet ones like she is." But, he assured me, she belongs in the class, isn't rejected. Then he concluded: "If she could work at understanding and ask questions, things would go much better." If only John Coombs could know how hard Nora Tarlow worked at understanding! But that would come. This was just our first communication.

Philip Archer, curriculum coordinator (the closest Dunbrook gets to a "principal"), teacher, and beloved friend of the students, wore many hats in this school with a limited budget and an unconventional administrative approach. At Dunbrook, the teachers all serve as a democratic, power-sharing, decision-making body who administer a curriculum and apply a philosophy disseminated from the geographically distant corporate headquarters of this worldwide educational organization. There is no designated administrative leader on campus. Dunbrook provides a true alternative choice for families seeking such unique governance.

A cooperative, perceptive gentleman, Mr. Archer was eager to talk about Nora. He noted that she often tries to sit at the back of the class and hopes to be ignored. He even teased her about her silence—"hoping maybe some day she'll speak." She's "tenacious in athletics, best softball player in the school, but she won't come for personalized help with her academics," even though he urged her to do so.

[Urging, unfortunately, is not enough, and a major responsibility of mine will be to help her know how to formulate her questions, how to interact, what and when to ask, and in her case, to write or tape-record the replies she gets from her teachers.]

The two teachers' apparent consensus in their appraisal of Nora's classroom characteristics was no real surprise. They confirmed my sense that there is nothing devious, fickle, or secretive about Nora. She is who she is—in every instance.

My third school contact was with Mr. Lionel Plant, the new visiting social studies teacher. He had come to Dunbrook on an exchange from a sister school in Europe, and Nora had already expressed her total panic about being in his classroom. I called to tell him I would be working with her, and since there was no textbook, I asked if he could give me some idea of the course outline or direction and overall content. Eager to be helpful after I had briefly explained Nora's difficulty in the most non-technical terms possible, he sent a letter about Nora's new Learning Block, "The History of Architecture," to facilitate my remediation.

I read the letter in double horror, especially this excerpt about the course:

> Overall ideas [about the course] include a) the emancipation of human consciousness from inspired instinct during the course of history, b) the transition of structural systems into decorative motifs especially when adapted by a subsequent cultural center. For instance, the Romans had the arch as structure but employed columns and architraves from Greece as decoration. The Romanesque builders used walls but had radial arcades as decoration, and so forth, right down to the present day, when structural steel shapes appear in bronze as part of the curtain walls of public or commercial buildings. c) a related generalization from b) that the new emerges from the old in accelerated revolutions, but always taking with it central elements from the past. Therefore the true artist architect will innovate without losing touch with reality, etc. etc.

He then went on to comment about Nora:

> As far as Nora herself is concerned, it would seem that she needs more words in her notes. She is not the only one, needless to say. She seems to have such satisfactory outlets for her energies in non-verbal activities that are in themselves not only legitimate but laudable. Therefore the pressure put on her to achieve verbally is most likely limited to separate episodes of inspiration rather than the steady stimulus of competitiveness. Please feel free to contact me about Nora at any time.
> Yours sincerely,
> J.W. Plant

First horror: Most of us write letters in the style in which we speak. Clearly, Mr. Plant was a knowledgeable and brilliant generalizer who loved his subject. But if this was the style in which Mr. Plant spoke, as well as lectured, Nora was doomed.

Second horror: The realization that Mr. Plant had absolutely no background in learning disabilities, nor had he understood my capsule explanation of Nora's. I would have to make my own communication more clear, or, if the teacher was "unmodifiable" I would have to help Nora to somehow survive his style.

The following Monday, before the situation could deteriorate, I visited Nora's Learning Block lecture to hear Mr. Plant for myself, to take notes, and to compare my notes with Nora's during our session later that day. The classically educated and erudite Mr. Plant did indeed lecture in the same style in which he wrote, frequently interrupting his discourse with quick sketches on the board, sketches that Nora felt compelled to copy, attempted to copy, failed to copy because the flow of words continued, and her effort to catch the words took every atom of energy, every millisecond of her time.

Since I had no background in the history of architecture, nor had I, myself, yet cultivated a strategy to cope with the complex syntax and speed of delivery of Mr. Plant, on that day, for that one agonizing hour, I felt a tiny fraction of what it must be like to be Nora Tarlow.

* * *

That afternoon, a furious Nora arrived at my office, ready to vent her anger at this man whom she perceived as "putting her down." She was unprepared for my chorus of agreement, my own expression of anguish, my total empathy for why she felt so lost. I paused there for an explanation of "empathy" and a momentary defense of the lecturer. "No, Nora, I don't believe he was putting you down. That was just his style of intellect, and he earnestly believed he was giving his students his best knowledge. But Mr. Plant is a challenge to anyone."

We compared our notes. Mine were even more sparse than hers, because I had given up trying as soon as I realized the enormity of the situation. Instead of frantically writing, I used the rest of the hour to watch how Nora and her classmates were operating under such stress. Interestingly, Nora was the only one who seemed stressed. In fact, some of the students in the back rows were whispering, not writing, and apparently not paying attention at all. Most likely, I speculated, those were the kids with "insider information," the kids who used their intelligence to find ways *around* conventional study, the kids who seemed to know, almost instinctively, when they did or didn't need to worry. Unsophisticated Nora was not only language-deprived but was unaware of the network of survival strategies which so many high school students employed. Obviously, these back-of-the-room whisperers had other means of getting by in Mr. Plant's class, perhaps by trading the notes of others. I knew that some high schoolers were stealing exams, or (for those few with the greatest nerve) even altering grades before they got to transcripts. Every generation has some individuals who abandon scruples. Indeed, kids learn all kinds of things in life and in school, and not necessarily what the teacher is teaching. Language-challenged kids like Nora know as little about such crafty deception as they do about academic vocabulary. Besides, Nora had no time to "read" classroom behavior; she had to be totally consumed with note-taking.

Our first goal was clear: we needed to craft a survival plan. Nora needed something visual to which she could anchor her thoughts and inquiries. Since Mr. Plant offered no textbook as a resource, we turned to the *World Book* for some context about architecture and its history. [My work with Nora was pre-Internet, so the encyclopedia was still a vital source.]

I showed Nora how to use the main headings, photographs, and outline at the end of the entry to give herself a framework in which to fit all the details. The snatches of information in her notes were remarkably helpful because she always managed to get the main headings. In addition, those main headings followed a temporal order so that, together with the encyclopedia, we could build a coherent body of information generally similar to that presented by Mr. Plant. As we studied the sections on Greek and Roman architecture, Nora's innocent face glowed with each recognition of a word she remembered or had written down in the classroom.

Arches and vaults were easy, but she bowled me over when she remembered the Cyclopean Wall (a clue to her capacity for memorization of detail). She was a whiz at Doric, Ionic, and Corinthian columns, and correctly explained the Ionic fluting in the Christian churches. Between our efforts and Nora's consultations with teacher and friends, the project evolved into a whole, and the completed Learning Block book was turned in. With trepidation, she awaited the verdict from Mr. Plant.

* * *

Nora burst into my office waving the pebbly white folder of her Learning Block book, flipped open the cover to reveal its bold title in upper-case letters—A R C H I T E C T U R E— and two inches below, in brilliant-yellow China marker, a large letter grade: "B". Her first at Dunbrook.

It was whoop-and-holler time. A "B" for Nora from Lionel Plant! This was a day to remember. She directed my attention to the comment, written in precise longhand on the final page of the bound project:

> The fact that you not only consulted your book but also dealt more fully than others with the ideas in the course, which you could not have gotten elsewhere in the same way is impressive, and I appreciate the work and the improvement it represents. I'm sure that your tutor is also proud of you.

[At that time, and even now, most folks regard an educational therapist as a tutor—part of the reason for this book.]

I noticed then that, unbelievably, Nora was *not* proud. Apparently, Mr. Plant had first given her a C, leading her friends (who had used her notes and got better grades than Nora did!) to protest to Mr. Archer, the administrator, who pleaded the case to Mr. Plant. He reconsidered her efforts against the odds of her learning struggles and changed the grade to a B—the bright yellow one I had cheered so loudly.

Given her low level of self-esteem, Nora did not believe that she had earned the B until I spelled out for her that *she had delivered 42 pages of text, illustrated and correctly organized, in her own home on her own time, without my assistance.* Only then was she able to see that perhaps that "B" belonged to her.

When Nora left that day, I reviewed what had happened over these past weeks. First of all, the scholarly Lionel Plant had "joined the team" for Nora with caring words that acknowledged her supreme effort. Second, Nora had reaped a coveted reward for that remarkable effort. Third, she had learned to adapt to a totally incompatible teaching style by using compensations and applying her greatest strength—organization—to produce a better-than-average product. Fourth, we had lots of work to do on her sense of self-worth.

Regrettably, just when Nora was adapting to Mr. Plant's style and he was learning about hers, he ended his brief tenure and returned to Europe, never becoming a full-time player on Nora's team. But for that Learning Block, he came through as something of a cheerleader.

* * *

Testing had revealed the holes in Nora's mathematical concepts, particularly in the area of basic measurement, so that essential topic became the focus of our Organic Curriculum at the end of the architecture learning block. Nora had never mastered the mysteries of pounds, ounces, feet, yards, pints, and quarts. We began with the linear measures, using body parts to keep it interesting. We started with the first joint of her thumb, an approximate inch, and the width of her pinkie finger, a near-centimeter, as units of measure. Using nothing more than those two body parts, she measured small objects in the room, comparing her estimations with actual measurements by ruler. She was thrilled with this new discovery about the "inch-ness" of her thumb and the practicality of body parts for measurement.

Next, we measured the office by feet, using her own feet, of course, and speculated how it was that the 12-inch ruler was called a "foot," giggling that the guy who named it probably had some humongous shoe size. We speculated *when to use what*, a fundamental skill usually taught in elementary school (but not to Nora)—when to measure by centimeters, inches, or feet. She learned to feel the distance of a yard by making 36-inch jumps around the perimeter of the office carpet and then out on the lawn, pretending she was the referee at a football game, pacing out the 15-yard penalties.

When she understood the words, acted on the distances, felt the lengths, and jumped the widths, Nora became a learner of linear measurement. She practiced drawing line segments of different lengths, using her fine visualization skills to internalize the length of a one-inch, one-centimeter, or on-millimeter line. Making a personal connection to the size of a millimeter—the thickness of a dime on its edge—she squeezed the dime sideways as I told her the story of an old cigarette commercial that boasted it was "a silly millimeter longer" than others. She suddenly understood how silly that millimeter was. Nora was a smoker.

The following week, we moved on to volume and mass measurements—the pounds, ounces, kilos, cups, quarts, and so on, weighing everything in cupboards, pouring water or rice into different sized containers, studying cartons and cans of grocery store products to understand their measurement markings, and estimating without looking so that she could guess the fluid ounces in a Diet Coke or the ounces of weight in a package of hamburger, an apple, or a cookie. The key to her learning was in the doing, feeling, estimating, and finally, generalizing.

The real-world reward came that day in the market, when Nora's mother casually asked her to "go get a half-pound of bacon from the case." Nora panicked as she looked at the pound-sized packages and two different kinds of smaller ones. Suddenly she connected the meaning of the "8-oz." package to her newly learned fact that 16 oz = 1 pound. She proudly delivered the package to her mother's cart, pleased about what she had just figured out. Still, the full impact of her joy at that mini-victory had to be muted until she reached the privacy of my office. Who, besides Mom, can a 17-year-old tell about such a "trivial" victory as understanding the meaning of a half-pound of bacon?

[In time, this would be the kind of example that could be used to help Mrs. Tarlow expand Nora's life skills. I noted the incident, to be shared in a future parent conference where we could discuss real-life ways to build Nora's familiarity with "common knowledge" that remained uncommon to her.]

4

AN ATYPICAL FAMILY MEETING

*I had already gathered the history data from a previous meeting with the Tarlows.
The bracketed information below offers guidelines for family meetings in general:
effective ways to connect and attain the most useful exchange of information. This
meeting's more atypical goals were: (1) to meet the whole family, see how they
interacted as a unit, and learn how each one perceived Nora; (2) to explain the
nature of Nora's problems and enlist family members' help by teaching them how
to communicate with her in a different way.*

Tonight is my first meeting with Christine and Walter Tarlow since our initial history
gathering. This time, the whole Tarlow family, including brother Rob and sister Carrie,
are here at their parents' urging so that all of them can hear my thoughts about the nature
of Nora's learning struggles. It's been a challenge to find a meeting time to accommodate
all of their schedules. And most reluctant of all, of course, is ambivalent Nora, who always
dreads the unknown.

[Parent meetings are usually for information gathering, goal setting, and trying to
build some working relationship so that we are all in agreement about the path we will
be taking and the purpose of our work together. Whenever possible, it is essential that
both parents be there. This even works for amicable divorce situations. Usually, I begin by
asking both parents what they like about their child—what they each see as strengths
and admirable qualities. Then I ask what are their concerns and the things they wish they
could change—what they see as weaknesses, troublesome patterns of study, and learning
issues. Next, I ask about developmental, health, and school histories, probing for further
details under each topic. For the developmental history, I look for anything out of the
ordinary —any exceptionality of precociousness or delay, infant sleep and eating patterns,
favorite preschool play activities, and social issues. The health history questions probe for
problems with vision, hearing, allergies, serious illnesses, surgeries, chronic ear infections,
or accidents.

Also during this meeting, we will go over test implications both from my own testing and
test reports from other specialists, simplifying any professional jargon the parents don't

understand. The goal here is to try to explain the client's strengths and weaknesses in understandable language, all the while gathering information from them about their perceptions of their own youngster. **The cardinal rule, too often forgotten, is that parents are THE experts on their children.** No professional has logged the number of hours most parents have put in, and any professional who forgets that or fails to respect and listen carefully to these incredibly valuable reporters is bound to lose the most essential allies in the helping process.

Many educational therapists send out extensive questionnaires in advance of this meeting, so that they can read the responses beforehand and prepare additional questions. I have found that many parents leave out a great deal of information, especially if the questionnaire is very long, so I prefer an open-ended interview session based on my basic list of questions to ask. This allows me to pursue topics as they arise—ones that may never have been anticipated for inclusion in a standard questionnaire. This meeting also provides the opportunity to observe the parents' relationship with each other and whether they both support the same positions about the client. Sometimes, although rarely, siblings are included in these meetings if there is a particular purpose, as there was in Nora's case.]

The Tarlows arrive on time—all but Nora, that is, who has decided to come separately. Christine and Walter introduce 20-year-old Rob and 13-year-old Carrie, who look mildly irritated at having to give up their evening to attend. They look around the room, then take seats in chairs across from the couch where Mom and Dad have settled.

I banter a bit, first with the conservatively dressed Rob and delicate-looking Carrie, sensing their apprehension, asking how *they* do at school and if they wish they could do better in certain subjects. After some moments of silence, Rob shares that, even though reading is easy for him, he doesn't like to study. Carrie admits shyly that she has trouble with tests—all kinds—and then falls silent.

A knock at the door interrupts us as Nora arrives, apologizing for being late, and avoiding the family's glances.

"Come in, Nora. You're not late. We were just getting acquainted. Come join us. We were just talking about people's different strengths and struggles."

I switch attention to the parents, directing it first to Christine Tarlow. "And Mom, what kinds of things do you wish you could do better?"

Everyone starts to giggle, the family's laughter implying that Mom has lots of things to work on.

Mrs. Tarlow, unflappable, gives a hoarse laugh and, with certainty, says, "I need to be organized."

Nora breaks up at that, and they all agree that Mom has a major organization problem. And finally, "Dad, what are your thoughts?"

Getting the floor for the first time, Walter Tarlow seems to relish the opportunity, perhaps using me as a witness to be sure his family hears him. "I wish I could run my family! I don't really know how to express it. . . ." There was an extended pause as he searched for the words.

Filling in, I asked, "Do you mean to get everybody together so you're all following the same plan?"

"Yes! So we're all on the same antenna." [Antenna: I noted the interesting word choice and wondered fleetingly if Mr. Tarlow shared some of Nora's struggles with word-finding, a problem that often runs in families.] He shared his frustration about the general lack of cooperation, the constant battles about who should do what, and the elusive wish of almost every parent for a calm household.

With that, I explained the purpose of our meeting: for me to clarify my perspective of Nora's learning problems and for them to describe how they perceive her, and how we could work together to help her function more successfully.

I started by explaining her unusual kind of a problem. "It's one that you can't see just by looking at her. She has a problem giving meaning to language that she is receiving—that's spoken to her—especially when it comes in too fast, or if there's too much of it at one time. Some diagnosticians call it an 'auditory processing problem.' That means how the brain gives meaning to what the ears hear. Maybe when I explain some of these things to you today, the kinds of interactions you've had with Nora over time may make more sense—like those times when you got really mad and annoyed with her, and you couldn't understand why she didn't get what you were saying. Maybe she didn't ask for help, and maybe she just yelled and screamed and everyone got angry."

Everyone nodded in recognition, except Rob, who was rolling his eyes.

"Rob, does that ring a bell? Does that sometimes happen—that Nora doesn't seem to understand the point you're trying to make?"

"Oh, no, no, no . . ." Rob sounded annoyed then. "Look, I have no idea what's with Nora. She tries a lot, but I always thought her problem was that she tried *too* hard and got frustrated easily, and I noticed . . . I'm not putting you down for this, Nora, but it's a fact that if you walk in her room and she's typing something, there will be over 50 pieces of paper rolled up on the floor and you open one and look at it and it's a perfectly fine piece of paper. There might be a little smudge mark on one of the e's or something—and she'll throw it out and get frustrated."

"Got any idea why she does that?"

Rob quickly hypothesizes, "I think she's a perfectionist."

Checking out Nora's take on that: "Nora, do you think you're a perfectionist?"

Nora concurs with a barely audible "Yes."

Mrs. Tarlow joined in on a topic that touched her. "I think that's very interesting what you brought up about the paper, Rob. She knows she *can* type perfectly, but if it doesn't look perfect to her, she crumples it. And when she draws, too, she does the same thing—she will throw away a pile of sketches until she gets one that looks right to her."

Rob went on with his interpretation, describing his attempts to tutor her. "There were some times when I could get a point across to her, but there were too many times when I'd try to be as careful as possible in how I explained it, and she would still be too erratic, and when she doesn't understand something, it's like it just drops out of her system and she just forgets it all."

"That's really a helpful description, Rob. When these things happened, did you ever consider that it's not because Nora wasn't trying to understand?"

"I know that she tries, but . . . well, I have had some very successful times tutoring her, like math homework—division or fractions or something like that."

"She mentioned that was very helpful. And she mentioned that you tried to help her with the Constitution. How did that go?"

Nora, suddenly animated, jumped into the conversation. "You had a lot of trouble, remember?" She reminds him of some word that she didn't understand. "And you kept giving me the meaning of the word, but I didn't understand it."

"Yeah, but I didn't know you were having problems with it when I gave you the definitions."

"I did! I kept going back to the book and looking at it."

"But you never came back to me!"

"I did! But you kept saying the same thing, and I just didn't get it."

Their dialogue provided the perfect example to help the whole family understand the breakdown points for Nora's learning.

"Nora, you just hit on the answer to what you need. Rob kept repeating the same explanation over and over, without finding different words that might have worked for you. That's what we want to be sure everybody hears tonight. *You need things said in different ways—not just repeated.*

"Let me explain what I've learned about Nora's style and struggles, so that, hopefully, it will help you. She can understand lots of words, especially the nouns—the naming words that label all the 'real stuff' of our world. But the abstract stuff, those words that stand for emotions or things we can't see and touch—and the way those words are used in sentences—none of that has real meaning to her unless she can *link it* to something she already knows or a situation that's given her some *experience* with the word."

I then shared with the family our lesson on the words "luminous" and 'illuminated," the exercises we did with real objects to help her visualize the concepts. After that, Nora could understand that a star is hot and luminous and that the moon, just like the planets, is cold, and is illuminated by light from somewhere else.

Rob wondered aloud: "Are you saying that she understood it after you did all that?"

"Yes. Absolutely. She really did understand it, but only after we went through the whole hands-on process. When she reads it in a book, it just doesn't have any meaning for her. Once she *gets* it, though—really owns it in this experiential way— she's able to understand it in the text. And best of all, we don't have to ever go through that process again, because she really remembers it!"

Rob grew quiet, thinking.

I went on with the presentation I had planned for this meeting. "Now let me just share some basic information that may help. You need to know something about brains. You may already know some of this, so please be patient with me for a few minutes. Every brain is different. And every part has a different job—whether it's being in charge of language, seeing, hearing, singing, coordinating movements in paddle tennis, driving a car—in other words, everything we think and do. The key is that all of us do better or worse in some of those brain parts than in others. All of us have different areas that give us trouble. For Nora, her area of trouble is in grasping the meaning of language as it comes at her fast— every day in every situation—and *it affects every moment of her life*! It makes her feel separate from friends, and even from family, when everyone tries to explain something to her and give her more words than she can comprehend in that instant."

All of them were listening intently, so I used that moment to bring out Fred Gwynne's marvelous children's book, *The King Who Rained*, an illustrated collection of children's misconceptions about language. The cover had a picture of a king with rain coming out of him to illustrate the title. The opening page, "Daddy says there are forks in the road," showed how the young child pictures a fork, the eating utensil, just sitting in the road. In another illustration of the mother's body as a bridge over the creek portrayed the child's interpretation of the expression "Mommy says not to bother her when she's playing bridge."

Christine Tarlow really laughed at that one, because she remembered sharing with me that exact experience of Nora's misunderstanding about her home bridge games during our first meeting.

I needed to explain why I had chosen a children's book for my mature audience. "I'm not showing you this to have you think of Nora as a little child but to feel what she might have been experiencing at any age when her world of language was like this book—when she misunderstood words that most of us use with clear understanding . . . when the meaning of what she's hearing becomes all mixed up." Out of the corner of my eye I could see Nora relax her posture and sit back in her chair, giving a barely audible sigh, showing relief that this information was being exposed to her family.

"The point that I'm making is that if you don't understand these kinds of things, all the language around you is a confusion. Nora says she doesn't remember hardly anything of her early years of childhood. Now, there may be a lot of reasons why she doesn't remember. Your parents have told me, Nora, how they really thought you were hyperactive and that you used to have a lot of accidents. And I really believe, just in the little time I've known you, that you believe nothing you do is ever good enough. You just confirmed that truth, Rob, with those 50 pages crumpled up—that Nora really doesn't think very highly of herself."

"That's her problem," Rob concurred with a new level of agreement.

"Yes, that's her problem, but I believe it's not just an emotional problem. It becomes an emotional problem, but it didn't start that way."

"I don't understand what you mean," Rob challenged.

"I believe it only becomes an emotional problem after *years* of feeling different, years of feeling wounded by never understanding what other people understand."

"Are you basing that on one example, like that luminous stuff?"

"No, no. That was just an illustration of the kinds of word struggles she has *all the time*, in every situation in life. She gives most words a literal meaning, whether it's in a textbook or a teacher's lecture, on TV, or in a conversation with her friends. When she listens to her friends or to all of you in the family talking about something and says, 'I don't understand,' she reports that, all her life, almost everyone always told her, 'Oh Nora, you never understand. Just stop with the questions already.' So she stopped asking. I don't know exactly at what point she stopped asking, but once she did, she got herself into even more of a hole, because she stopped building her vocabulary."

They all grew silent, seeming to consider the theory I had just presented, perhaps feeling guilty about their role in it, a feeling so many of my clients' parents had expressed over the years. Dealing with the unspoken, I said it for them. "There's no need for guilt because no one can be guilty for what you never knew. Let me give you some more examples of potential frustration for Nora. Think for a minute about the language of *instructions*. Instructions or directions usually come in a sequence, one after the other. You know, like when you're lost and you go into a gas station and ask for directions and they start rattling off one cue after another to look for? You have to hold on to what's told to you first and then second and so on—and it's really tough for all of us." Everyone nodded in acknowledgment of that common situation we've all faced.

"For us it's a challenge. But for Nora, with her tricky wiring, it's a nightmare. And it happens *every day*—like all the instructions by teachers when they're explaining a procedure or a lesson or a concept. For Nora, she gets lost after the first instruction. But it's very hard to admit that to anyone."

Drawing Nora in then: "Nora, can you remember incidents, either recently or in the past where this kind of thing happened? Maybe your examples will help the family understand better."

For the first time, Nora joined in the conversation with a new sense of importance. "Yeah, I can. It happens all the time! Everywhere, with everything! Like when my Spanish teacher asked me to get the infinitives of the verb, or something, and I asked her to explain because I didn't understand, she retold me and retold me until the bell rang and she had to leave and I went home to try to do what I thought she said and I did it all wrong. And I looked up 'infinitive' in the Spanish book that Rob gave me, and I still didn't understand it so I couldn't go on, and Rob offered to help."

I had Rob explain, if he could recall, what he had said to Nora about infinitives that day. He plunged in proudly with his recalled instructions: "The infinitive is the full state of the verb . . . OK, take the verb 'to run.' If you say 'He runs,' you're taking it out of context. The term 'to run' is the infinitive. When you change it and say 'He ran' or 'He's running,' that's basically a verb."

"Thanks, Rob. Nora, did you understand that?"

"Uh-huh," Nora responded very softly, feeling challenged now.

I asked her to explain it as she understood it, and saw that she could repeat almost his exact words—"an infinitive is the complete form of the verb"—and she could name two or three infinitives—"to run," "to hop"—but when asked what "hopping" was, she said, "It's a verb form."

When asked how "to hop" was different from "hopping," she said it was the infinitive.

Finally, I asked, "What makes it the infinitive?"

"The 'to' in front of it," she declared.

"Yes, you've got it! That's the rule."

"That's all?" Nora exclaimed, smiling.

"That's it. Nora, you said the words, but you didn't make the *generalization* about all infinitives—that they are the verbs in the 'to' form. 'Generalization' means the rule that works every time, with every different kind of verb. The missing step, Rob, was to ask her for four or five other infinitives that you hadn't already given her to see if she understood the 'why' of the rule.

"And *this* is the thing that I'm after—that every one of you can help Nora to learn *so that she can give it back to you* and make the generalizations in different kinds of situations. Not just infinitives. This was just one small example, but I wanted you to see how to slowly help her make self-discoveries. I know it takes time, but when she understands the rules, she can apply them and move on. Just like she made the rules about things that are luminous or illuminated."

Rob defended himself: "But the information I just gave her she gave it all back!"

"Yes. She did, Rob, and thank you for showing us how you did it. I just want you to stretch it a bit, not just give her definitions. Help her look for what *features* all the infinitives had in common. You did a fine job and gave her a great start, but I want you to go the next step. At first she was just repeating your choice of words, but she didn't really own it until she could say the *rule* that fit all infinitives.

"This is a hard example and not from everyday life, but what I'm hoping is that, for all of you, any time you explain something, whatever it is, ask Nora to teach it right back to you and to apply it to different examples from the ones you gave. Then you'll know she got it.

"Please understand that none of you has been unfair to Nora. There's no blame here—not for anyone! It's just that *you* never understood either, and of course, neither did Nora, so she didn't know how to ask for what she needed. Last week she told me about her early tutoring, and she said, 'They taught me how to read but never how to understand.' Can you imagine that? Just reading words, but not understanding their meanings?"

Christine and Walter were both distressed with that revelation about the limited nature of the "help" they thought Nora was getting. [**How could they have judged the tutors when they never knew what questions to ask or what kind of help was needed? They had never even been given a diagnosis for Nora's learning problems.**]

Time was running out for our meeting, and before we stopped I wanted to give them some insight into the impact of these language issues on Nora's *social* interactions—her difficulty with the way her friends discuss different topics.

Nora explained then: "It's not the things they talk about. It's the *way* they talk about them, the words they use. I'm afraid to ask what they mean, and I think they'll tell me to shut up, so I just keep quiet. If we go to movies together, there's so much I don't understand that I hope they won't ask me about if I keep quiet. And that usually works."

"And what about at home? You told me that if you ask Mom, she gives very long explanations, and you get lost."

"She does." Nora directs her answer to Mrs. Tarlow. "Mom, whenever I ask you a question I know you always want to help me, but I'm so frustrated because you know so much about it that it keeps unraveling, and I get lost in your words."

I cut in with a question: "But, Nora, is there a way that *you* can help Mom understand how much you can handle?"

Before Nora can respond, Christine answers my question: "She just says, 'Stop, that's enough.' And then she says she understands, and I hope she's telling the truth."

"You see, Nora, you have responsibility, too, to help Mom know which parts you didn't understand—or to slow her down."

Turning then to Carrie, to include her: "Carrie, how about with you? Can Nora ask you to explain something?"

Carrie thinks for a few seconds, and then offers that she tries to help with the homework, but she usually doesn't understand it either.

We all laugh then, acknowledging that the stuff from Dunbrook is awfully tough language for anyone. I share with them my trip to Dunbrook and my own struggles in taking notes from Mr. Plant's lecture.

Drawing to a conclusion I cut to the final reason that I wanted them all to be here.

"Look, everyone, Nora and I need your help. There's no way in the two hours a week that I see her that I can begin to help her enough, and every one of you needs to be a part of this, if you're willing. The more she can ask, and the more clearly and simply you can answer her questions, the more likely she'll get it. What I've already learned about Nora is that she doesn't forget once she really understands. But she puts the label 'stupid' on herself. Nora is anything but stupid. It's really the opposite—she is hungry to learn. If all of you can be a part of the team—and I know it takes patience—if she comes to you with a question, I would like you to try to find a way, by using different words, to make your answer clear to her."

Walter Tarlow, previously listening but not participating, suddenly spoke up. "I think I have the same problem. As you were explaining a couple of things I could relate to them. Really, I think she's inheriting the problem from me."

"It's interesting you say that, Mr. Tarlow. Many times, fathers and mothers will say just the kind of thing you're saying, sort of a sudden realization about their own personal struggles that were never explained to *them* during their own growing-up years. Often, these kinds of problems with language and other learning issues run in families, and that's why we usually ask if anyone else in the family had similar struggles or diagnosed disabilities. Again, there is no reason for guilt or blame here. It's just the way styles and strengths and weaknesses get passed between generations. And usually, people with struggles in one area tend to have exceptional strengths in another. Once we understand our own patterns we can do what we need to do for success, just as you did, Mr. Tarlow, in your career.

"What I'm hoping for, after tonight, is that some important changes will come out of our meeting. For one, that Nora will be able to ask and will slow you down when she doesn't understand, and that you'll all try to simplify what you're saying to her and explain in different ways."

Walter Tarlow adds, "And that we'll basically understand Nora's frustrations and how to help her cope with it."

"Absolutely. But the reality is that Nora is 17, and she and I alone can't help her move as fast as we would like, so we need all of you on board."

I thanked them for being so patient, so willing to listen to all the information I'd been sharing and suggested we schedule a future meeting to discuss progress, answer new questions, and fine-tune our teamwork. I urged them to call me if any questions arose.

And, with that, we said our polite goodbyes.

* * *

[From this one interlude you can see how parent conferences require all the skills which an educational therapist works to develop—listening, teaching, explaining, interpreting, simplifying, and encouraging. So, when the office door closed behind the exiting Tarlows, my head filled with questions:

Did I make myself clear?

Did they feel at ease confiding their thoughts?

Did they trust my explanations about Nora and feel some beginnings of an alliance with me in helping her?

Do some other Tarlows have trouble understanding complex language?

Will there be a change in how the family communicates after this brief encounter?

Will Nora feel more comfortable asking family members questions, and will they know how to modify their answers?

The questions were mine. Only the ensuing process of our work together will give me the answers.]

5

FEBRUARY

Goal-setting, Present and Future, in a Safe Haven

For secondary school students like Nora, the goals must be qualitatively different from those of elementary-age youngsters. Time is running out before college, and it must be used efficiently to address not just academic but lifelong needs—career and survival issues, the pros and cons of college. In this chapter, the door is opened to serious conversations on future planning, balanced with needs that surface from her school math and language assignments. She also begins a "new word journal" that will be a critical tool.

With the family conference behind us (and survived by Nora), we continued our pattern of the Organic Curriculum for addressing her progress on school assignments. She was having rather remarkable success in class with her specific new patterns of study for mastering the vocabulary as it arose. Acknowledging her increasing independence with her studies I began to delve, casually at first, into her hopes and dreams for the future. Nora, like many older teens with learning disorders, had been sheltered for longer than most from any serious discussion of such a plan. The questions had to be asked. I had to start with a few broad ones. Just by asking, I was beginning to plant the seeds for her thinking about the future:

    Did she want to go to college?

    Did she hope to have a job?

    Did she plan to live alone or with a friend in an apartment?

    Did she hope to manage her own money?

    As always, her face—transparent window to fears and joys—revealed alarm at such adult, as-yet-unasked questions. The only one that brought a definite "Yes" was college. College was what her friends did. Even though her parents didn't expect it, college was an expectation of her community and the circle in which she moved. College was the key to *respect*, the most sought-after of all human responses that Nora coveted. The job-and-money questions were beyond any answers at the moment, but now they were on the table. From this moment on, Nora knew our hours together would probably be reapportioned to address both remedial curriculum and practical life goals.

"College" had to become more than an abstract fantasy. First of all, where did she want to go? She didn't know—but maybe, she pondered, the place where her brother went. The local community college. I was familiar with Rob's college and told Nora about their very forward-thinking program for those with special needs. She was amazed to learn that there was such a program, so I showed her the latest Peterson's guide, *Colleges with Programs for Learning-Disabled Students* (Mangrum and Strichart, 1989) and the even larger (1,568 pages!) Lipkin *Schoolsearch Guide* (1990) that described the kinds of assistive programs available in colleges across the nation.

[Before the availability of computer searches, these kinds of guides, often upgraded annually, not only provided contact numbers, names, and statistical data about the programs at universities in every state, but they explained the specific services which each one provided. Most interesting to students was their system of ranking the relative importance for admission of grade point averages, SAT scores, transcripts, and other student data. There was significant variation in these rankings at the different schools; some saw the SAT as most important while others didn't even require a SAT. There was also a great range of requirements for grade point averages, so that a student who was a late bloomer or who had one disastrous year might look for a school that only required a GPA of 2.0, or one that didn't even ask for numbers at all, such as many community colleges—open to everyone for a chance to start afresh. The guides also catalogued which schools offered which services and accommodations, so each student could consider his or her strengths, weaknesses and particular needs, and then search for schools that met those requirements.]

Nora was pleasantly surprised to read the lists of special services that most claimed to offer, including textbooks on tape, special courses, subject-area tutoring, priority registration, technology, alternative exam arrangements (such as extended time testing), and even note-takers. We studied the index, looking for schools with such programs in our state and even in our city. A smile flashed as she came to the words "Santa Lucia"—confirming what I had said. Rob's college could indeed be a place for Nora to consider.

* * *

More out of a need to please me than herself, Nora faced her fear of the unknown, fought her reluctance, and actually made an appointment to visit Santa Lucia. I'd referred her to a colleague who was the special services program director, a compassionate, highly competent professional whom I'd prepared for Nora's arrival. She welcomed her openly. Nora felt the warmth, really liked my friend, and expressed hopefulness about the program. Her account sounded wonderful. Too wonderful.

The very day after her visit to the college, Nora suffered a freakish accident. She cut her finger, fainted at the sight of all the blood, got a concussion when she landed on the bathroom floor, and stayed home from Dunbrook all week.

I had to wonder: was there a connection between these two events in February or was it just an unfortunate coincidence? How would I know? I recorded the incident in my session notes, linked it to my memory of Nora's accident-prone history as described earlier by her mother, and tucked it away in my mind.

[The goals of educational therapy covered a broad and multi-faceted domain, but it was not my role to explore Nora's subconscious. However, this incident was a warning for me: Don't move too fast. Be careful not to presume connections of cause and effect. Be aware of

potential minefields that would present themselves as we take on the process of transitioning to adulthood. And be prepared to refer her for a different kind of therapy if the need surfaced.]

Regardless of the reason for Nora's fall, we would use the untimely accident and the luxury of an unscheduled week without school (it was the winter break) to get on with our academic pursuits and fill in some holes in her learning. During a previous math assignment, I'd observed that Nora couldn't read multi-digit numbers. This was a perfect time to address such a basic topic that was relevant to school curriculum and life needs. I knew, even if she didn't yet, that the adult world was becoming more and more filled with numbers. Not only would she need to read them, but she would have to develop ways of writing them in correct sequences without succumbing to her earlier reversals, omissions, and inaccuracies.

We tackled the system of numeration by using graph paper for writing each number in its own box and keeping numeric place values in aligned columns. For this lesson, I kept language to a minimum by using "color talk." Using a black marker I drew 15 zeros, each in its own box in the top row of the graph paper, color-coding them in five groups (three per color) by tracing over the zeros representing the hundreds in red, the thousands in green, the millions in blue, etc., and separating each group with a comma. The system, I explained, was really simple: if she could read any numbers expressed in hundreds, such as 435 or 982, then she could read *all* numbers. She just had to know what word to say when she came to each comma.

We talked very little, but went right to the practice of reading real numbers. I wrote 342 in red and she read it perfectly. Then I wrote a six-digit number by rewriting the 342 in green, adding a comma after that in green, followed by three zeros in red, to make 342,000. I explained that commas were always placed between every group of three numbers, counting by threes from right to left, and the very first comma told her where to say the word "thousand." She practiced saying "three hundred and forty two" followed by the word "thousand" where the comma was. After that, we practiced lots of combinations of thousands that we took turns making up for each other until she felt expert at reading and formulating her own six-digit numbers with one comma.

Systematically, we added the next set of three digits and the second comma in the series—the one representing "million," this time in blue. By now, Nora was generalizing the rule she'd learned so well for thousands, and, with very little practice this time, asked to go on to the "billion" group, for which she chose the color orange. I stopped her at trillions, suggesting that might be as much as she'd need to know, "practically speaking." A few minutes were spent explaining *that* expression, and then we took turns testing each other, constantly shifting our roles as teacher and learner. We wrote huge numbers for each other to read, lots of them with zeros in weird places, trying to trick each other with the toughies like 3,040,004,201,100. But she understood it!

She asked how high the numbers could go, speculating that this trick of adding groups of three could go on forever, and was delighted to learn that her speculation was correct—that numbers were "infinite" (with that, I made a huge gesture with open arms and she deduced the meaning of that one herself). However, I added, the wise men of mathematics had arbitrarily decided to stop naming numbers after a specific group they called "googolplex"—the word, at that time, for the highest number group ever given a name, representing ten to the hundredth power.

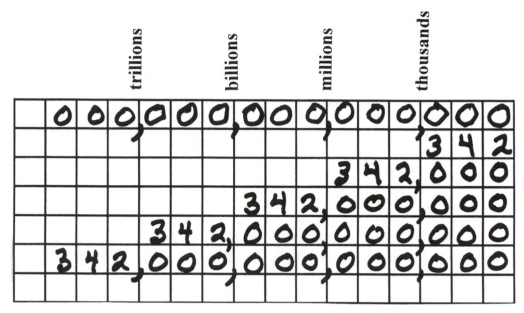

Learning the system of reading multi-digit numbers

And what was "power"? Shifting once again, we explored the meaning of exponents. "Exponents tell how many times we will multiply that number by itself. Ten to the hundredths power means $10 \times 10 \times 10 \ldots$ a hundred times!" She knew it was big, huge, not a number we could write with ease or begin to work with in our life experience. But it was a number that scientists would use to explore things so infinite, like the stars in the universe, which we couldn't even imagine. And so our "organic" tangents of knowledge grew out of each other, connected by context. In that hour's lesson, Nora mastered the reading and writing of large numbers and had taken a brief peek at the concept of exponents.

At our next session we returned to the multi-digit numbers to explore why numbers often had those zeros, the legendary placeholders, scattered between them. I pulled out a box labeled "place value cards," a homemade favorite for this concept. The box contained packs of inch-wide number strips of varying lengths, made from large index cards and held together with paper clips. Each group of strips represented a different set of denominations in the place value system—the ones, tens, hundreds, thousands, ten thousands, hundred thousands, etc., ending for this exercise with millions. The lengths of the strips were determined according to number size, i.e., the cards for ones were one-inch squares, the tens were two inches long, the hundreds three inches long, and on up to the millions, adding inch by inch as the numbers grew. They were designed to be placed in layers, one on top of the other. I had Nora make a set for herself, using one-inch graph paper and taping some strips together as the numbers grew longer than the graph paper. After she had made all the numbers, I had her make a red line on the right-hand edge of each number strip.

The cards were laid out on the table in vertical columns, one column with all the ones, another row for tens, a third row for the hundreds, etc. so that Nora could see the entire array of numbers in each group. Then I asked her to pick one card from each group, layering one atop the other, from largest denomination on the bottom of the pile to smallest on the top. The red lines at the right-hand edges were used as guides for placing each strip on top of the other in proper locations to keep the values aligned—each red line on top of the one below it. For example, she would put a 1,000 card on the bottom, a 400 card on top of that (placed over the "empty plates at the dinner table"—the three zeros in 1,000), a 30 card on the two "empty plates" of the 400, and a 6 over the single zero on the 30 card, until she had created the numeral "1,436." For fun, I had her close her eyes and I'd slide out the 30 or the 400 very carefully so as not to disturb the location of the other number cards. When she looked at the numbers as they were altered, she saw the 0 where the number had been, such as 1,406 or 1,036. (See Appendix B, Place Value Cards, Instructions, and Template.)

And then we'd talk about Why. Why did it work that way? What was the purpose of placeholders? What did she think? Guess, Nora. It's OK to be wrong, but the more you guess, the more you'll learn to be right.

[At every opportunity in our work together, I would encourage Nora's risk-taking to get past her fear of being wrong. Once she realized that she often had a 50 percent chance of being right, the possible success was worth the risk.]

For place value lessons, she learned to be right. One session to learn, one session to review, and the sporadic checking throughout the ensuing months established that Nora could both read and write multi-digit numbers on demand—and understand them. Best of all, she knew what those missing numerals meant, the ones whose spot was reserved by the zeros.

Leaving numbers for a few sessions, we switched to incoming language from her daily life, returning to words and comments she was hearing from friends, from family conversation, from the TV—all the mystery-stuff that surrounded her in every social and recreational situation. I'd given her an assignment to take notes as best she could on the nightly world news from TV, a very difficult task for Nora, and one that provoked her first signs of resistance. However, being an approval seeker she was still willing, reluctantly, to do what she was asked, so she brought in bits and pieces of her unknowns. This week, the "bit" was the news report that the Santa Lucia pier, near her paddle tennis club, was "in danger." How could a pier be in danger? It wasn't human. We speculated on how the existence of a non-living thing might also be "in danger," and the light of meaning came through. Of course! The pier might be broken, destroyed. But by what force? The pier's danger led to talk of tides: high tides, low tides, and the why of tides, returning to our month-old "friends," the moon and gravity. From there we diverged to examine the globe in my office to allow Nora to consider the earth in global form, the globe as a ball, a sphere.

"Try to picture, Nora, that more than half of that sphere is water. As the earth turns and the moon pulls with its gravity forces, what happens to the watery parts? Do they stay still like the mountains and land masses?"

The questions provoked that fine, curious mind to get a whole new picture of the continuous up-and-back rhythmic flow of ocean water sloshing on that sphere, from the western shores of our continent to the eastern shores of Asia, from the western shores of Europe and Africa to the eastern coasts of North and South America. East, West, North, South. Movements of oceans, movements of planets, movements of moons—we connected it all again to our earlier discussions about planetary movement when we had explored the physics of light. We looked through a wonderful picture book about the nature of the universe to refresh her memory of previous discussions about heavenly bodies and planetary movements. Now we could add tides to the mix.

In this way, Nora newly applied the recently acquired "old" (one month old!) knowledge which she'd stored in her brain and which was now available for her to use for this new level of learning. I learned more about her thought processes when I thumbed through her mini-spiral Notebook of New Words with its lists of words, questions, and observations. In that telling journal, I noticed the double entry for February 24:

> When you are standing in one place staring at the moon, could you see that the moon is *really* in motion, or just in your imagination? I ask because I thought that maybe because the moon is so many thousand miles away that maybe you couldn't really see its revolution.
>
> Stars—are they illuminated objects because they give off light that is reflected from the sun? Is the moon illuminated?

I was blown away by the entry—her struggle with concepts, the questions based on observation, the wonder, the risk-taking, whether correct or not, the effort to use the concepts we'd been studying to reveal what was or was not understood—a real gift for this teacher.

And best of all, another truth had surfaced: *Success is not necessarily measured by correct answers to questions, but by the questioning itself.*

6

MARCH

Alternate Routes to Word Mastery, Engaging the Teachers

Nora and I discuss why her SAT scores don't have to determine her future. We acknowledge the vital nature of her journal writing to the direction of our work, and I seek visual sources for vocabulary and concept development, since she is a visual learner. Two movies lead to unexpected surprises and the necessity for field trips for more clarification. Nora's new self-motivation leads to an unexpected action, and our Organic Curriculum ranges from the purpose of tears to the complex language of the Constitution. My quest for teacher collaboration is expanded through a meeting with her faculty to clarify Nora's diagnosis and hear their own observations.

Nora is distressed by her SAT (Scholastic Aptitude Test) scores from the tests she took in the fall semester before our work together. They just arrived in the mail. The 300 on the verbals and 340 on the math seemed to confirm the worst that she believed about herself. She knew that the possible maximum on each score (at that time) was 800.

[How often I had seen the devastating effect on my students of that fateful "Envelope," the rite of passage of the "killer" 11th grade year, with its confluence of SAT testing and beginning applications to colleges. Eleventh grade is also the time when many in high-pressure schools are expected to be taking at least two AP classes, the advanced placement, college-level courses now being taught in high school. Theoretically, the acceleration of these college courses into high school would allow ambitious students to finish college in three years rather than four, saving time and money to allow them earlier entry into the working world. In reality, its purpose has become a test of endurance under extreme pressure and one more competitive measure for college admission.

Saddest of all, the "AP expectation" has institutionalized anxiety in the brains of 11th grade students and parents. Fear and doubt about required qualifications and individual competitiveness is epidemic. A whole new industry has been spawned: multiple companies offering SAT classes, test prep books, training DVDs filled with strategies and practice tests, specialized tutors and "essay consultants" to help students survive the essay requirement for college admission. All this occurs simultaneously while the student is trying to meet the academic demands of the 11th grade and AP curricula—and to satisfy the terror in their parents over concern that no college will take them.

Another job for us educational therapists is to fill in what most parents don't know. Most parents don't know that there are (at last count) 4,140 colleges in the United States! Some are private, some public, some two-year and some four-year institutions—all wooing their children to come and learn, all wanting their money and often willing to make remarkable accommodations to lure students into their programs. Most parents don't know, and it is our job to inform them, that the two-year community colleges in many states will even admit students who failed to get a high school diploma. These "second-chance" institutions allow those who may have rebelled as teens or been in trouble, with issues like failing grades or substance abuse during a turbulent period of development, to make a fresh start. There is no SAT requirement or scrutiny of a grade point average at these colleges. An added plus is that students can often proceed at their own pace, self-determining the number of courses they can handle in each semester. If the students do well in those two-year colleges, they have a further opportunity to go on to the four-year colleges or universities, and some states even guarantee university admissions to those who maintain a B average in the two-year institutions.]

Nora had taken the SAT without preparation, in 12th rather than 11th grade, without private courses, and without the benefit of strategy training (what is often called "test-wiseness," i.e., being wise to the tricks of test-taking). Now that the scores were in, I tried to explain why this kind of test could never really measure Nora in the same way that it did others. I reminded her again of all those years where she was not picking up vocabulary—of her lifelong struggle with words flooding her brain at full speed. Only now, when she had *time*—to think and question and inquire and define—could she categorize word groups with their proper meanings. I tried to comfort her with the fact that even those who never had her language-processing struggles have a dreadful time with the extremely sophisticated language of the Scholastic Aptitude Tests.

All my explanations fell on deaf ears, however. Nora was never comforted by hearing information about others, so we put away the SAT report and moved on. I had just seen a fascinating film, *Quest for Fire*, a film about prehistoric times that was made completely without dialogue other than the indecipherable noises of the early humans featured in it. Because of its unusual nature, I thought it would be great for Nora—thinking, without thinking, that she would understand its visuals and be relieved by the lack of language.

Nora's distressed facial expression from the mere mention of the title told me that something was wrong. I learned then that she was not only familiar with *Quest for Fire*— she had already seen it. Stifling some anger at my mention of it, she let me know that it held absolutely no meaning for her.

Then the truth struck me: Of course she wouldn't be able to give it meaning! Nora had no internal vocabulary or any familiarity with the concepts of prehistory. Another truth is that stories told in pictures require the background knowledge to interpret the visuals. Apologizing for my lack of awareness, I saw Nora become very quiet, perhaps reconsidering whether she wanted to face the unknowns of this movie or just run away from it.

I asked if she might like to talk about it—if I might clear up some of the questions I imagined she might want answered. Questions like "Who *was* 'prehistoric man?' And when *were* prehistoric times?" Her response confirmed that she had no idea.

How totally confusing then to see these grunting violent "animals" that looked like people but behaved like wild beasts! Their open sexual behaviors must have frightened her. When I expressed my thoughts aloud, she confirmed those suspicions, and by then she had put aside her anger and become engaged in the learning. We turned then to some picture books about prehistory to give her the critical background.

Our inquiry led to the question of fire, the "quest for fire" that the title implored us to examine. Nora had never thought about a people that had no knowledge of fire. I asked her to try to imagine what fire would have meant to someone at the first discovery of it—of the total awe those primitive people must have felt when they first accidentally created sparks, perhaps by hitting two rocks together. And imagine, too, I further challenged her, what they must have thought the first time those sparks ignited some kindling material nearby and burst into a flame—a never-seen-before flame. Imagine them feeling the heat on their faces. Imagine dropping something into the fire and watching it turn to ash. We both laughed aloud at imagining them accidentally dropping some raw meat into the fire—and discovering the first barbecue! I attempted, through my enthusiasm in the telling, to re-create the sheer marvel of that incomprehensible moment in human history.

Nora was spellbound by the imagining and revisualizing scenes that previously had been so frightening to her. In the new context, giving new meaning to the images, her face brightened as she responded to imagining this scientific wonder—the miracle of a human's first exposure to a phenomenon so matter-of-fact to us moderns. It had never occurred to her that fire wasn't always there or that the knowledge of fire was something that had to be discovered.

The conversation somehow led to another film, *Gandhi*, which was also popular at that time. At the mention of Gandhi, Nora instantly let me know that now I'd gone too far. Flushing, she shouted, "Geez, Dorothy, you're not going to ask me to go out in the world, are you? I saw *Quest for Fire* and I didn't have any idea what it was about. How could I sit through three-and-a-half hours of *Gandhi*? No one will explain anything to me, and I can't ask! Don't you understand? I can't ask!" Then, a brief pause, and another, previously unspoken fear was shared.

"And I'm even afraid that you'll let me go, too."

Where did *this* fear come from? Was it connected to something she had concluded during our family conference? I absorbed this ruptured secret in a few moments of silence, realizing then the range of thoughts that generated pain for Nora every day.

Slowly, I asked why she believed I would end our work together when we were just barely getting started. Slowly, too, she began to describe her past experiences with tutors and various "helpers" who tried for a while but usually gave up after a short time. Of course, she blamed herself for failing to please them by asking "dumb" questions or by not learning fast enough, or not remembering for long enough.

Then she explained the real source of her worry. Her mother would always ask, "Are you still learning?" and if Nora replied "No," Mrs. Tarlow would stop the tutoring sessions. Perhaps she feared saying the wrong thing and there would be another termination.

As she confessed the story, I felt the moisture rising in my eyes (the dreaded, involuntary, unprofessional plague of tears inherited from my family genes). I looked away, hoping Nora wouldn't notice, but she did. Not surprisingly, she was frightened by seeing me, the professional, with visible emotions. Once again, life becomes lesson. The Organic

Curriculum, adjusted to emotions. We have to deal with whatever comes. People feel. And people talk about feelings.

[**It was my turn to model the behavior of feelings. From that point on, I knew that explanations on every subject, whether academic, social, or life-driven, needed elaboration and examples in order for her to process them.**]

I apologized for frightening her but explained how, in those few emotional moments, she had helped me feel her years of pain and humiliation. "Do you know how hard it is for those of us who haven't experienced such pain to know what it means to you? Nora, your words teach me what it's like not to be able to ask when you don't understand. You gave me a few minutes to be *you*, to try to feel what *you* feel! Just like I did when I was trying to take notes in Mr. Plant's class and imagine what you were experiencing. It's that thing called 'empathy' again. Do you remember that? As for the tears, Nora, all my life I've had this problem with tears when I'm moved by something. When I feel too happy or too sad or too sensitive to someone's problems, they just sneak up on me. It even happens when I watch all kinds of movies. It doesn't bother me anymore, it's just who I am, but I'm sorry if it upset you.

"And, Nora," I came back to the issue she had raised, "I will not 'let you go.' This will be your haven, your safe place to ask anything, for as long as you need my help. *You* will be the one to let me know when we've achieved our goals and when you feel more comfortable in the world on your own—more ready to try to deal with challenges independently. We'll talk about it together and see if we both think you're ready, but when we do stop, it will never be sudden or a surprise, and it won't be a one-person decision. Do you understand what I'm saying?"

She nodded in the affirmative, still wide-eyed at all that I had told her.

"And even when you're ready for that leap into independence, Nora, I'll be just a phone call away if new things come up at different times. Many of my students stop for a while and then call, sometimes three years later, when they need some help on a specific new problem that comes up in school or even on the job. I like to tell them they can come in for an oil-and-lube—just like you get a tune-up on your car—as needed."

[**I often tell my clients that, when they're ready to go on their own, I'm putting them on "Will Call," meaning they will call as needed. I explain that no one ever feels he or she has all the answers to whatever schools and life bring. In fact, we are all "still in the oven, not done yet," and that learning goes on every day, in every situation. The trick will be to try out new skills and see how far they can go on their own but always knowing that they can call on me for help as a safety valve if they really can't find answers. This advice maintains a connection without fostering over-dependency, and it softens the end-point of the educational therapy because there is no final closing of the door. It helps clients feel that I recognize the growth they've achieved, and that I have confidence in their capability to problem-solve on their own. By leaving the door open, so to speak, they know that they have not been abandoned.**]

As always, Nora listened very intently, but I couldn't tell, from her face, if she believed me in that instant. Fortunately, I had asked Nora to write summaries of each of our major lessons for homework, including thoughts and reactions to issues discussed. I learned that she is more comfortable writing in private, and in this way she lets me know what she has understood, or misunderstood, and where I've failed to clarify concepts. Her writings that night, shared at the following session, told me that she hadn't been upset by the tears. Quite the contrary. She'd been deeply moved that someone heard, understood, and felt what she was feeling. And she speculated by using one of her new words:

"I guess Dorothy has empathy with me."

* * *

The following week Nora arrived, grinning and holding up a list. She had rented *Quest for Fire* and watched it again! Only this time she slowed it down on her VCR while she wrote down questions—questions about each and every thing she didn't understand. The notebook became the curriculum as we began our own quest for meaning—beginning with a discussion of primitive man and how the combined sciences of *archaeology* and *anthropology* (two new words) sought evidence to re-create some idea of life in those times before civilization as we know it. Nora was fascinated by our search through reference books and magazines for pictures that would help her understand each new concept. As always, the conversation brought up more misunderstandings that led us down divergent paths— warm- vs. cold-blooded animals, 32 degrees being the temperature at which water freezes, Fahrenheit and centigrade, frost and why it was on the ground, dreams, and the concept of "inner language."

Quest for Fire, in spite of its fearfulness to her, had proven its redeeming value. When I used *that* expression, of course, Nora needed an explanation.

That night, in her word notebook, she penned the following:

1. Redeeming value: Quest for Fire—its redeeming value, in spite of the violence and sex, was that it taught us how people lived before, in prehistoric times.
2. Survival of the fittest (Charles Darwin)—it means those creatures survive who have the best qualities for survival in the times in which they live (also the "fittest" survive competition with sports, in college placement, in the arts and music, etc.)—the most able to survive. For example, Athletes in smog—survival of the fittest—the athletes who are used to smog will be more qualified to do well than those who aren't [related to the Olympics in Mexico City].

* * *

I scheduled a group meeting at Dunbrook with the principal and Nora's faculty to try to explain further, this time in person, the nature of her language and processing problems. I also planned to advocate on her behalf so that their latest graduation requirement— mastery of the Constitution—doesn't become the obstacle to her high school exit. My goal, of course, was to help them understand more explicitly that this young woman, soon to graduate from their school, is of normal intelligence but suffers from impaired auditory processing that affects her language acquisition, her comprehension, and her sense of self. Her expulsion from Kingsley Hall had left devastating scars that influenced her perceptions of every teacher and school experience.

[I knew from years of teacher conferences that I had to carefully plan the way in which I spoke to them. Most teachers are untrained in the terminology, characteristics, and emotional toll of learning disabilities. In order for them to really comprehend my message, I had to plan a strategy for the meeting and to prepare real-life examples of specific

breakdowns in Nora's learning process. **More important, I knew from experience that it
would require tact, diplomacy, and personal passion about Nora's potential under the right
conditions for them to understand enough to actually modify their approach with her.]**

Armed with anecdotes from our work together, I wanted Nora's teachers to feel some
of the confusion that Nora feels daily and to experience language through *her* ears for just
a brief time. If I could win them over in this way, perhaps they would be motivated to make
some accommodations for her so that she could succeed in their classes. Even more
important, they needed to understand why Dunbrook, a school where almost all academic
content is delivered orally, was especially formidable and overwhelming, given her problems with auditory processing.

How *could* they believe that all this information was just coming out when the young
woman was in the 12th grade? **[It was the very question I asked myself, but Nora's handicap
is so commonly undetected. We can only guesstimate how many others are out there, never
properly diagnosed, going through life believing they are "just stupid."]**

I had rehearsed the presentation so that I felt prepared. The meeting opened with the
perfunctory introductions and proprieties. After thanking them for being willing to give
me this time I presented Nora's case, speaking slowly and simply, with a bare minimum of
professional terminology, using examples instead so that it would be real for them.

"Nora has a rarely understood learning disability that's hard to identify. It's an *auditory
processing disorder*. Are any of you familiar with it?" I paused to see if they had, in fact,
heard the term, but no one confirmed any knowledge of it, so I continued.

"She has difficulty holding on to information that comes in through her ears. She loses
the words before she has time to interpret their meaning. She can *hear* the words and sounds
just fine. Hearing isn't the issue. It's the perceiving—giving *meaning* to what she hears—
that's the problem. She might understand isolated words but lose the meaning of the whole
sentence depending upon arrangement of the words—the sentence structure—so that
unfamiliar words, sequences of words, and sentence variations can leave her totally lost."

Then I went on to give them a specific example. "One test that I gave her had a question
about the Great Wall of China. It was worded like this: 'For hundreds of miles, what
condition is the wall in?' Nora was baffled by what they were asking until I paraphrased
it more simply without the introductory phrase. 'What condition is the wall in?' She
understood that question instantly and was able to answer it. When I tried giving her a
series of long instructions for an activity in my office, she was lost after the first instruction.

"Given this problem, perhaps you can guess that note-taking is nearly impossible for
her. She can take simple notes in strings of short sentences, but serious note-taking like the
kind required for your Learning Blocks means she would have to hear, hold in memory,
comprehend, synthesize, extrapolate the most important ideas, and write—all simultaneously and all under pressure of time—because, of course, you keep continuing on with the
lecture." I paused to allow the enormity of such a problem to sink in. "Can you see why
note-taking is probably the most highly integrated task in the whole school curriculum?
And that kind of integration just is not in the realm of possible for Nora, although I know
most of the others can probably handle that lecture style of learning."

They seemed truly interested, engaged. Some nodded, showing a definite kind of new
understanding. I continued, trying next to give them a feel for her literal interpretations
of abstract figurative language and the impact of such misunderstanding even in social
situations.

"Let me tell you what happens outside the classroom. For example, Nora's friend talked to Nora about her father being angry with her for coming home late. But that's not the way the friend said it. She used the words, 'My father hit the roof!' Nora pictured this father literally striking the roof with his hand, and she was completely puzzled, but of course she said nothing to her friend—just listened and nodded, pretending she understood. Then she came and asked me what the expression meant. This happens for her dozens of times every day! Can you understand now why she's always so quiet? Quiet is safe. Quiet lets her hide what she doesn't understand, at least for a few moments."

It was their turn to be quiet now.

"She's completely lost, too, with the sentence variations of grammar. If the sentence, 'The woman brought the boy' was transformed to the passive, 'The boy was brought by the woman,' Nora just wouldn't have a clue that the meanings were the same. And those incredibly long and complex sentences and paragraphs in the handouts you give her, like *The Physics of Light*, might as well be in a foreign language. She tries! Oh, if you could only watch how hard she tries, and the process she goes through! She'll try to analyze, word by word, or sometimes phrase by phrase, looking up each unknown word in the dictionary, writing the definition above the word, then reassembling the pieces to try to decipher the *whole* sentence or the *whole paragraph*. Sometimes, after hours of this, she might, with luck, go on to make sense of a whole chapter." I then briefly summarized our session with the two words *luminous* and *illuminated*, to bring the example closer to home for them. Through these anecdotes, I hoped the faculty could begin to imagine the toll on this conscientious young woman and the hours spent in her tedious segmenting tasks to extrapolate meaning from every bit of language in her academic and social worlds.

They began to question how this could have gone on for so many years, and I explained that no one had ever given the family an explanation for her school difficulties. Since early childhood, when she kept saying, "I don't understand," people grew tired of answering her questions, and so she just stopped asking. She had also learned how to "trick" the test process by reading paragraphs and looking for words that answered the test questions. She got good at it. By guessing pretty well, she could achieve average scores without comprehending anything. She had outfoxed herself, depriving her of the help she needed so desperately. And here we were, talking about it in 12th grade!

I assured the teachers, then, that Nora was definitely capable of and, in fact, very hungry for learning, real learning, when given the time and the means to understand. Then I asked them about their own observations and perceptions of her in their classrooms and whether my explanations helped them to better understand what they were seeing.

Each teacher related different anecdotes, usually offering more evidence in support of my own findings. The ethnography teacher was particularly responsive, noting that Nora didn't really participate, was always very quiet, politely smiling, and saying she didn't know the answers. But she had begun to open up recently with her own life observations. [**I was pleased to learn that our work on "ethnography" had actually generalized to the classroom. Such application of new skills from the individualized setting is a crucial test of the effectiveness of the educational therapy.**]

They all concurred that she never demonstrated much competency verbally in the classroom but seemed to be paying almost painfully close attention. Now they were beginning to understand *why* she took so few notes and never asked for help in the readings. To ask would have revealed the extent of her confusion with this mass of incomprehensible language. The science teacher shared her own observations of Nora's trouble with abstract concepts in contrast to her ability to remember the more concrete facts. All agreed that she had "no high opinion of herself," but again they were starting to understand why. It was interesting, and hopeful, to notice that they were finding the examples themselves that fit the profile so perfectly.

At the end of our meeting that day, three of the four teachers seemed to have new enlightenment and were willing to work with me and Nora to establish a compensatory plan. The fourth remained unconvinced, having come to the meeting already believing that "learning disabilities is a crock," an excuse used by rich families to justify the poor efforts of their "dumb" or "lazy" kids. Three teachers out of four was not a bad percentage, as these sorts of appeals go, especially at the secondary level of schooling. Nora and I would have to work around that fourth teacher in any way we could.

Best of all, we'd won over the school's version of an executive director, Mr. Archer, and the channels of communication had been opened. I couldn't know in that brief meeting what changes would actually be made, but through ongoing contact with the teachers in the ensuing months I observed how they responded to her, what accommodations they made, how they really tried to clarify some of the language they used in their interactions with Nora, and best of all, how they showed new compassion.

* * *

I told Nora my strategy for explaining her learning difficulties to her teachers—her note-taking problems and her difficulty holding information when it came in too fast or comprehending such antiquated handouts as *The Physics of Light*. When I told her of their willingness to work with her differently, she seemed glad but doubtful. She'd been there before.

This talk about the teachers led her to talk about her friends who also don't understand her, and I commented on how *vulnerable* she must be to their criticisms. "Vulnerable" was a new one for her, and we looked up its possible meanings (there is always more than one) in the dictionary to see whether "susceptible to injury" or "unprotected from danger" made any sense to her. She knew about injury because of all her knee problems. Her knee was vulnerable to injury—weakened, easy to hurt—but feelings could be vulnerable too. Her feelings were vulnerable to criticism and teasing. It was easy to hurt her feelings, just as it was easy to injure her knee. With that analogy, she understood "vulnerable." Perhaps her friends could learn more empathy for her struggles. She smiled at that one, hearing her new word applied in yet another new context.

The month of March had brought new challenges, and words like "vulnerable" and "empathy" were easy compared to the formidable task of making the Constitutional amendments comprehensible, one by one, phrase by phrase. We drew upon lots of examples from life, starting with the Second Amendment, because it was about "the right to bear arms." We chuckled because it was such a perfect example of what Gwynne had been talking about in *The King Who Rained*—was it "bare arms" or "bear arms"—and how they were different.

The Second Amendment was one of the briefest, but even then the language was beyond Nora: "*A well-regulated militia, being necessary to the security of a free state, the right of the people to keep and bear arms shall not be infringed.*" "Arms" in this case meant armaments, as in armies, and Nora knew that armies fight with guns, so arms was readily connected to guns. A brief clarification of "infringed" and "militia" was followed by my own paraphrasing of the whole amendment: "This amendment gave the states the right to form their own citizens' army that could carry weapons in case they were needed." We talked briefly, too, about its meaning today. "No, Nora, this amendment doesn't mean that everyone has a right to pack a pistol in his or her purse. That's a misinterpretation." Up came questions about "misinterpretation," and then talk led to the National Rifle Association against the Handgun Control folks, as we moved up and back between the 18th and 20th centuries on this issue of guns and rights.

[Whenever we studied in this manner, words like "misinterpretation" were used deliberately by me and then restated using more common synonyms. I might say, "That's a misinterpretation, a misunderstanding, or giving the wrong meaning." In this manner I was constantly feeding Nora adult language and its meanings simultaneously, in context. Her absorption of language in this fashion, and her later use of those words in our subsequent conversations, never ceased to impress me. It proved, at least for those who learn like Nora, that memorization of vocabulary lists is a futile exercise, but those same words used in meaningful context and connected to real life can be learned—and owned—for use over time.]

We paraphrased the other amendments, starting with her *guessing* about them. In that way, I would know what Nora already understood and not waste time unnecessarily. Time was always our enemy. Twenty-six amendments had thousands of words. Reality dictated that we find a way to talk about broad meanings and connect code words to those meanings so that she could use the mnemonic memory devices that seemed to work so well for her in mastering the Second Amendment.

Nora was constantly teaching me how to teach her. We experimented with all kinds of approaches, and because I kept notes of each of our sessions I had a running record of those that worked for her, forming a body of evidence to define her learning style. This evidence by interaction with real academic challenges was more meaningful to me in predicting her potential than any of her standardized test scores had been. We learned together that the best plan for learning huge numbers of concepts, such as the Constitutional Amendments, seemed to be from the whole amendment to its phrase-by-phrase parts, and back to the whole again. Nora was also helped by the writing process, keeping notes or formulating charts or sketches that she could then review at home in her own time and at her own pace. This she did willingly, this tireless Nora with her inborn passion to *know*.

[Nora's zeal made me think of how often I'd told my clients' parents: "My job is to determine if your child is unwilling or unable. The unable, if they're willing, can be taught anything—we just have to find the right road to get the knowledge in. The unwilling will remain so until someone can light some spark that makes them want to be partners in their own process of learning. Lucky for me, Nora was the Queen of Willing.]

* * *

We planned a trip to the Dinosaur and Prehistory Museum to flesh out her understanding of the questions raised by *Quest for Fire* and, undoubtedly, create more questions for study. We talked en route to the museum to build her anticipation and give her some verbal preparation.

The museum evoked excitement, shock, and fear in Nora. She was a total innocent in regard to every sight there, from the massive skeletons of the extinct behemoths, to the tar pits bearing fossils, to the remains of "Lucy," the prehistoric homicide victim, and most of all, to the extraordinary film explaining the whole period. Sadly, the film was as confusing to her as *Quest for Fire* had been. That truth was apparent to me the moment the lights went on at the film's conclusion, revealing her look of horror. Once again, an entire film had been one continuous question. I asked if she'd like to see it again, but she was too upset.

We left the amphitheatre and went over to study the fossilized Lucy. I read aloud the information plaque next to Lucy's remains. Nora hadn't ever heard the word "homicide" but was fascinated when she learned its synonym, "murder." She was trying to imagine what murder might have meant in those days to those people. She wondered aloud: "Did they feel fear of violence like we do today? Did they punish people who murdered? Why did they name this fossil 'Lucy?'" Nora's endless desire for answers left me endlessly seeking ones that I, myself, didn't have—by reading the information plaques and pamphlets the museum provided, or asking questions of the guides who worked there. This field trip gave me the chance to let her see that no one, not even teachers, can know everything, and to model ways in which we can all learn *how* and *where* to find answers.

We drifted over to the museum's research department, the area where they sorted and catalogued all the fossil bits that were currently being excavated from the dig outside that very museum. Peeping through the picture window, Nora was spellbound by the walls full of cabinets with hundreds of little drawers, each marked with numbers and coded information. She expressed an intrigue so intense that I suggested off-handedly that she might want to volunteer there sometime, since they always needed help. Then I quickly changed the topic, not wanting to pressure her on so delicate a subject as work, something she still believed she was too inept to attempt. The McDonald's incident remained an indelible reminder of her "personal worst."

She was pensive on the way home, giving me no clue of the surprise plan formulating in her brain. The following week, a glowing Nora presented me with an essay about the museum.

[Her spelling, punctuation, and capitalization are as she wrote it. Often spelling errors are increased when one is concentrating on the excitement of new ideas and trying to hold them in memory. More importantly, her errors in what are called "the conventions of written English"—spelling, punctuation, capitalization, and grammar—help me realize her strengths and needs in this area. Rather than correcting her journal entries, I used them to guide me as to instructional needs. The number of correctly spelled words was a testimony to her superb visual memory skills (note how close she came to spelling "paleontologists" correctly). Her errors were "good" errors, meaning that misspelled words were readable as what they were meant to be and in phonetically correct sequence. Nora had no problem with this aspect of auditory processing—she could hear the sequence of sounds in words. In fact, these variations in strengths and weaknesses in different subskills of auditory processing are the factors causing teachers to be suspicious that, in fact, there is no such syndrome.]

The Tar Pits and The Museum

By Nora Tarlow

There are cracks beneath the surface of the earth and hot tar would erupt and create puddles of tar (tar pits). The dinasors went into the tar thinking it was water and be traped. Other animals would get traped also, while the vultures watched from above, until the animals were dead and eat them.

Then more tar woudl erupt and cover the bones that were left there.

Paloentologists don't know why these dinasors and other prehistoric creators are extinct now. But they think it could have been the changes in tempature, meaning that the animals that are most able to survive in the times in which they live, do survive.

Archeologists can determine the types of animal skeletons which they find and catogorise them by studying modern skeletons of its living relatives to the ancient ones.

To find the appearance of an extinct animal is found in the study of biology of its living relatives.

Lucy, The Woman in the Tar Pits

The only woman found in the tar pits at La Brea. Because their was a hole in her skull, they could observe that she had been hit in the head by a ston, rock or club. There she was a homocide victum (murdered). Carbon 14 tests indicated she died about 9,000 years ago. They could tell how old she was by her new wisdom tooth that was left in her mouth, that she was 30. Her pelvis bone indicated she was female, and her upper leg bone could tell her height.

Nora's essay left me dumbfounded. She had not only understood, but she had *remembered* everything we had discussed. How was this possible? When I marveled aloud she grinningly revealed the surprise. She had returned to the museum on her own, to view the film three more times, each time writing more questions as they came to her during the showing. She earned my most enthusiastic "Bravos," not only for her repeated viewing of the film and writing down her questions, but for the extraordinary act of initiative. She had acted on her own, from her own motivation, and without any suggestion from others—real growth for this budding thinker, usually so frightened and tentative in every new situation and fearful of risk anywhere except in the athletic arena. For Nora, it was a "personal first."

From my positive feedback to both the product of her work and the self-motivation and persistence it took to produce such an essay, Nora absorbed another lesson: there is great value in knowing what you want and going after it. Best of all, you can give *yourself* permission for such pursuits.

Nora had never earned praise for taking an action based on her own wishes. This new "first" would be the beginning of future braveries as yet unanticipated.

7

APRIL

A New Use for Soap Operas, Journal Writing, and Dreams of the Elephant Man

More frequently, Nora's essays express her needs and conflicts—both academic and social. Our sessions are varied: the use of the TV soap operas for lessons on non-verbal communication; the effect of two movies on her sense of self and retardation; different aspects of government as "organic" outgrowths of her school assignments; and a crisis over a borrowed encyclopedia. I refer her to colleagues for further evaluations this month to assess her intelligence and language/auditory processing issues. Strategic preparations for another parent conference and a more serious consideration of her possible need for psychotherapy make for a full agenda.

Nora continued expanding the form of her journal from questions and isolated paragraphs to short essays. One of her first essays addressed her questions about learning disabilities, particularly about the origin of her problem. She formulated her own "attribution theory": the cause. She blamed herself:

> Are learning disabilities a handicap from birth or can they be cured in early grades? If a child is born with a learning problem if he is taught in an early grade, will it affect him all his life? Is there any way Nora Tarlow could have not had problems in her teenage grades, if she had paid more attention in her earlier grades?
>
> Why can she understand now what she couldn't before?
>
> Who makes the separation between someone who is stupid or someone who has learning problems?
>
> What's the difference between retardation and a learning handicap?
>
> **[Referring to a page in a textbook about language problems that we had studied together.]**
>
> When they talk about adults who have language problems who become a professional athletic something or a politician, do they mean that the adult who has the language problems should not pick a career in something with languages that are hard for them, because their problem will *never be solved*?

With these writings as a catalyst for our discussions, I sensed some signs of melancholy in Nora this month and speculated on the source. Has she misunderstood some of my remarks to her? Is she still concerned that I will "let her go?" Is she worried about the influence of the family conference on my impressions of her? She told me that her mother wonders why Nora "listens to Dorothy's advice but not to mine," even when Mom advised the same things. In response, I explained that many teens and young adults have that kind of conflict with their parents because it's easier to take advice from a stranger at certain times in everyone's life. I offered to have another meeting with her mother so that we could all be working together, but Nora rejected that suggestion.

Nora's next writing further exposed her continued confusion about this conversation:

> Last time I was at Dorothys, as I was leaving she was telling me something about my parents not being real happy that I confide in Dorothy. She tried to explain that a lot of teenage parents have that same feeling, but that it wasn't a big deal at all.
>
> To me, thinking about a possibility of maybe not getting Dorothys help, scares me so much. I always feel scared and alone when I encounter new situations, just as everyone else dose, but when I'm at Dorothys I feel that I'm not alone (*sic*).

Nora had misunderstood the main message of our discussion—that it was natural for parents to sometimes feel a bit left out when their children turn to others for advice. But the Tarlows had never given me any indication that they were planning to end my work with Nora, and I tried to reassure her about that fact.

Other remarks by her parents were also being misunderstood. Her father, probably jokingly, commented one night to his wife that *she* should see me because maybe she has the same problem as Nora, since she often didn't understand *him*.

Nora interpreted this comment literally, of course, missing the double meaning of her father's comment. I explained that married couples often complain that they're not being understood by each other. It was just a kind of joking threat and that I didn't believe her father really wanted her mother to start educational therapy with me.

To probe another possible source of Nora's misinterpretation, I asked if *she* thought her father was joking and whether or not she could tell by reading his *facial expression*. I learned then that the concept of "reading faces" was completely foreign to her, that she often avoided eye contact and missed facial expressions altogether. [**Misreadings of non-verbal means of social communication, especially facial expressions, are commonly described struggles for individuals with learning disabilities.**]

Often, I worked to move Nora away from the heavy talk of fears to some practical skills for mastering them. Specific strategies like exploration of body language and facial meanings might relieve so much of her anxiety. She had been missing a whole dimension of social understanding.

To do this, we went to the TV set and turned it on without sound so that she could study faces in a daytime soap opera for the next 10 minutes and see if she could guess the emotions the actors were expressing. She gradually became more adept, enthralled at finding a purpose for studying faces for unspoken messages. We added "the meaning of faces" to her list of learning goals.

Watching the TV screen reminded Nora of having watched the movie, *Charly*, at the weekend. From her demeanor, I sensed that this film may also in some way be connected to her current worried state, so I asked her to write down her thoughts about it right there in the office. Her essay revealed that she was convinced, through distorted logic, that she, like Charly, was retarded. During the course of our many discussions, Nora was often obsessed with the word "retarded" and let me know she wondered if that adjective applied to her. I had tried to explain how diagnosticians distinguish students with learning disabilities from those considered to be retarded. One distinction I gave was that retarded children may learn differently but may not realize that they are different. They may wonder why people laugh at them but not ask the kinds of WHY questions or engage in the kind of direct exchange of thinking-based ideas as Nora does.

Nora didn't buy my explanation, as her writings the following week revealed:

> Charly was bothered by the kids laughing at him. Dorothy said retarded kids don't know they are different. Since Charly was bothered by the laughter, Dorothy must be wrong. Retarded children *do* know they are different. So I must be retarded, too. Just because I know I'm different doesn't mean I'm smart.

Back to the drawing-board. Nora always drove me to do more research for answers and facts. She needed *proof* of her intelligence. The proof must come as I provide daily feedback about the quality of her questions and her growing capacity to generalize new knowledge. Nora's journal was crucial in keeping me honest about my conclusions as to what she did or did not understand. I also realized how carefully I must choose my words, or at least ask her for immediate feedback before damage is caused through misunderstanding. As always, I pondered which of us was learning more from this intervention!

* * *

Something must have worked during that last session, because Nora was lighthearted again. *Charly* and retardation did not return to the discussion. We could turn our attention to new concepts arising from the school curriculum and from our discussions. Next up on the table was a whole new list: (1) the five senses (she had never learned them); (2) compensations ("to go around the problems"); (3) all kinds of terms related to her unit at Dunbrook on energy—fuel, wood as energy, the gas stove and the light bulb as direct and indirect uses of combustion; (4) carbon dioxide and water as products of combustion; (5) polyester made from oil; (6) solar energy and "decomposing" as energy; (7) wind and windmill farms; and (8) fission and fusion—the wonders and hazards of each. Somehow we wandered into (9) labels for feelings. Following our discussion, she defined some new ones herself—sarcasm (the act of making fun of a person to hurt their feelings); tact (to be tactful is to say things very carefully so that you don't hurt people's feelings); respect (consideration, honor); and envy (dislike for a person who has what you want).

In subsequent sessions this month, we discussed at length the terms related to her government unit. Nora learned that political parties are a whole new class of parties different from the social get-togethers of her world. Using a "compare and contrast" model in two columns on the page, we listed the basic philosophies and differences, such as they are, of Democrats and Republicans. We made schematic drawings coded in three colors to represent the parallel three-branched structures of state and federal governments. The colors helped her to see the similarities between the two levels of governments as well as the differences between the executive, legislative, and judicial branches, shown in red, blue and green. Each branch was fleshed out with its component parts so that she learned such terms as chief executive, cabinet, secretaries of each cabinet post, Senate with senators, House of Representatives with congressmen, legislation (*legis* meaning laws), Supreme Court, justices, and all the numbers and terms for each branch of the governments.

Nora is marvelous at memorizing details like this, especially when introduced so visually, and in subsequent sessions she showed how much knowledge she had retained. She was opening up more and more, feeling confident to express her opinions on these subjects once she knew what ideas they represented. She even raised questions and expressed opinions about the meaning and possible reasons for separation of church and state!

During this period, I referred Nora to a psychologist, Dr. Dixon, for specific testing on intellectual functioning and language evaluation, seeking some objective additions to my own testing and impressions.

[Educational therapists, unless specifically trained and certified, do not administer intelligence tests or psychological tests done by psychologists. They often refer to speech/language therapists for more extensive evaluations of all aspects of receptive and expressive language. We marvel at those diagnosticians who offer explanations that are a perfect fit for the very behaviors we see in our ongoing clinical sessions, and even more when their recommendations are also a perfect fit to apply in educational therapy. The field of diagnostic testing is in a constant state of change, not just with the myriad new tests, new functional brain imaging, and new diagnostic terminology, but also with a change in the style of reporting which now focuses on client strengths and avoids making long-term predictions of future potential, giving families a more hopeful prognosis whenever possible.

At the time of Nora's testing, however, reports were less sophisticated and testers had been trained to come to very definitive conclusions. Many would often make rather dire predictions about a client's potential, providing a dilemma for the educational therapist if impressions and conclusions about the client by the evaluator were not in synch with her own. The following two consultations provide examples.]

When the report on the intelligence test came back from Dr. Dixon (see Appendix D for scores and excerpts), his findings confirmed my own regarding Nora's preference for non-verbal activities, her low fund of information and memory, and the presence of "chronic anxiety which has further depressed her verbal comprehension." I was less sure of his conclusion that "she is a global learner," better able to see the big picture and not getting mired in details. From my perspective Nora was a detail person, but his comments caused me to reconsider my own evidence.

Still, I was concerned about the "flat" test scores—called "flat" because there was no range of highs and lows, just all the same lows that would make a flat line on a graph. More troubling was the fact that there was no accompanying disclaimer about reasons why those scores might be so flat—no speculation that her limited language acquisition and auditory processing problems could have impacted upon her performance in many areas of the test. My work with Nora certainly showed highs and lows, definite strengths and weaknesses. As I read some of the report terminology, the kind used so routinely in the diagnostic reports at that time, I tried to imagine what these written declarations about Nora would have meant to her parents, and more importantly to her. The jargon of the report spoke of her overall "intellectual functioning in the 16th percentile."

[Would they know that this meant that, out of 100 students, she was only better than 16? Would it help them if they didn't know that fact? Would it help more if they did?]

The report went on about "the absence of significant inter- and intra-subtest scatter," referring to those flat scores, "which adds a measure of evidence suggesting that her 'true' intellectual capacity is not significantly higher than the functioning level she attained." In other words, he says that this is probably quite an accurate assessment of her low potential. Summing up his conclusion, "Nora Tarlow is a young adult with a low average capacity for schooling."

The sound of it was so absolute! I knew the *words chosen* to describe Nora's percentiles were a correct fit for her *numbers* according to the testing manual. Indeed, my own testing of Nora had yielded low numbers as well. But the numbers were definitely *not* a correct fit for the Nora I had come to know over these past months. Our work together was building a different "measure of evidence" to prove that Nora's capacities were much more than those numbers. Now I would have to interpret this report for the Tarlows and challenge its implications with my own observations and real evidence.

This month, I also sought some professional input from my colleague and friend Jennifer Allen, a highly experienced, expert speech and language therapist, regarding my own findings and impressions about the source of Nora's disorder. I gave Jennifer examples of the types of auditory processing difficulties that I had observed throughout the year as well as my findings on specific standardized tests of auditory processing. I explained that I did not want to ask the Tarlows to pay for another extensive and costly evaluation.

[Many families either cannot or will not undertake the financial challenges when their children need multiple types of costly evaluations, and the educational therapist has to prioritize what is most necessary as well as to engage her network of colleagues who might be willing to help informally and who possess significant expertise to gain valid insights from abbreviated testing and skilled observation, i.e., "the informal evaluation." Such insights enhance the educational therapist's understanding and build new knowledge from other fields with which we interact.]

Because we had shared and consulted about many clients over the years, and because Nora's case sounded so challenging and provided her with an opportunity to expand her own knowledge, Jennifer agreed to conduct a partial evaluation at no charge. She used selected subtests from her battery while also observing Nora in informal conversation.

She called the next day to give me her impressions.

"Dorothy, you were right on with your conclusions about Nora's auditory processing difficulties. She's low in three areas: auditory segmentation, auditory synthesis, and auditory processing of oral commands—the underlying skills necessary for divergent production. Those are the technical terms, but what it means is that she has difficulty breaking down the incoming stream of words in a sentence into their individual units—that's what we mean by "auditory segmentation"—and then trying to process the meaning of each word in the sentence. Segmentation and synthesis work together, like segmenting syllables of words and putting them back together." She gave the example of pronouncing individually (segmenting) each syllable in the word "in-ter-est-ing" and then synthesizing into the whole, "interesting." She explained that Nora has trouble with segmenting phrases and groups of words in a sentence so that she can first understand the segments and then give meaning to the entire unit. She just cannot hold all those parts together and understand what each word or word group means in relation to the whole sentence. Yet often she can memorize the sentence and repeat it perfectly, word for word. She just cannot under-stand it.

She clarified further: "So you can see why hers is a problem of auditory processing of *meaning* rather than straight auditory retention of incoming information or sound sequences. [**That explained to me why she was able to spell words phonetically and sound out words in reading.**] This difficulty is compounded when she has to draw inferences through reasoning about information that isn't even stated in the text but only implied. This makes her ability to understand subtleties of language, like idioms and innuendoes and abstract or implied expressions, almost impossible.

"As I see it, her primary deficits, then, are in *semantics*—that is, the meaning of lan-guage— and she is troubled further with what we call 'peripheral meanings' of words, such as word associations, and categorization. The reduced auditory segmentation skills cause trouble when processing vocabulary, and limited vocabulary adversely affects her ability to segment incoming speech.

"However, her strength is in syntax, or sentence *structure*, and she learns best experientially."

[Jennifer's analysis was so confirming for me, and it explained, in diagnostic terminology, the reasons behind all the signs that I had observed in Nora's daily performance—the constant quest to understand language surrounding her but always unable to hold the segments of meaning long enough to link them to each other and comprehend the whole messages. Now I was more prepared for another challenging role in educational therapy—the demystification of reports from collaborating professionals. Parents often get 20- to 30-page reports and their eyes glaze over as they try to understand the overall message: what it means about their child, what should be done, and what it predicts for the future. Today, diagnosticians are much more aware than they were then of the importance of pointing out strengths and explaining possible causes for the areas of low performance on tests.

For my interpretation of Dr. Dixon's report to the Tarlows I would need a very clear plan: (1) emphasize the findings on Nora's non-verbal strengths, her visual and memorization skills, and her capacity to learn best through experience; (2) help them understand that her low memory scores were from years of not understanding the language of the curriculum, but that when she learned through experience and had new concepts introduced in context, with practice and repetition she proved that she could remember very well; (3) focus on what I had learned about her performance in our sessions in order to soften the hard edges of IQ scores that, in this case, revealed very little about Nora's potential for her future.

Jennifer Allen's findings had confirmed what I had already discussed with them in more simple language, but I would try to help the Tarlows and Nora understand the processes of segmentation and synthesis in simpler terms. I knew that they could never use such professional terminology to explain Nora's needs to others.]

* * *

My meeting with the faculty at Dunbrook was beginning to bear fruit. Nora's government teacher actually took the time to rewrite the test questions for her so that she would understand them. She had studied with a friend and thought she really knew the material, but now she's not sure how well she did. The despondent face returned as she wondered aloud whether her language problem would ever be solved and whether she could ever hold a job that would require proficiency with language.

I showed her, with specific examples, that she *is* able to remember, but in different ways—not by listening, but by experiencing, and that all knowledge is "cumulative" (we discuss that, of course), but that she must learn *how* to ask people to re-explain by using different words and examples when she doesn't understand. **[This is easy for me to say; not easy for Nora to apply. The real world is *not* all that caring, and very impatient with those who need extra time for anything.]**

* * *

The all-telling notebook once more informed me that we were still not done with Nora's thoughts of retardation:

> The difference between retarded children and children w/ learning disab. is that retarded children no something is wrong w/ them but they really don't want to know what it is. They know people laugh at them and look at them different but they don't know why and they don't care to know why. They also don't have the care to want to learn, therefore they don't learn. Most children w/ learning disabilities want to learn. There are 2 choices in life—either to put your head into the ground, or to do it and master it (*sic*).

Nora had certainly picked up on some of the ideas I had presented, but clearly I must find a better way to explain. I turned to Jack Westman's *Handbook of Learning Disabilities* (1990) for clues about distinguishing characteristics. Westman described the limitations in the population considered "mentally retarded" (currently referred to as "developmentally disabled"): a lack of direct exchange of ideas, impaired self-help skills, and impaired generalized ability to learn both in daily life skills, academic learning, and social adjustment. He gave his thoughts on the problem of "tests designed to measure the ingredients for intelligence" (p. 24) in these two populations: "This testing approach does not consider the extent to which children can be taught to develop their intellectual powers, only their limitations" (p. 25).

That profound line from Dr. Westman made me think about Nora's scores and proclamations about her limitations from the intelligence testing. No test could predict how she was flowering with the experiential, contextual approach to learning.

I shared a watered-down version of Westman's information with Nora and will have to wait for future journal entries to see if she feels more clear about what is and isn't "retardation."

* * *

Nora's class was starting a new Learning Block, and she asked if she could possibly borrow one volume of my *World Book*. She had proven so trustworthy with everything I'd loaned her that I broke one of my rules (I never loan out encyclopedias), and agreed to the loan, jokingly telling her she'd have to sign it out in blood (and then quickly explaining the origins of the expression).

Just as she was about to leave, Nora shared her concern again about our upcoming parent conference to talk about her repeated problems at home. The constant yelling by family members makes her so frustrated that she cannot concentrate on her work.

Ten minutes after Nora left the office, the phone rang. It was Nora calling from a payphone a mile away to plead with me not to see her parents. Once more she stated her now-constant fear that they would stop our sessions. I assured her that that won't happen and explained why it was so important that we resolve this fear with some reality.

[The idea of worries and fears, particularly the analysis of the causes behind them, is more the domain of psychotherapy than of educational therapy, and as they came up at various times during our sessions, I would use those occasions to advise Nora that it might be very helpful for her to get some counseling. (For some reason, the word "counseling" itself has proven less threatening than "therapy" for most clients.) At the same time, I noted that Nora's range of fears seemed exacerbated by her misunderstandings of language in every aspect of her life, so that the demystification of those misunderstandings often allowed her some relief from the anxiety that came from the unknowns. Clearly, she would have benefited from psychotherapy at this stage of her life, and the issue needed to be addressed, hopefully at the upcoming family meeting. As various emotionally based issues arose during our sessions, I frequently repeated my recommendation that she could be helped to deal with these in counseling therapy, not in educational therapy. She refers to this advice and her responses to it in some journal writings, but the seeds are being planted with the hope that, at the right time, they will come to fruition.]

* * *

Nora arrived for her afternoon session, her face ashen. I thought someone had died. To her, the accident that had occurred the night before was worse than death. She'd been standing at the top of the stairs in her home, had somehow stumbled, and not she, but my borrowed *World Book* had tumbled down the entire flight, suffering a major fracture of its binding. There was no question about the degree of utter despair Nora suffered in that awful moment of confession. I could just imagine the thought process in her mind: I had trusted her, broken a rule for her, taken a chance on her—and she had failed me. Her self-flagellation must have lasted throughout the night, and she'd spent the morning locating a bindery that might rectify the damage. But nothing could rectify her feeling of shame at disappointing me.

Now the shame was mine for my own compounded errors. Searching for the right words that would let her know *my* responsibility for this outcome, I first cajoled her back to the fact that *her* safety and well-being were far more important than the binding of a replaceable book. Then I apologized for making such a big deal out of loaning her the book, realizing now how seriously she had taken my joking about "signing out in blood."

[She had completely misunderstood the exchange. My interpretation of the misunder-standing was her misreading of the subtle humor in that comment. In my mind, I had put aside any worry about breaking the book-loaning rule owing to Nora's very responsible nature. In my mind, I knew that if anything happened to the book it was just a book and it was correctable. I thought that she had taken me at my word. Years later I learned that I completely missed the real reason for her extreme upset. She had grown to believe that, in my office, the second most important source of our learning, besides our work interpersonally, was the encyclopedia. And she had damaged this treasured object. She was unforgiving of herself and equally upset that I had so badly misinterpreted her devastation.]

During the course of this sensitive conversation, she brought up the topic of the evening meeting with her parents, making a natural shift in the discussion and leaving me wondering about the connection between the two topics. Why was she so frightened about this meeting?

"You don't understand," she said. "I've never had anyone to talk to before—I mean, really, to talk. . . . *Bad things happen when I try to talk to friends.* Once I did—about dreams. You see, I have lots of dreams, but there's one dream I have a lot, the same one, over and over. It's about the Elephant Man [another film she had rented about a grossly deformed man with a huge head, causing this nickname, Elephant Man]. I dream that I'm the Elephant Man and everyone can *see* what's wrong with me, and then they understand. I had one friend once, and I felt I could trust her. She was the only one I told about this dream. And after that . . . she stopped being my friend. She just stopped seeing me."

So . . . two other missing pieces in the puzzle of understanding Nora emerged. First was her longing to have a visible, tangible handicap—even one of such sheer horror as the Elephant Man. And second, Nora had concluded that if she confides she will lose people. She was generalizing again, but alas, incorrectly this time. From one painful rejection, she had concluded that confiding brings rejection. The endless horror of constant misunderstanding of the spoken word tormented her every day.

Then she shared an afterthought: "And by the way, you don't have to tell my parents that I'm real upset about your going away."

There was the third piece to the puzzle! I had told Nora I would be leaving the country for two weeks in mid-May for something that couldn't be postponed until the summer: the birth of my first grandchild who was to be born in a foreign land, and that I would find someone for her to work with while I was away.

My trip was her verification, i.e., If Nora confides, people leave her. And if I share her concerns with her parents, perhaps she will be forced to leave me. I had become her rock, her support, the keeper of her safe haven, and the potential loss of that was too terrible for her to contemplate.

More than ever, I knew that the parent conference *had* to occur, be *survived* by Nora, and have a *successful outcome*. To ensure success, I had to address two crucial realities: first, to respect her anxiety in advance of the meeting, and second, to reassure Nora that I had every intention of returning from my trip to be there for her all summer. Then I suggested a plan for her to be able to tolerate this meeting and come out a winner. Together, we wrote up a "List of Promises to Nora" about the only topics to be discussed that evening. The topics addressed the issues that had originally provoked the suggested conference: her often-expressed frustration over her parents' inability to agree on the discipline of her brother, the turmoil their dissention caused her, her feeling that she was being taken advantage of in the family constellation, and her fear of termination of the educational therapy. This list became our agenda for them to discuss:

1. Nora's wish for her parents to be in agreement as father and mother.
2. Nora's wish that if Mom disciplines, Dad should back her up.
3. Nora's feeling that the family has been abusing her niceness.

4. Nora's wish for assurances that she will continue in educational therapy, and that no one else in her family will come to this office for these services.
5. Other issues that may occur to Nora (and only Nora) during the meeting.
6. Nora will control the agenda.

Agreed to and Signed by Dorothy and Nora

The conference happened. Nora's agenda was strictly observed. The Tarlows, somewhat surprised by the topics of Nora's concern, acknowledged that son Rob's problems were a source of major turmoil in the family. However, they had been unaware of how much their disagreements regarding the solutions had been upsetting Nora, whose family role, they verified, was indeed the nice, helpful protector and guardian of her parents' emotional states. At the suggestion that they might want to seek family counseling, both parents instantly and almost simultaneously said they "had been that route" but the results were ineffective, and they were not open to trying again.

I respected their stated position. The issue had been raised, however, and I knew that people's circumstances change. At a later date they might reconsider, if not for their family, then perhaps for Nora. I would keep a list handy of potential referrals if and when they changed their minds.

[Parents are often threatened by the suggestion of psychotherapy or the less threatening "counseling." They are either reluctant to open up the whole unknown world of emotional issues and interrelationships, or they may have been unhappy with earlier therapeutic interventions. They may also be guarded about yet another financial undertaking.]

The Tarlows assured Nora that they wanted her to continue to work with me, and they laughed at the idea that either one of them would be entering into educational therapy. No, she did not have to worry about that. Nora forced a smile after that item was addressed, but was it really resolved in her head?

Once Nora's list had been addressed, she granted me permission to explain in more depth what I was learning about her style of learning and the impact in school of her specific learning disabilities. This meeting was also my opportunity to summarize some points from the psychologist's evaluations, as I had planned. I used the parts that lended support to what I was explaining, while, at the same time, I ignored the specific numbers, the flat scores, that had so concerned me. Interestingly, the Tarlows never asked further questions about the evaluation. They may not have understood it or not wanted to, but they seemed relieved by my summary and accepted the information.

I went on to provide further examples, developed since our previous conference, of how Nora's struggle with auditory processing of language was affecting her understanding of lectures in school, conversations with friends and even family, and dialogue in movies and on TV, working into these examples a simplified version of Jennifer Allen's interpretations about segmentation and synthesis. As we talked, Mr. and Mrs. Tarlow began to share some of their own examples of behaviors at home that had puzzled them, but they thought they were beginning to understand them a little better now.

Then I brought them up to date on our current work together and how it was constantly changing as the school demands, and her desire to build knowledge, changed. Using examples of her work, I showed how Nora had mastered the history of architecture, sharing some of her insightful questions and her curious wonder about issues that arose in everyday life.

The conference served its declared purpose. Although Nora was not quite a legal adult, I never would have considered meeting with her parents without her permission or presence. I explained to the Tarlows that future meetings would follow those same constraints, but I asked Nora, then and there, if she objected to her parents calling me about issues of concern.

Nora's response reflected her pleasure with her new power: "Not if they tell me first what they're calling about."

They agreed, and the dreaded conference came to an end. I invited the Tarlows to stay in touch if they had questions about my work with Nora or with misunderstandings they might observe at home.

As for Nora's response to the whole meeting, I knew that she would let me know soon enough.

When the family had left, I thumbed through my own log on Nora and realized that, in retrospect, April had been an extraordinary month for all of us.

PART TWO

Employment and Continued Education

Living the Organic Curriculum

8

MAY

Job vs. Occupation vs. Career—and Lessons on Worry

In preparation for Nora's entry into college, we explore: the need to have long-term goals that would guide her choice of studies; the topics of independence and risk-taking; and the difference between job, occupation, and career. New strategies are introduced for mastery of her unit on zoology. The month of May brings an abbreviated number of sessions owing to my brief departure out of the country. Adjustments are necessary for her working with a colleague, leading to a spontaneous lesson on the topic of worry itself.

Something good happened. Nora's parents heard her. She reported that when they came home from our conference, her mom yelled at Rob about not doing his laundry, and her father backed up her mother. Both parents were saying the same thing, at least in this instance while it was fresh in their minds. Rob was shocked, even more so because Nora was thrilled that, at last, there was action, not just talk.

She was so much more relaxed today. I hated to intrude on her new tranquility, but it's May, and we must talk about the "scary stuff"—my going away this month, her summer plans, and, of course, the dreaded word JOB. My departure out of the country could not be postponed since I was going to assist my daughter in the birth of her first child. The timing, immediately before graduation, would be difficult for Nora, but I assured her that I would be back before that big day. I had arranged for a caring and competent colleague, Bonnie Runken, to fill in for me during these two weeks.

[Separations and reunions were as much a part of life as our academic curriculum, so this was an opportunity to add those topics to our ever-evolving Organic Curriculum.]

This seemed to be the right time to share a poem I had received, written on his 25th birthday by my son, who had no learning disabilities but still suffered the universal doubts that come with the unknowns of growing up—separation from home and moving on to beginning adulthood without much to show for it yet. **[The use of something from a family member may be considered controversial by some educational therapists or other clinicians, but I had weighed this carefully in favor of the human lessons involved. We are professionals but we are also members of families sharing common dilemmas during phases** of development. **My personal belief is that this universality of the human condition may also be incorporated into the Organic Curriculum if and when the examples are relevant to the needs of our clients and do not cross any boundaries of confidentiality. My son had given permission for the verse to be used.]**

He ended the verse with an unusual choice of words that I wanted Nora to hear:

> Songs of life are born of living;
> Only leaving breeds of your return.
> From my life songs rise—
> You will know me as you are willing to see me fly:
> Not to say goodbye—
> To see hello from my own eyes.
>   (J. Ungerleider, 1983)

We spent a lot of time guessing what he meant, especially by that last line—"To see hello from my own eyes." Her puzzlement persisted, so I offered my own interpretation, paraphrasing as I went, but making it clear that poetry can have different meanings for different readers. This in itself was a new idea for her, a right she had never dared to exercise. I explained that, to me, his words meant that all humans, whatever their age when they first set out to test themselves—to separate from their families—walk gingerly, cautiously forward into the unknown, and they all have to face the fear and excitement in their hearts as they begin to see the world through their *own* eyes, their *own* perceptions. It's scary because there are no clear answers if they are right or wrong. They will take risks, and sometimes they *will* be wrong, but they'll learn from that, just as their parents and others did before them.

Nora was fascinated, not only by the discussion but by the idea that my son had these same anxieties and doubts that she had to face. Clearly, she had grasped the message. I eased the conversation back to my pending trip and reminded her that my absence would actually be very brief, expressing confidence that she will feel comfortable with Bonnie Runken and will have much to tell me about her self-discovery when I return.

We reopened the third sensitive topic—Nora in the work world. Her reluctance, bordering on terror about the uncharted waters of job-seeking, was rooted in her one brief disaster at McDonald's. I suggested she might need to have "trial jobs" in many different places for her to find her "fit"—a place of employment with *needs* that fit her *skills*.

This provided a perfect time to discuss the difference between "job," "occupation," and "career," a distinction I'd heard described so clearly by a colleague of mine in his book on the subject (Phoenix, 1985). I summarized his explanation for Nora. A *job* is something you do for money, and you may or may not like it, but you'll be getting paid for doing it. An *occupation* is a whole group of jobs that share the same kinds of demands, like being a cashier or a clerk or a mechanic. Each one of those occupations will be doing that same work, no matter where they are. A *career* is the most complicated. A career includes your job, your occupation, and your values. You may start with a job as a sales girl in a department store and then decide to go to school and study marketing. After school, you may work your way up as a buyer or manager in the store and that could become your career— if it makes you feel needed in the world and if it fits your values about what is important to do with your life.

She listened intently, intrigued by the distinction between these three forms of employment. This led to our talk about the importance of risk-taking and the kinds of goals that may be set for all different job situations. She had to understand that the risk itself was part of the lesson, and that "sometimes you'll succeed and sometimes you'll fail, but if you never take the risk, you'll never grow, never move forward."

[Risk is so important to keep discussing with Nora because of her ever-present fear of failure, a common fear among young adult clients, many of whom are averse to risk.]

Her notebook entry following our discussion that afternoon signified a breakthrough. For the first time there were no distortions between what I had meant to say and what Nora heard. **[Besides that, her spelling and punctuation were near-perfect, except for those compound words and troublesome homonyms "no" and "know" that still needed our attention.]:**

> Part of growing up is doing things that are hard for you. By not doing them you're putting your head into the ground and will get nowhere. You must learn how to do things and master them. But by avoiding these different responsibilities, and other things you don't no about, you are being babied, by who ever is doing them for you. If I don't go out and take different jobs, by experimenting with my future I'll never no what I want to do. And part of taking different jobs is taking the risks of not only being rejected at first, but also by failing, Dorothy says its not the end of the world if I fail.

Nora's new Learning Block that week was zoology, so we reached again for the *World Book*, which, thankfully, was no longer a threat. On to coelenterates and mollusks and how they operate. Never before did a common backyard snail get such attention, such piercing examination of its juices and movements under magnification. Tides came up once more in this lesson, and now Nora could examine their relationship to a new application: animal life in tide pools. We developed charts on characteristics of phyla—she's wonderful at that! She was able to re-visualize the whole chart and, in that way, "see" the facts in her mind's eye. Indeed, the memorization of facts was a genuine strength for Nora, something very useful to observe because her career directions might tend toward fields that demand memorization skills.

Tomorrow will be our last session before I leave the country. Zoology was put on hold as we discussed her uncertainties about the plans I'd made for her in my absence. She has met Bonnie Runken, but her reluctance about starting all over with a stranger was evident. Trying to reassure her once more, I asked her to write down her concerns so that we could discuss them in our next session.

* * *

Nora walked in, grumbling about her hatred of news broadcasts in the car because she can't understand them and then took out her latest writings. They moved from her summary of our talk about tides, gravity, and the moon to the fears related to my leaving:

> If I really like this Bonnie, which I do, will Dorothy send me to her permanently, will she just shine me on, like everyone else has done in the past—will she just forget Nora when she returns and goes to reschedule clients?

She doesn't like to talk about stuff that psychiatrists [**her word, substituted for mine about "counselors"**] are there for 'cause she is a tutor. But she doesn't understand, I don't gain anything by talking to her about my problems, I gain from her the encouragement she gives me. My Mom encourages me not to give up, but she is going away, like Dorothy everyone is going away.

Nora's journal disclosure shocked me because she had neglected to mention that her parents were leaving town at the same time that I'd be gone. Both support systems disappearing at once—this was a cause for some concern. Given this new information, I spent even more time talking about Bonnie—how much I respected her work and knew that she would be an excellent "substitute teacher" while I was away for these two weeks. Then I took out the calendar to reschedule her for the weeks following my return so that she would see herself "written into the schedule" and not worry that there would be no place for her.

Since worry was the order of the day, we turned it into a lesson, hopefully to reduce some of its power over her functioning, so we took turns sharing worries. All kinds of everyday worries.

"You go first," she said.

"OK. Worry about the dark—ever since I was a little kid and my sister told scary stories in our bedroom. And deep water—ever since that camp counselor pushed me in the deep part of that black lake in Wisconsin, and, as if nearly drowning weren't enough, when they got me out, I had black leaches stuck all over my body. Ugh!" [**Time out to talk about leaches.**]

Now it was her turn. Fire was a big one. Ever since 6th grade when the fireman came to school and talked about all the dangers in her house that could cause fire. After that, always being afraid to go to sleep from thinking about fire. And burglaries. Always hearing sounds in the house and thinking someone was breaking in, like they did at her neighbor's house. Fire and burglaries were her big ones.

Sharing and listening, in turn. The human condition. Life brings fear and worry just as it brings joy and success. No judgments, no advice. Just sharing. The hour had been a catharsis—and a drain. We both decided to have a Diet Coke, say our goodbyes, and wish each other good luck over this two-week break. We promised to keep journals to share when we would reunite in June.

* * *

[**I believed that, by remaining as lighthearted as possible, I was creating an expectation of normalcy about the separation, wishing, perhaps magically, that Nora could handle this time without me and her parents for the two-week span. Part of the intervention with adult clients involves preparation for independence, but readiness for such new status is always uncertain until it is tested. Two weeks could seem like a lifetime.**]

9

JUNE

Traffic Tickets as Curriculum, and Other Misunderstandings

With my return in June, Nora's revealing narrative about events during my absence defined our pre-summer "curriculum" from the social proprieties of reconnecting to the language on a traffic ticket, the U.S. Constitution, social issues of graduation, and, last but not least, pumping gas.

I returned just one week before Nora's graduation ceremony, and we had so much to discuss that we scheduled an extra day. Nora had developed a habit, even when I was in town, of calling my answer machine and then hanging up without leaving a message. She didn't want to bother me but just liked to hear the little quotes I always had on my message machine—a link to her support system from a distance. From the 35 beep-and-hang-up signals that greeted me when I returned from Israel, I realized the importance of that familiar connection to me in my absence.

We greeted each other with a mix of delight and restraint, a "reconnect" process after such a long break. So much had transpired for both of us. Small talk was the cover for whatever traumas might have transpired during my absence. Politely, she asked about my trip and the new baby, but I knew that she needed to talk, not listen, after this long separation.

I filled her in briefly on the basics and joy of the baby's arrival—then quickly redirected the conversation to how well she looked with her new bleached Levis with multiple patches and zippers, her rosy suntan, and her noticeably trimmer body from all the summer sports. Pleased by my observations, she shared some of the latest paddle ball successes, and then admitted to liking Bonnie, filling in the specifics. They worked mostly on Spanish and math, with some review of social studies. She said she "really knew" the Constitution material, but she got sick the night before the exam, felt awful that day, really "blew it."

First question: Did I think they'd still let her graduate?

Recalling the massive number of words in the Constitution, I told her that I would have a talk with her teachers and the principal. Maybe they'd let her take it again when she was feeling better. [Graduation was only a week away, and I felt certain that Dunbrook would not hold off such a milestone based on that test. Teachers often make threats that are out

of proportion to reality in their desperation to motivate recalcitrant teens. Nora, however, was certainly not recalcitrant, and by now the teachers knew that very well.]

It became clear that two weeks' suppression of discussing the range of life issues we often addressed had taken its toll. She could do the academics with Bonnie, but she couldn't risk anything more with a stranger. I acknowledged how hard that must have been but reminded her that she seemed to have managed remarkably well during our break.

She laughed at that. "Maybe you won't think so when you hear what's been happening." And the litany began.

The next woe was her latest traffic ticket—familiar territory for us. Another moving violation. Traffic cops and Nora were somehow always in the same locations at the same time. But this one, for her third moving violation, apparently put her over the legal limit for a minor and required a court appearance. She reluctantly relayed the details, coupled with her huge concern at the thought of telling her parents. In their and my absence, her friends had all advised her to wait until after her 18th birthday the following month, when she'd be a legally responsible adult and could go to court on her own. Then she wouldn't have to tell her parents at all. That's what her friends would have done.

For Nora, such emancipation was beyond her. Whether she was more frightened by the notion of being a legal adult or by the thought of lying to her parents was hard to determine. She had no practice at this business of adulthood, and she had never kept things from her parents. On the contrary, she'd always confessed to them immediately and looked to their counsel for solving all her problems. Torn between her friends' heretical suggestions and her belief that her parents would "kill her" from their anger at such disappointing behavior, Nora sat waiting for some specific solutions from me.

She paused for my response, but deep down she knew why I remained silent. Even though we had had a two-week break in our sessions, Nora knew that a major goal of ours was *her* development of decision-making and problem-solving skills. We had discussed this often, especially when we studied political parties and she wanted to know how to vote, rather than how to consider what the different candidates said—and which ones appealed to her *own* beliefs as they developed.

Breaking the silence, I reminded her of that premium goal of ours—problem-solving—in case she forgot it during our break in contact. I also reminded her of *my* goal: to hear her, to respect her, to recognize her anguish, and above all, to teach her *meanings*—meanings of words and language, meanings of faces and looks, meanings of expressions and customs—and laws. Once she knew meanings, I truly believed, she would be capable of deciding and solving issues on her own.

I hadn't expected the smile that followed, but Nora seemed pleased with where she sensed we were heading. Back to the Organic Curriculum. Yes, she had raised the issue. Now, the traffic ticket, with its stated language and unstated implications, would become that day's topic. The vacation was over. We would face the problem head-on, analyze everything about it until she became a mini-expert, and then work toward a rational solution.

And so, from the language of the ticket, we lifted our "study guide" for the day:

- What *was* a "moving violation?"
- What were the codes that were listed?
- How do you read them and what do they mean?

- Did the officer write down the correct code to describe what you had done?
- Do you think you were guilty of the charge?
- If so, what were your options, your choices, for solving this infraction, this breaking of the law?
- And finally, what did the commentary about "insurance" mean on the back of the ticket?

Nora relaxed her posture, comforted by the familiar format. The first few questions on the ticket seemed easy for her, probably owing to frequent prior experience, but the word "insurance" brought unexpected interest. Just what did "insurance" mean? When I explained it to her, with living examples and words like *liability, premiums,* and *policy plans,* that "Aha" look came on again. So *that* was why her parents kept talking about "premiums" going up and having to "take your brother off the insurance." They had warned her, too, about how they'd "added her to the policy." She didn't know what in the world they were talking about, but the way they said it, she knew they presumed she understood. Everyone always presumed. But she never knew. No way would she expose her confusion on that one. The "stop asking" mantra from early childhood still played its tune at almost 18.

After our discussion, I asked her to write an on-the-spot essay about her understanding of insurance, and I couldn't help smiling as I read her refreshing description:

> Insurance is a type of protection for you. You pay a premium yearly so that if you don't need the protection one year, say, then you still blow the money that year. Insurance companies have different charts for different insurances and they have all different plans and they tell you which particular plan you are eligible for. If someone wants to sue me for 1 million dollars, yearly, I would already be paying liability insurance so the liability insurance would pick up the whole bill.

She had the details exactly right. I couldn't bear to tell her the unwritten realities of dealing with insurance companies and fighting the "fine print" details. Enough was enough on insurance for one day.

We turned our attention then to the legal orders and choices which the ticket gave her, weighing up all the pros and cons of her court appearance, with or without parental knowledge. With her parents still away, she had some time. Growing up was not always fun. We both agreed that maybe Peter Pan had the right idea. She knew about Peter Pan. The hour ended with her finally being able to manage that smile which was so unique to Nora—open, aboveboard, completely guileless.

* * *

Nora left me her journal to read, with the new entries of thoughts and happenings that had occurred while I was away. This journal recorded her good relationship with Bonnie, her disappointing progress report, and the distractions in her house while trying to study in spite of Carrie's loud music, her worries about burglars if the door wasn't locked properly after Rob came home late, and her feelings of inadequacy to take on responsibilities while her parents were away.

She further chronicled her ongoing car troubles and her in-the-moment solutions, made even more remarkable by her persistence to problem-solve on her own. Here was the sequence: Car wouldn't start . . . push it to the gas station . . . take her parents' car instead (since they were away) . . . then, same day, *that* car breaks down . . . late arrival to school . . . very angry teacher from her late arrival . . . late again for a meeting . . . decision to try the third family car—old, with faulty brakes ("Well, I'll just drive extra slow") . . . discovery of a traffic ticket on the windshield . . . and on and on. She wrote, "I couldn't think of anything that could possibly go wrong today that hadn't except someone said, Nora this day isn't over. So I'm trying to laugh without crying." It was a fabulous, creative report revealing something new: Nora's strength in spite of adversity.

* * *

At our next session, Nora expressed embarrassment about her journal, worrying in retrospect that it made her look like a fool. I assured her that she was *never* a fool for expressing real concerns, and, on the contrary, I cherished this booklet, was impressed by her solutions on her own, and appreciated her giving me the privilege of reading it.

[This was another opportunity for me to broach the subject of psychotherapy. Each instance of our clients' constant growth in many directions may open doors that were previously closed to other kinds of help.]

"You know, Nora, as I read about all those upsetting thoughts, I wonder how you can wake up sometimes in the morning. You must be exhausted!"

"Sometimes I am, but I try not to think about any of that when I'm awake."

With that, she gave me an opening. "And you know what I'm going to say, but I need to repeat it again. Understanding the meanings of deep fears is really the business of psychotherapists. You can try not to think about these thoughts, but if they're in your head and keep coming up, they may keep bothering you."

Nora got that "Dorothy's trying to get rid of me" look I'd seen before, so I responded as if she had said it.

"Don't worry, Nora, we'll still work together." I spoke slowly and deliberately to be sure she would understand me without lots of repetition. "I have lots of clients who go to counselors and therapists. One thing has nothing to do with the other. My job is to be your teacher and support in your world of learning—to help you understand the things you don't understand so that you'll stop feeling like you're dumb—so that you can start to like yourself better." I paused to give this time to register.

"Sometimes, those good feelings and successes in school and in jobs help people feel so much better they can put aside their old fears and doubts. But sometimes the held-in stuff doesn't go away so easily. Sometimes those things may need a different kind of help getting resolved."

I studied her face to see if she was ready to bolt the topic. She was silent but listening.

"So you think about it," I went on cautiously. "Talk to your parents, and if you decide you want to see a counselor, I'll be glad to help you find one."

Nora mumbled something noncommittal, but she didn't freak out this time. I knew I'd have to wait for more journal entries to know what she was really thinking.

* * *

Two days before her graduation I discovered another instance of Nora giving me only partial information when describing a personal problem. Her distress about needing a white dress for graduation had been unfounded. There had been no color requirement at all, just some friends who decided, together, to wear white. She'd gone to a thrift shop, found a dress she liked but couldn't decide, so she did nothing. She shared that fact with me.

"Nothing" I pointed out without much thought, "is sometimes, but usually not, a solution, Nora." My comment was meant to be instructive that day, but apparently my tone was not the usual, patient one. The discussion was over quickly since Nora didn't respond one way or the other.

Months later, I learned of her hidden fury at this advice and her interpretations of my "tone of voice" from this angry journal entry, written, but not shared, at the time:

> Well I just got back from running around all over Hollywood for a stupid ugly thrifty type costume dress. Well I did get it, after talking with Dorothy today, she kind of knocked *some* sense into my head. She was just getting me so angry today, I wanted to just tell her to f**k off, and walk right out of her office. She was getting angry with me because of the fact that it seemed that I enjoy when things don't work out because I was smiling when I was telling her what was going on.
>
> I surely don't need her to just tell me how stupid and hopeless I am and then tell me I enjoy being a loser. I need her encouragement so I don't keep on giving up. She seems to think I enjoy giving up. She just doesn't understand, my friends all have other things to do, my mom and Carrie aren't here, so I have no one to turn to. I just need someone to tell me or stop me from giving up. I'm sertinly not proud of the fact that I've given up on a lot of things lately, I *want* to succeed so I can have people proud of me.
>
> Dorothy is kind of furious with me. She never yells but her tone of voice and her choices of words she uses, i can tell, that she's far from being happy with me at all. That's why when I left her office I rushed to get my costume, so I can at least be taking the first step. (*sic*)

[The expression of her fury was an important step for us. To be real, the educational therapy sessions had to offer a safe place to express not only agreement but disagreement. To be real, both teacher and student sometimes show human frailties, and Nora had not anticipated my potential for impatience or disapproval in contrast to the almost constant support. Interestingly, she channeled the anger into action and actually addressed—and solved—the problem, never letting me know at the time that her anger was the catalyst! The lesson she offered me: constantly being patient and understanding is not always the best way to promote real change and growth.]

* * *

In actuality, June ended with a string of plusses in Nora's life. She passed her Constitution exam somehow, celebrated the remarkable milestone of high school graduation with family and friends, looked lovely wearing the elusive "white dress," and resolved her traffic problems in court—*on her own*—at the emancipated age of 18.

We celebrated all this positive news with a graduation lunch at a local eatery, discussing the graduation and how exciting and scary it was to be finished with high school and on the path to a whole new passage of her life. On the way back to the office after lunch, since I was low on gas, we took a brief detour and stopped at the gas station. Nora was stunned to see me pull up at the self-serve pump, and I was equally surprised to learn that, in spite of all the hours she spent in her car, she had never pumped her own gas! She explained that she had been too frightened to try, afraid she'd spill it or start a fire or something, so she'd been paying all that extra money just to avoid the risk.

Consequently, Nora had a different kind of lesson that day—her first in the art (or is it a science?) of pumping gas. With intense concentration, she watched me model each step in the process, adding another skill set toward her path to independence. I looked forward to hearing from her on the day when she would actually fill the tank by herself.

10

JULY

Lessons on the Job, Lessons in Literature, Headlines, and Fairness

Nora takes a surprise volunteer job at the museum, but conflict between job and paddle tennis leads to a lesson on the issue of quitting—when, why, and how. Strategies for teaching literature and creative writing are used in preparation for college English courses, while newspaper headlines lead to comparisons of religious beliefs. One more speeding ticket offers an opportunity for assessing a judge's fairness in contrast to her need to self-assess her own responsibility.

Free from the constraints of a school curriculum, Nora announced the exciting—and astonishing—news of the day. She had taken a job! On her own, she had returned to the Dinosaur and Fossil Museum and volunteered to work there over the summer on their fossil cataloguing. She reported that her first day proved successful in two ways: she understood and accomplished the tasks given her, and on her way home, filled her own gas tank at the self-serve pump! Following our shared celebration of these milestones, our Organic Curriculum headed in two directions that she selected. First, she wanted to get a handle on how to study literature and maybe even try her hand at creative writing. Second, she wanted to learn better how to deduce the meanings of cryptic newspaper headlines and to use those new words for our "knowledge trails."

Creative writing was virgin territory for Nora, but since she was showing a real strength in expository essay writing she felt that creative writing might be a natural extension of that skill. In her mind, she imagined stories, but she had no idea how or where to begin committing them to paper. Since she had become an avid fan of Rod Serling's *Twilight Zone*—tales of the supernatural and unexplainable—so popular on television at the time, I suggested she begin reading some of Serling's stories in book form to see how writers might construct short stories. I hoped to use her keen interest in Serling as a bridge to deal with interpreting the settings, form, and structure of literature. The fact that these TV stories had first been committed to print was in itself new to Nora. [**How many students never connect the fact that stories they see dramatized on TV originated in the written form?**]

The Serling stories were difficult to read, so I modeled one for her, reading it aloud with the correct phrasing and intonation, introducing literary terminology such as characters, plot, climax, and story line. We used a synonym finder rather than a dictionary for unknown vocabulary to give her more choices of synonyms that may be both familiar and fit the meaning of what we were reading.

[The demands of reading literature are enormous for individuals with reading and language disabilities. Unlike textbooks, which usually provide a skeleton like the table of contents and chapter headings from which to begin seeking the big picture and the overall sequence of the material, literature is a trip through No Man's Land. It gives no bold paragraph headings, no chapter summaries, and no structural clues for plots, themes, and characters. Because of these missing cues we would read the first chapter aloud together very slowly, discussing and predicting the "who, what, when and where" that the author is trying to establish in the beginning. We would stop after each one or two paragraphs to discuss what we think is going on. What is the setting—the "where" of the tale? What time in history—the "when"—does the story takes place?

I ask the students to keep two pieces of paper next to them on the desk, the first one to record the "whos"—the name of each character as he or she appears, clarifying each one's role in the plot and the relationship of one to the other. The second sheet of paper is for writing a two- or three-sentence summary of the action of each chapter as we finish it. These very brief, very informal summaries, without regard for grammar or conventions of writing, are to be used as reference for the reader only. These summaries provide a trail of the plot and help the reader rethink the big picture of each chunk of the book. Most important, summaries demand the ability to synthesize—always an essential skill and always a challenge for struggling learners. I encourage many of my students to use Cliffs or Spark Notes, in spite of many teachers' warnings against them because they fear the students will never read the book. On the contrary, I have learned that these note systems serve as fabulous aids to set their minds to the overall plot, the various themes, and the key roles of characters, so that they actually become interested. Then, once they begin the text itself, they have already made friends with the book, know where it is going, and even look forward to seeing the plot unfold just as they were told it would in the Notes. At the same time, they are less intimidated by the old-fashioned sound of much literary English and the convoluted sentence structure that loses their attention. Classical literature, with its unfamiliar word usage and daunting, 14-sentence paragraphs, is often like a foreign language to twenty-first-century teen minds that are used to five-word sentences without punctuation and the even more bare-bones communication of the text messaging that abbreviates the words themselves.]

After reading two more of Serling's short stories at home, Nora decided to start on her own fiction. Choosing a name for her main character, she came up with "Martha Quisenberry," a name intentionally selected by thumbing through the multitudes in the phone book. Nice choice, a little Serling-ish, suggesting another time and place somehow. We played with lots of plot-mood-action-climax discussions to try to have a working plan, but I sensed her reluctance. This was supposed to be pleasure, but these strategies were stifling her enthusiasm. Ignoring the conventions of writing then, I told her to close her eyes, picture the scenes she imagined, and then try to describe them in written form. By removing constraints on the creative process, Nora started on the story but lost interest at home. Since this was a self-chosen pursuit, her change of mind had no consequences for any course work at the time.

[Some goals become postponed or even abandoned when the rewards don't match the effort. They can be revisited if college courses make the skills more essential to achieve a

passing grade. This was an example of an effort without fruition, how it was handled, and how it was abandoned without guilt.]

We turned then to some headlines for fresh vocabulary challenges. One story about the Pope opened up a flood of unknowns: atheism, sin, the Old and New Testaments, Jesus as Messiah, Poland, communism, and world leaders in the news. Her own pursuit of religious studies had tapped Nora's deeply spiritual side, and she longed to understand her religion as sincerely as she did her school curriculum. Atheism was easy for her to comprehend because she had heard some friends use the term in expressing their doubts about God's existence. "Sin" was pretty easy too, but "Original Sin" needed some connections to her study of Adam and Eve and the Garden of Eden story.

This use of newspaper headlines took us through vast amounts of content because Nora was now so comfortable and familiar with the pattern. We discussed the jobs of words (Nora always laughed at the notion that even words had jobs!), examining those "functions" of the same word in different forms—from naming to doing to modifying, using examples like "concept" and "conception" and "conceive" and "conceivable." She grasped this quickly, and I noted a subtle change in our interactions. Nora was generalizing information that we hadn't visited for a long time and asking fewer and fewer questions about the meanings of the language I used. *She was beginning to automatically understand my vocabulary.*

* * *

One day, Nora surprised me by sharing her interest in "sayings to live by," which explained further why she loved to call my answer machine with its quirky or famous quotes that I recorded and changed weekly to soften the coldness of answer machines. Without ever telling me where she found the quotes, Nora had made her own list of favorites and presented it to me. I could hardly express the full joy this gift gave me. Her choices were a revelation, a peek into her values and beliefs:

1. "When you are ready to learn, a teacher will appear."
2. "Without risk and failure, there is no new learning."
3. "Anger is one way of getting control when you are afraid of being vulnerable, but to allow yourself to be vulnerable opens the way to affection and tenderness."
4. "The door to learning and love opens when we see and hear without fear."
5. "Sometimes I'm so clear, I realize how great my confusion really is."
6. "Fear concerns the future and the past. In the eternal now there is no fear."
7. "Life is not humorous, but there is humor in everything."
8. "Pay attention to your friend's feelings; it is a cure for self-centeredness."
9. "I remember in order to forget."
10. "Laughter is one way towards health and enlightenment."
11. "If you don't take yourself too seriously, others will take you more seriously."
12. "I asked a friend when she began to laugh. She said, 'I began to laugh when my life was in a state of total disaster."

As I read her selection, I wondered if she might have hit upon a new form of projective test—particular sayings that resonate in personal ways for the selector. How I wished the creators of psychological tests could have read Nora's choices in forming new conclusions about her potential.

* * *

During July, Nora received yet another speeding ticket. This one made me wonder about the cause behind such frequency. Was there some deep emotional reason for the pattern, or didn't she really understood the driving laws? Did she become so preoccupied by her thoughts while driving that she paid no attention to the speedometer or to her rear-view mirror (a common ticket-avoidance behavior of mostly-law-abiding citizens) to see if she was being followed by the police? More importantly, I was concerned for her safety.

A little prying disclosed what had been on her mind when the infraction occurred. She had made two commitments for the weekend—one, to play in the paddle tennis tournament as defending club champion, and two, to work at the museum. Naturally she wanted to be at the club, but she now believed that wasn't the right thing to do. Her journal clarified the source of her confusion:

> Y'know, I commited myself to work at the museum every Friday and Saturday, well last week was my first week and the very next week I need to cancel. I know I made a comitment but I'm in this paddle tennis tournament, and people don't no how come that's important. For sure Dorothy was disapointed that I wasn't really acting responsible when deciding over things I have to do and things I want to do.
>
> But the tennis tournaments that I can be in, I take the oportunity to be in them. Its kind of like as important as teaching is to Dorothy, the way I feel on the court. The people watch you when your playing and they route you on and you get real positive input from the people. Some people down at the club say if I just practice a little more, I will some day be the best women player down there. It makes me feel real special when I'm on the court. But on the same token I don't want the museum to think I'm flaking out on them. (*sic*)

So, now I knew that my voice (like so many others) was in her head, confounding her reasoning. When I'd first learned of her volunteer job, I'd said something about what a fine opportunity it would provide for her to prove her responsibility and generate good references to use for an eventual paying job. Hearing this old "tape" in her mind, she was torn. If she cancelled her Saturday job at the museum, would it spoil her record? And would it be disappointing to me?

This entry was a perfect lead into a discussion of her decision-making and her right to openly disagree with my suggestions—a right that she had never considered, and probably never would have dared to, without my permission.

"Nora, only you can decide if and when you're ready to quit at the museum. My comments are to help you consider the pros and cons in making decisions. But they have to be *your* decisions. Paddle tennis is your world of success. What you accomplish on that court is phenomenal! I'm not asking you to give that up. What I am asking you to do is to think and plan *before* you schedule your work hours. Then you can avoid the conflict, play as much as you want to, and be responsible about work commitments."

She heard my permission to disagree. In an immediate breakthrough, she challenged me with two powerful comments:

"Maybe *you* care about my work more than the museum does. Maybe *they* don't care when volunteers come or if they cancel."

Wow. Her words forced me into my own "maybe"—Maybe she's right. Since I'm not there, I don't *know* how much they need her or whether it matters to them. In trying to help her be prepared for the world of work, I'd brought my judgments about conventional work behaviors to this very unconventional situation. Respecting her new courage, I responded to her very convincing points.

"Nora, thank you! You've really made me think about this. Every work situation is different, and I'm not always right. Don't give me, or any human, that much power. I just react to the information you give me, and I don't know all that's going on in your life outside my office. You have to help me understand. *I* never suggested that you work on weekends—that was the schedule you arranged for yourself. If you hate the schedule, revise it, change it. But my advice is to do it in advance so that you give your boss notice.

"Now I'll give you *my* WHY, just the way I'm always asking you the 'why' of what *you* say and think. Remember, when you first took the museum job, we planned that it would be kind of a training experience for a paying job? Like a rehearsal, to learn how to behave in the world of work. You may feel ready to quit this job now. I just don't want you to quit because of fear or self-doubt. When conflicts come up in situations like this, please don't feel attacked when I suggest that some of your decisions may need rethinking."

"Does that mean I can never quit a job once I start, even if I don't like it anymore?"

"Of course not. But what I want you to learn is how to quit from a position of strength."

"What does *that* mean?"

"Look, you're at an age where you take jobs to learn the business of work and to find out what you like or don't like, what you're good at or not good at. This is a *job*, not a career or an occupation. And it's not even a paying job. There are *healthy* reasons for you to quit, but you have to know when—and why. A healthy reason for you to quit is because you've learned all there is to learn at this job, and—for you especially—because you've mastered the fears you had when you started—all those skills you thought you couldn't perform. Can you understand that?"

She nodded and looked hopeful for the first time.

"Nora, when you think I'm wrong, you have to tell me so! I won't be mad, I promise. Oh, I *will* hold you to the reasons WHY—you know that—and then I'll be proud to have you argue your case and win. That's what all this 'growing up' stuff is really about."

And right then and there, Nora did just what I asked. Not at home, in the privacy of her journal, but face to face. Buoyed by permission to disagree, she did something wonderful. She championed her cause for paddle tennis and against work on weekends. For the first time, she shared formerly withheld dialogues between herself and her boss during which the boss assured her that she could cancel when something more important came up. [**No wonder she was confused by our two diametrically opposed messages! And no wonder I was confused by my lack of inclusion in this information.**]

When she had finished this passionate defense of her case, I applauded and bravoed her for one long minute. And this time she understood WHY.

* * *

Nora played in the tournament that weekend. She and her partner won the mixed doubles. They played three sets and won them all, the only team undefeated in their division. In women's doubles, she and her Mom won second place. After winning two trophies, she said, "I almost feel like a real champion!"

She continued working at the museum, arranging her own schedule without compromising her paddle tennis exploits. Here is what she wrote in her journal about the difference between quitting a job and leaving:

> I learned that *quitting* is leaving a job without mastering what I needed to learn at that particular job, and *quitting* would be an easy way to avoid learning the particular task. *Leaving* a job is mastering the learned tasks of the job and then *leaving* the job, to therefore learn other tasks of another job. I'm trying real hard to keep going.

* * *

Now, seven months into the educational therapy, we did some new testing, with Nora's mindset more free of anxiety about the process and its purpose. [**A routine practice for educational therapists is a schedule of periodic retesting to assess academic improvement and provide accountability to client and family through quantitative evidence of the effectiveness of the educational interventions. With younger clients this kind of standardized testing is essential, coupled with portfolio assessments that use dated work samples in all subjects to compare progress over time from the starting point (baseline) over each school year. For Nora at 18, assessment was more portfolio-based, comparing her basic achievement levels with continuing areas of new mastery. Formal tests were used when I felt that I or Nora needed more information to clarify unanswered questions from earlier assessments and to measure progress.**]

We started with a separate test of visual memory and planning, the Rey-Osterreith Complex Figure Test, that had not been given during our early sessions. I felt this test would verify my impressions of her superior visual memory and provide insights into her planning for a graphic test. First, she was asked to carefully copy a very complex, detailed figure, and then to draw it from memory (see Appendix D).

Her copy and the drawing from memory were nearly perfect in every detail and reflected her strong organizational strategies for attacking the task. This test gave more objective support to my clinical observations that Nora learned in a visual systematic way, especially when the task was hands-on. This time she saw the proof herself, comparing with some pride her reproduction of the original pattern. Such concrete evidence had more impact than my words, helping her understand why she absorbed information best at Dunbrook when it was presented in some visual form.

An alternative test of general information, the Peabody Individual Achievement Test, disclosed some other specific holes in her base of knowledge. For one thing, Nora didn't know that fire requires oxygen in order to continue burning. The fire season was just beginning in California, and there had been a lot on the news about taking precautions, so it was a perfect lead into this topic. It was the right time to expose her to a basic science experiment, namely covering a lighted candle with a jar and watching it go out, this time focusing not just on fire's need for oxygen but on the word "smother," another unknown from the test. A stream of questions guided her thinking.

"When we smother a fire, Nora, what do we do? How else might we have smothered it than just putting the jar over the candle? How would we smother a fire in a frying pan, or on a person's clothing? What other way might the word "smother" be used? Oh, you saw something on a murder mystery? Right, the woman was smothered. How could a fire and a woman both be smothered? What do they both need to live? Oxygen." Deductive learning at its best.

Nora then asked about a "fire storm" which she had heard mentioned on the news. Looking out at the brush-covered hills we could see from my office window, we speculated about dry brush and its "combustibility." Since this word needed more realness for her, we headed for the kitchen. Using a deep pot, we played with various materials and saw firsthand which ones were combustible. As the flames rose out of the pot, Nora could see that fire could have a life of its own, making a thought-leap to a fire in the hills that had no pot to contain it. Could she imagine such an out-of-control "storm of fire," what they called a "fire storm," rather than a storm of rain? She could. And why might the news-casters talk about a "fire season"? Why would August and September be "fire season" in Los Angeles?

At that point, Nora made the links and guessed all the correct answers. We both laughed then, knowing she could now hold her own at a party when the discussion turned to the fire season in California.

* * *

At the next session, Nora arrived in a state of fury. The source of her rage—she had lost her appeal about the speeding ticket, leading to her uninhibited name-calling of the judge. His Honor's ears would have burned if he had heard himself verbally crucified by his victim of gross injustice.

In that moment, my feelings about the whole scenario were mixed. I was delighted that Nora could let out her frustration in the office, not just in her penned journal confessions. At the same time, I had to help her understand the system of laws and the factors deter-mining "justice." Using specific questions, I prodded her to think in new ways:

"Nora, what do you think the judge thinks about *you*, the 'traffic offender'? Why do you think they have traffic tickets? What's the purpose? How can a judge, who was not at the scene of the crime, know what is a fair or unfair consequence of an action?"

(And the most sensitive issue for her) "What do you think is, or should be, the *driver's* responsibility?"

She hated the questions. But she thought about them. Attributions of cause and blame were rarely objective for Nora, and this was a ripe chance to hit a topic we could no longer ignore: Fairness. Having felt victimized throughout her entire life, Nora was fragile about fairness. She perceived her world as one endless criticism. Clearly, she'd learned from her friends that it's safe to swear about judges. Not only was she "pissed" at the judge, but another injustice bubbled to the surface as a "by the way". By the way, she added paren-thetically, she's thinking of quitting at the museum because the people there won't talk to her.

And so another hour went by, revolving and resolving—from the impersonal courts to the highly personal workplace. If she's pissed at the judge, can she quit the job? Her connections defy logic, but they are all part of the same problem—*the fog of words, always in new contexts, always clouding meaning. One cannot adequately reason and problem-solve or correctly assign blame, even one's own, when the capacity to communicate, even to self-communicate, is impaired by limited language mastery.*

At the month's end, Nora did quit the job at the museum, but, as she explained, given her new permission to defend her reasons, she was quitting "from a position of strength." She had mastered all the tasks assigned to her and learned what she went there to learn.

I certainly couldn't and wouldn't challenge that decision.

11

AUGUST

College in Summer, Field Trip, and Videotape as a Learning Tool

With fewer sessions this month because of the August school break, we meld the academic with real experiences. Art courses call for exposure to real art in the museum, but failings in exhibits provide opportunities for letters of complaint. We take advantage of history being made—the Democratic convention—using video-tape in a new way. My attempts to stretch her to a new level of independence are misinterpreted—offering another chance to clarify, resolve anger, and create awareness of misunderstood communication. To relieve too much seriousness, we change the pace by conducting some simple science experiments.

Nora enrolled at Santa Lucia City College for a six-week art history course which both intrigued and frightened her. She wasn't interested in art as a career, but she had decided to try it to please her mother, who thinks she has a gift. She brought me the course outline and syllabus so that we could do a pre-course preparation and vocabulary survey. As we studied the materials, I suggested something that might inspire her interest and motivation—a "field trip" to the county art museum. The trip might make the art course come alive. Nora loved the idea, and we put it on our calendars.

The following week we arrived at the museum, which was huge and overwhelming. As we began to explore the first gallery, Nora noticed that there was very little printed information next to each painting, so we decided to rent the audio-tour of recorded commentary about the individual artworks. The plan seemed perfect, but the reality was a catastrophe because, once again, Nora's auditory system failed her. She couldn't rapidly process the unfamiliar vocabulary and sophisticated sentence structure on the recording, and it kept advancing to the next painting before she had understood the information about the last one. After a few minutes of frustration we returned the audio rental, continued on at our own pace, and tried to find artworks by artists she will be studying—Seurat, Monet, Renoir, and other Impressionists.

We took our time, and I encouraged Nora to study the styles and color use of the artists as well as to consider her "gut reactions" to each painting—which ones she liked instantly— and then to think about the reasons for her preferences. She tried this for a while but still remained upset by her helpless feelings during the audio-tour. Seeing her distress, I suggested she might want to communicate her thoughts in writing to the museum director during one of our sessions. This idea both excited her and sustained her interest for the rest of our tour.

When we met next in my office, our agenda, of course, had already been set, so we got right down to work. We brainstormed and prepared a four-part outline for a "masterpiece" letter, establishing the courtesies and form necessary for a letter of criticism to be respected by its recipient:

1. Reason for the letter and general comments.
2. Positive things about the Impressionist exhibition and the existence of a recorded tour.
3. Disappointments: no written descriptions, hard to understand exhibit, problems with recorded tour.
4. Comments on recorded tour itself.

The heart of her mission, of course, was No. 4. She wrote that, although such a tour seemed to be very necessary for understanding the exhibit, the language was too difficult and it moved on too quickly. She added that it was unclear why only a few paintings had explanations, and the exhibits were not designed with children or teens in mind, but rather for an older, very sophisticated audience.

Her conclusion: "Even if the recorded tour had been included in the price of the ticket, it would have been no help because those who would understand the language on the tape probably wouldn't need it, while others who needed it most couldn't comprehend it."

After careful editing, the letter was mailed. Thus, Nora began a path to the empowerment of letter writing, a journey that would serve her remarkably well in the future. But not this time. Regrettably, this time, she never received a reply from the museum director.

Busy with all the work facing her for this art course, Nora never noticed the lack of response to her letter. [**Perhaps I was the more disappointed one because her letter was only half of the mission; the reply would have demonstrated how this kind of action should work. There is always the hazard of counting on others to be partners in a remedial plan of which they have absolutely no awareness!**]

* * *

Meanwhile, the Democratic convention had been on TV, distracting us somewhat from the art history course. I videotaped a famous governor's keynote speech so that Nora and I could watch it together. Nora took notes, and when she got lost we had the privilege of rewinding the tape to play again and pause on command. Such a wonderful tool, the pause button—too bad she couldn't do that in her classes! [**Some students do, in fact, record teachers' lectures, but for most, the time required to listen again, pausing and repeating the tape, becomes too tedious to be practical.**]

We analyzed everything about this remarkable oration—his word choice, his eye contact, his tone of voice—all the ways one can try to read the meaning of a speech and the character of the speaker delivering it. During this exercise I learned, by observing Nora when she took notes, that she never looked at the speaker. She explained the reason: she was distracted by the visual features, giving her even more trouble processing what she was hearing. Thus, the videotape allowed her to take in everything by doing separate viewings.

At the end of this session Nora was filled with questions about politics, candidates, and of course how one decides which way to vote. The national convention filled our summer days with lots of new directions for investigation.

*   *   *

I observed a new behavior in Nora this month. She began to change a lot of appointments, and I became suspicious of the reasons, asking if something was wrong, or if perhaps she was wanting to stop coming over the summer. Many students want or need a summer break, so the question seemed logical to me, but not to Nora. She looked agitated when I asked this but denied any dismay and changed the subject.

Her newest writings, however, revealed the sources of her changed moods: her frustration with the art history course, a crisis with a best friend who didn't understand why she wasn't more open with her, and my recent prodding for her to increase her independence in both academic and personal management. The prodding was misperceived as criticism and anticipated anger.

> I couldn't believe on Friday Dorothy thought I didn't want to continue with her, I mean with all these problems I have now. I'm totally freaking out. I'm suposed to study about 50 slides of paintings. Well that's fine, except I can't study them unless I can see pictures of them in our Art History book, but no! I looked in the index, the contents and even under the artists name, and I still can't locate any pictures so I can't even study. I bet if I said that to Dorothy, she would give me a 15 minute lecture on the idea that I am giving up. I made a point of not telling her what was wrong Friday because I did not think she cared. It seems like she is so pissed off at me, its like she's only one more inch, then her temper is going to just fly.

This entry verified for me that, when Nora feels stress or pain, she presumes that everyone around her can see it, feel it, sense it. In the same way that she misread incoming language communications, she often gave out false messages to others, hiding her pain behind silence, noncommittal facial expressions, or unexpected outbursts of unclear origin. Was this why her friends were acting confused and unclear about what she was thinking? Life can become more and more lonely when communication breaks down in the social world as well. But her conclusions about my anger left me very confused until I continued reading her entry and found the source:

> I almost think Dorothy didn't want to re-schedule in the fall because this week I saw her Monday and when I left she didn't say: when will I see you again, she always says that and we schedule are next apointment but she didn't say anything. And later I didn't want to call her to reschedule, because I figured thats a hint, but I realized the Art History final was thurs. When I called she almost sounded like she was *so* angry that I wanted to schedule a second apointment this week.

[Now I understood. Nora had come to depend on my little verbal rituals or greetings delivered almost automatically at the beginnings and ends of hours without real awareness on my part—throwaways like "Hi, there, how was the day?" or "What's doing?" or "When will I see you next?" Unknown to me, these comments were a kind of "security blanket" of certainty for Nora, and alas, potential signs of rejection if unspoken when the hour ran late or another client showed up to interrupt the rhythm of our leave-taking. That was why the question as to whether she might want to take a break for the summer, so innocently asked, was so completely misinterpreted. Now I understood why Nora would not want to "have the summer off." And now I would have to clarify all the misunderstandings but also use the information about her study problems to keep us on the academic track.]

Immediately addressing her lack of adequate pictures in her textbook, I shared my collection of fine arts books to help her locate the artists and paintings she would be studying as part of her course. Being such a visual person, she began to grow comfortable looking for features of the paintings that her instructor had discussed.

One fact was certain: Nora was on the road to change, and I had become an increasing threat to her status quo—always stretching her to the next level, presenting new expectations, always believing she was capable of learning them. I included Nora in the need to revise our goals, explaining that for our "Stage Two" educational therapy we had to begin to put aside that comfortable, familiar hiding place that avoids life management skills.

[The constant revision of goals is essential to every educational therapy, especially with young adults who are used to being dependent on others for all decision-making. So many have "learned helplessness" over years of this automatic dependency. But the weaning from that dependency can be painful and take time.]

I told her I felt proud that she was beginning to assume some financial responsibility while pursuing her college goals and also revisiting the world of job/occupation/career—huge steps toward growth. She needed to acknowledge the changes, embrace them, take pride in them, and yet I knew that each change was very unnerving for her.

Could I assure her that the successes would be worth all the pain? It was a delicate time for our working relationship. The following journal entry showed me just how fragile it was. I had just learned that she had left the museum job, her own decision, and one that I'd perceived as an act worthy of pride, but now I learned that the decision was not prideful but guilt-ridden, and she still saw herself as a quitter:

> I never could understand why people always said growing up was so hard. Because I never was in a position where I was faced to "grow up" and experience that hard pain. I could avoid the situations, so often because I was never forced to. But then Dorothy was telling me that she was not going to take that bull.
>
> Nobody ever really said, Nora "stop running away, or hiding" except my parents. Dorothy is trying to give me a push. But why?
>
> I mean I am not proud of myself for quitting the job, because I knew that I only quit the job to run away from another opportunity to grow up. I don't want to keep running away, but I'm so scared to think about attempting another job situation because its so hard for me to sometimes talk to people.

When we met again, Nora said nothing of this written outburst, even though she had shared it willingly for me to read. It was up to me to address the writings directly. So I gave her my *real* thoughts on the topics she'd raised: that I feel *respect*, NOT disappointment, with her work. I feel *respect* for her really remarkable progress at the museum—the fact that she kept the job for almost the entire summer, even though I knew that she always wanted to stop. And especially, I feel *respect* that she made the decision and took the action all on her own to *leave* (not "quit").

She listened intently, not sure whether to be relieved or doubtful about my honesty, but something must have connected for her because, unexpectedly then, Nora took control of the discussion, switching the topic to her art class at the college. She thinks she is failing.

On the topic of failure, I sought a more objective appraisal. After all, this was Nora's first real college course, and she had lost sight of what she *had* achieved in this past month. It was another list-on-paper moment. Seeing things in black and white always allowed her to grasp the significance of real change. Written lists seemed to have that kind of power, and this list impressed both of us:

Nora's Accomplishments
She has enrolled at the college, by herself.
She has attended the classes regularly and on time.
She has taken careful and quite thorough notes.
She has studied the text and learned from it.
She has learned about the paintings of the Renaissance.
She has even tried to pass the tests (and maybe she did, since we don't know yet).

In a dramatic stage whisper, I said, "Nora, every one of these represents *real* learning, *real* milestones of change and of growth. This was your *first encounter with a college!*"

Once again, my hushed tones and the graphic evidence helped Nora change her perspective. She laughed and put aside the high-pitched voice and worried face. Best of all, that sheepish grin let me know she got the point—maybe she had finally done something right!

* * *

Nora passed, not failed, her art history class—with an unexpected C! The teacher was amazed at how hard she tried in the exam, asked her to come and talk personally about what she understood, and gave her the grade. Still, the girl who had expected to fail now had a different kind of disappointment: "I wish it was a B!" Never good enough.

In that moment, I realized that I should stop giving Nora options to consider other than college. She wasn't about to quit this quest, no matter how long it will take to get those first letters—Nora Tarlow, AA—after her name. Let that be the major goal, and then we will see what follows.

We discussed her schedule of classes for fall. She had met with my friend, the counselor in Santa Lucia's special services program, and was pre-enrolled in introductory psychology plus two labs in writing and "study skills for special students." The prospect of a psychology course had her excited and interested. However, she was less enthusiastic about any class with a "special" classification.

[At this age level, most students with unique needs are very offended by this word and any class that makes them feel identified as "different." Most have had many years of tutoring, special classes, and accommodations—often welcomed by some students, but others long to be "regular" and blend into the crowd. Though they may still need the slower pace and modified curriculum of these preparatory courses at college level, they also need

a new identity, a new beginning, and a wish that they can finally manage the demands without these compensations. For some, they can. For most, they need that boost, especially in their first year.]

* * *

It was the end of August. Nora arrived at the office after another student had been making a miniature volcano, and the smell of burning chemicals filled the room. We took out her folder to revisit our discussion of the three "isms" of government when she complained:

"Why does everyone else have fun in here and I don't?"

We laughed about that truth and decided to put aside the "isms" and get into experiments today—she deserved an occasional respite from growing up.

It was a perfect time for her to enjoy my favorite starch experiment. We headed for the kitchen, and found, peeled, and grated two baking potatoes. Then we put the gratings into a handkerchief, which we twisted closed at the top, and dunked the wrapped gratings into a bowl of water—dunking and squeezing out the water three or four times. We let the water in the bowl settle for a few seconds, then carefully, slowly, poured it out, and there, on the bottom of the bowl, was a smooth coating of white starch, perfectly separated from the potato pulp. We scraped the pure powdery starch on to a paper towel. I brought out my iodine bottle and had Nora touch a drop of it to the small pile of starch, and Voila! Nora observed with amazement as the iodine, which is a cinnamon-brown color in the bottle, turned a dramatic black the minute it touched starch.

We talked about the meaning of chemical reactions for a few minutes, and then she was ready for the best part—testing samples of different kinds of foods from my kitchen to see which ones contained starch. I had her speculate first, giving me some reasons behind her educated guessing, and then we checked her accuracy with one drop of iodine on each of the bread-cracker-apple-cheese-bologna-rice-lettuce-pita, etc. morsels. I loved the drama of this experiment, especially the surprise when even the apple turned a little bit black. Yes, apples contain a little starch! She gradually made the generalization connecting grain and potato products as starchy foods. However, when she asked if starch was the same as fat, I saw that she was still a little fuzzy about the basic food groups. So nutrition took its well-deserved place on the day's and the month's intellectual "menus"—a practical conclusion—and a welcome relief to our summer schedule of widely diverse topics and mini-crises.

[Balance was so important to keep in mind during this difficult crossroad into more independent adulthood. Nora had trouble even acknowledging her successes, so respites of fun were essential.]

12

SEPTEMBER/OCTOBER

College Texts and Morning Papers—
A Whole New Path

The long-anticipated, full-semester college enrollment will involve planning, strategies for survival with textbook demands and workload from multiple courses. The mass of vocabulary in Nora's psychology course alone leads us to consideration of a very unconventional plan. Other questions arise about more general survival in adulthood. She is finally reading the morning newspapers, and the result is a whole new, profound interest in autism that stimulates an independently produced academic project.

Traditional back-to-school month was an exciting one for Nora this year—her first real, full semester of college. Armed with confidence from her success in art history, she was open to guidance about how to proceed in her next course, introductory psychology. To prepare her in advance for the new vocabulary she'd be facing, we used one of the "(*Subject*) Made Simple" series, this one called *Psychology Made Simple*, to introduce the lingo of "psychology-speak" in preparation for her real textbook work. As we had done in the past, we surveyed the Table of Contents and did a quick page-turning through the book so that she could understand how the chapters had been organized. By paraphrasing what she thought the major headings of the contents meant, she disclosed what terminology was already familiar (e.g., "clinical" and "experimental"), what words were totally foreign (e.g., "ecology," "forensic,", "perception," and "stimuli"), and how much worrying would be legitimate.

Then Nora proudly shared her own personal study plan for academic survival in college: to read every page with a dictionary next to her; to look up each word she doesn't know and to write the definition above the word in the book; then to try to figure out from context what each word means in the sentence, what each sentence, and what each paragraph means. In short, she would be moving through the text like an army scout surveying a battlefield—from smaller to bigger chunks. It was only a workable plan because Nora, a rare bird, was actually *willing* to put in that awesome kind of time and dedication.

In subsequent sessions, we transitioned from *Psychology Made Simple* to the real course textbook, applying her newly tuned textbook-surveying skills. One by one, systematically we addressed the multi-level challenges she must face in college—such basics as how to think actively while studying, how to organize notes by main ideas and details, and how to prepare for different types of tests. Capitalizing on her marvelous organizational and visual memory skills, we worked on expanding her ability to prepare graphic schemas and charts of major topics for each unit of the text as it comes up.

During the first week in the introductory psychology class at Santa Lucia, the teacher gave her class the *Learning Style Inventory* (Barsh, 1991) (see Appendix C), a self-admin-istered checklist to determine if one learns in a more auditory, visual, or tactual mode—or some combination of the three. Nora handed her checklist to me as she walked into the office and said, "How did you know this? You were right!" Her score was a 40 on Visual, a 24 on Tactual, and a dismal 5 on Auditory. I couldn't hide my smile at these results sup-porting my early testing and both of our observations about her daily style of functioning.

Nora was intensely interested in the topic of psychology, both personally and intellec-tually, but she was drowning in the amount of vocabulary. Observing her anguish, I proposed a possible but unconventional plan for her to consider: *Use the semester to master the language of the psychology course itself, whether or not you pass and earn credit. Then, if necessary, repeat the course for credit.* With that mindset, I explained, she could relieve some of the pressure, continue to proceed with her need to build vocabulary, and just see what happens.

Nora was silenced by the radical proposal—she was not sure how to respond, wondering aloud whether this would be wise or make her look foolish. Acknowledging her uncer-tainty, I suggested some key questions she might consider to aid in her decision. We both knew of her determination to achieve a college degree. But how long will it take? We can't know that yet. Does she need to graduate college by some pre-planned deadline? Is there a rush for her? Would it destroy her self-esteem if she had to repeat some courses in order to master the language well enough to pass the exams? How would her parents feel about this plan, since additional costs would be involved (although community college had very low fees at that time)?

She didn't know the answers; nor did I. But the questions suggested a possible alternative path. Scary but interesting, uncharted waters. Nora needed time to think about it. Of course, the decision had to be hers and her parents'. Much would depend, too, on how she actually performed in this first psychology course.

[I had learned to think unconventionally from many previous students who had achieved success in very diverse ways. Some had left high school at age 16 for different reasons, and the community colleges offered a whole range of self-chosen schedule options. One student had great difficulty functioning in the early hours of the day due to a sleep disorder, but by enrolling at the community college, he could sleep late in the morning, schedule his classes in the afternoons, and gain a respectable high school degree while enjoying the status of being a college student. In fact, this student ended up at the university, graduating a year earlier than his peers because the community college time options allowed him to combine his final high school and first-year college requirements and realize his true academic brilliance. Another very hyperactive, athletic student ended up at a ski college in Colorado where he had academic studies in the morning and ski team training on the slopes every afternoon. He became an Olympic skier, and after a serious accident decided on law school to become a sports lawyer. And that is what he became! Differences in learning needs often demand different solutions.]

At the end of this hour of provocative ideas, just before leaving, Nora announced that *she* had a surprise for *me*.

"Close your eyes," she commanded, and I could hear her rifling through her saddlebag purse, making sounds I couldn't identify.

"Now, look!"

When I opened my eyes, there she was, seated at the desk with her brand-new imitation leather checkbook, writing me her first very own personalized check! And another toe just got dipped into the pond of adulthood.

* * *

When we next met, Nora reported that she had discussed with her parents the option of possibly having to repeat a course if the new vocabulary took more time for her to master. I was pleased to hear that they had both agreed to leave the decision up to her. She seemed relieved, too, but there was another worry today. She continued to have problems with her friends, who insisted that she had no learning disabilities, that there was nothing wrong with her, and that she should stop being so hard on herself. They accused her of trying to prove that she's really "no good," advising that she had to start liking herself. She didn't know what to believe, and this inspired her to write a fictional tale about the feelings of a girl whom nobody understands. In the end the girl gets hit by a car and ends up in a wheelchair so that everyone can *see* her disability. We were back to the Elephant Man again.

Before I could even address this latest fiction, she raised other new questions, new fears about entering the adult world:

What will she do to earn money?

How will she support herself?

Can she make it in college? What if she can't? (The job option was still scarier to her than college pursuits.)

[Her problems are familiar ones—the problems of all young adults getting ready to be on their own, especially those like Nora whose parents have provided lots of comforts and security. They all feel terrified that they will never be able to provide for themselves what has been provided for them.]

I just listened, wrote down her list, and suggested that we could deal with these questions as they arise once she starts to seek job opportunities in the real world. Then we'll address those problems in the same way that we have been tackling the academic ones—one at a time.

She surprised me by accepting that simplified explanation, reminding me once again how much our progress depends on trust.

* * *

After months of my prodding, Nora had actually begun to read the morning paper on her own. She was drawn to an article on autism and brought it in for us to discuss. We analyzed the language of the article and the terms that confused her. She had discussed the article at home with her parents. Apparently, her interest was acute enough to remind her father of a specialist in autism, a Dr. Beltran, whom he knew at the university. He offered to arrange an interview for her. I encouraged the opportunity for her to talk to a real expert who would know much more than I. Then she proudly told me more news—that, on her own, she had arranged a visit to the Reynolds Center, the same residential and day program for autistic youth that was mentioned in the article. **[Another huge sign of growth—Nora was beginning to initiate actions on her own before discussing them with me.]**

Impressed by her initiative and the potential demands—and possible pitfalls—of these two interactions, I advised Nora to prepare a list of questions for both situations. She definitely wanted to be prepared, to know what to ask, and, she said, "to sound intelligent." She copied the symptoms of autism from the encyclopedia to prepare herself for her interview with Dr. Beltran, which she would schedule to take place before the visit to the Center.

Showing another kind of self-motivation, Nora had more surprises up her sleeve. Going way beyond the informal notes I'd recommended, she wrote an actual mini-research paper on autism:

What is Autism?

Autism is a lifelong developmental disability that usually appears during the first three years of life. Four times more common in males than in females. About seventy five percent of all Autistic children are males and has been found in families of all racial, ethnic, and social backgrounds. True Autism, which is called early infantile autism, occurs in about one child in thirty thousand. But the term Autism is used to refer to other severe forms of mental illnesses that resemble true autism.

What are the Symptoms of Autism?

[Words and expressions she did not initially understand but looked for explanations on her own are in italics.]

a) *Difficulty in mixing with other children*—doesn't realize he is a person. He appears to live in a dream world, withdrawn and distant.
b) *Resists change in routine*—extraordinarily intolerant of changes in his physical surroundings. The child may have a severe tantrum if books, furniture, or other objects are not in their correct place.
c) *Not cuddly*
d) *Uneven motor skills*—may not be able to kick a ball, but some are excellent Climbers—good use of hands and fingers.
e) *Musical skill*—love music, insist on playing favorite record over and over. Perfect pitch. Can hum or sing an entire song after only hearing it once.
f) *Inappropriate attachment to objects*—can become deeply fascinated w/a certain *inanimate* object and carry it w/them everywhere at all times.
g) *Speech*—can be mute or they utter a few words throughout their entire lives. If they speak, they *repeat* what they've heard, in a very robot like voice. At 8 or 9, begin to speak if not mute.

Causes (neurological effect)

Inborn disorder of body chemistry. Abnormal amounts of some chemicals in the blood and urine of autistic children. Although some believe it is caused by the attitudes and the way the child is brought up. The *Practices* of the mother.

* * *

This was a fabulous first for Nora—a paper researched and written completely on her own, motivated by her own interest, not some teacher's assignment, and remarkable in its structure and body of information. We spent some time discussing the terminology she didn't understand, and after that, formulating some specific questions for Doctor Beltran. Nora felt both proud of her research and prepared for her meeting.

For me, her whole effort and the end result was an educational therapist's dream.

13

NOVEMBER

An Interest in Autism Becomes a Saga

Continued interest in autism finds Nora facing her interview with Dr. Beltran and also enrolling in a home-care respite job. The disrespect and ridicule she felt during the expert's interview leads to a lesson on the challenges of human interaction. We analyze criticism itself and factors that can determine if it is real or imagined. Her writings describe the twin traumas of the interview and the unexpected events of respite care. Often in life, one has to "make lemonade from lemons," another task for educational therapy. For the college demands, she must work to refine her conventions of written English.

Nora's meeting with Dr. Beltran was less than successful, in spite of her intense preparation. My heart broke as I read her description of the encounter:

> Every time I asked him a question he made it seem like I was a complete fool and that I was wasting his time. As I sat there, I wondered what had happened to all the enthusiasm he expressed on the phone to my Dad. He'd say what questions do you have, and I'd gain just enough confidence to say, "Well, I don't really quite understand what it is. I've read things about it." And this doctor would just coldly say, "Nobody is clear what it is, what's your next question?" and I'm shaking in my chair thinking what will I ask next so I thought, "What are the cures, how do people treat autistics?" and even more coldly, he said, "There are NO cures."
>
> Every time he'd shoot down a question of mine, I'd acquire a certain amount of confidence and try again, until he shot that one down. When I left that office, I felt wounded like someone had just shot me down, literally. So on my way home I kept thinking about the Bobby Reynolds Center where I was supposed to visit next week. That's when I thought if Dorothy came with me, I'd feel more at ease. But I'd die if I got shot down in front of her. Somehow she seems to think I'm something I'm really not.

[When students can describe experiences and the accompanying feelings this clearly, it provides an extraordinary opportunity to address their misunderstandings as well as to

examine the educational therapist's role in the outcome. Nora had generalized her sense of failure, giving herself no credit for having enough confidence to persist with new questions. Then she generalized this negative experience to the upcoming meeting at the Center, wondering how to avoid "being shot down" again, not even recognizing the courage she had shown. Most sobering of all was her conclusion that she was not worthy of my belief in her. What a perfect example of how a belief in a client's capabilities can backfire if the client feels her failure to perform successfully will disappoint the educational therapist! It was a very important lesson for me—to temper my enthusiasm because outcomes will not always be successful, but it also clarified a missing piece in Nora's perspective.]

The pervasive self-doubt expressed in this journal entry called for a new direction. Our curriculum had never yet addressed specific strategies *for the realities of social interaction*— the fact that conversations take place between two (or more) people who each bring to it *their own attitudes and personalities.* These were very new notions for Nora to consider: Did the doctor really shoot her down or was his style simply at odds with her own? Did she understand about differences in personality and variations in temperament? Had she ever thought about how one must adapt to those differences when having a conversation? Had she considered that such people may not be expressing criticism of her but may just have a cold style of communication? Could she realize that certain types of people are unable to be patient or supportive of those with less knowledge than their own? Did the doctor sense her fear and self-doubt? If so, was he annoyed by it, or was he just an insensitive, unaware scientist?

Indeed, Nora had never before considered such ideas, and now that she did, some of the pain from that Beltran interview was neutralized. Equally impressive was her handling of the complex language itself in this sophisticated discussion. The new point of view buoyed up her courage to face the next experience. She had already checked out facts about the Reynolds Center—that it was a residential and daycare facility for children and young adults with autism, and that they trained individuals who wanted to baby-sit with this population in their own homes to give some "respite" (relief) to the parents. She used the word "respite" with pride of mastery. Listening to her that hour, I felt she would be much more prepared this time for the Reynolds Center—a very different setting that would be less intense without the one-to-one interaction. And this time, I was careful to keep my comments very low-key.

* * *

In the week following her visit to Reynolds, Nora crafted a superb essay buoyed by her readings and real experiences—qualitatively the best she'd ever done owing to her genuine comprehension of new and difficult concepts. In it, she disclosed a personal decision, made 100 percent independently, owing to the impact of the experience.

My Experience at the Bobbie Reynolds Center

After reading an article on autism in the Los Angeles Times, I suddenly acquired a strange curiosity about autism. "What is autism?" I thought. This article was about an autistic adult. After reading it, my curiosity still was not satisfied. I wanted to know more about this strange disorder.

I then went to the public library to check out books on this fascinating subject. Still I only got very abstract theories and definitions about the meaning. I wanted somehow to observe this particular handicapped population.

Someone then told me to investigate the Bobbie Reynolds Center for Autism. I met with the director of the center and was given a tour of the Occupational Training Center where the clients learn trades so they can make money from their abilities. The Reynolds Center has a sitter-respite training program which offers a home care relief service for the parents of these youngsters.

I decided to take this training program. The training included a visit to the Saturday Program that was designed for the handicapped population who live at home and come there on Saturdays to develop social, self-help, and recreational skills. They make crafts, popcorn, play and have lunch together, and go roller skating. I observed some of the characteristics of autistic children which I had read about in textbooks.

Because the handicap population have acquired higher rights, their conditioning methods have changed in a more civilized manner. Each client at the Occupational Training Program is on their own individual behavior program, which is listed in the client's notebook. The Training Program does not like to stress on aversive methods at all, which is punishing for negative behavioral habits. This program stresses on a strong accent on positive behavioral habits, and the rewards of this behavior.

Nora's disclosure here of commitment to both the training and the respite care, a real job for pay, caught me by surprise. She shared her excitement over keeping the secret, taking the job, and also making money to "make a lot of people happy, for instance my family." She felt that her parents didn't consider the museum job as work, even though they never pushed her to find a paying job.

As she explained her plan, I cautioned Nora that her acceptance of this job was a big step, a first step, a trial—and no doubt one of many that would come along. This trial would help her see where she belongs as she explores the world of work, moving "from job to career to occupation." Nora smiled at her familiarity with the meaning of that last remark, and I sensed that she felt she really had something to give in this job.

[Neither of us knew whether this experience would be successful, and this time I wanted to prepare her for whatever outcome may occur. This proved to be a wise caution.]

* * *

Nora's new job would not begin for several weeks. Meanwhile, on the college front, she was upset to learn that two of the courses she was required to take at Santa Lucia, along with her psychology course, were "prep courses for special ed students," one in basic English and one in human development. No grades or college credits were given for them, but she had no options to avoid them.

In the English class, the teacher's focus on the grammatical imperfections in her essays discouraged her. College English teachers are, rightfully, less forgiving, since their main purpose is to fine-tune the written output of the students. Consequently, we shifted our own focus from her job to the basics in English, and now the motivation to perfect her skills would be driven by her wish to succeed in her college course.

[Again we face the cleaved domain of educational therapy. As you have seen throughout these chapters, we must move in and out of the academic/affective worlds when the academic demands are waylaid by the social-emotional distractions of real-life issues. Once those are dealt with, the energy is available again for the academic path.]

Nora needed particular work on basic writing conventions—sentence structure and such fundamentals as the distinguishing features defining "sentence," "phrase," and "clause." Using Warriner's *English Composition and Grammar* textbook (Warriner, 1988) and a workbook geared to making sense of sentences, Nora began to get a feeling for the jobs of *groups* of words in the development of correct prose. She quickly grasped the notion that both a clause and a sentence must have a verb—that's the rule—so, consequently, every sentence is also a clause. It was a little harder for her to understand that every clause is not necessarily a sentence. She laughed when we diverged into a discussion of *dependent* and *independent* clauses—that "only the independent ones qualified to be called sentences." That pair of words had come up often in her own life, but she never dreamed that clauses could have the same requirements as she for functioning independently! We had fun with the phrases, using the prepositional ones to illustrate their job of putting things or ideas in different positions, either on or under or near or over or around, etc. She had to demonstrate her mastery of all this to me by analyzing her own sentences from previous papers, identifying her own clauses and phrases, underlining the one in red and the other in blue, and editing those that needed it. We reviewed some basic skills on sentence variations, sentence combining, and parallel structure to enhance and mature her style.

Teaching the mechanics of written English demanded the teaching of *awareness*. Particularly for spelling, in the days before Spellcheckers, Nora had to develop conscious awareness that there was more than one way to spell certain words, the homonyms, and the choice depended on the meaning of that word in the sentence. She needed permission to make the error when she was rushing through a first draft in order to get her thoughts down on paper without losing them, but if she had awareness of these demons, like her always troublesome "no" and "know," she could look for them during the editing process and ask herself if the word she used fit the meaning. For example, the word "know" comes from "knowledge"; she knew what that meant, and she was clear about the negative meaning of "no," so the goal was to get her to visualize "knowledge" when asking herself if "no" fit the requirement for her sentence.

She also had no idea that there was actually a set of rules regarding the doubling of consonants, but mastery of rules was a strength for Nora. She had just never been exposed to them, and after so many years of spelling these words incorrectly, it would take some time to re-program the "spelling centers" of her brain. The important truth was that she would be able to do so if she had *awareness* and if it was important to her. The same was true for learning the rules for commas, and I shared my user-friendly list of 12 (most students are surprised it's only 12, a manageable number) that I had fine-tuned many years before from a list in a Steck-Vaughn English Mastery workbook (see Appendix A, Rules for the Use of Commas). Again, awareness would create the active mindset that was so necessary for all proofreading skills. I became more of a "stealth observer" as Nora proved herself up to the job and felt comfortable with these very specific tasks. Now she would have to demonstrate the changes to her English teacher.

* * *

The time arrived for Nora to begin her new job from the Reynolds Center. She had completed the Respite Service training course and was assigned to her first placement with a handicapped child. However, to her surprise, this youngster was not autistic but had severe cerebral palsy—a condition Nora had neither expected nor been prepared for. The following, very touching essay gives her passionate account of this emotional experience. It also reveals her first awareness of the overwhelming responsibility she had accepted. She had stepped beyond curiosity into grim reality.

My First Job Babysitting a Cerebral Palsy Child

After completing my training at the Reynolds Center, I was eligible to babysit on my first job.

I arrived at a home where I met a mother and her cerebral Palsy Child. She gave me instructions to feed the boy and just sit with him all day. She told me that when I was to feed him, I was to keep him propped up or he would choke and die.

This boy was 7 years old, about 2 1/2 feet long with all of his extremities spasmed in a curled up position.

All day I sat with him watching TV, and holding him. I tried feeding him and after a few spoonfuls I got scared he might choke. I would carry him when we weren't watching TV and the whole time just praying he would still be alive and OK when his mom arrived.

The house was very dark. Curtains were all drawn and the house in complete disaray. I saw lots of pictures of a very handsome boy who resembled the boy I had spent the whole day with. But the pictures weren't of a cerebral Palsy boy. I walked around the house and got curious to see beyond the moth-eaten dirty curtains in the livingroom. I opened them, and to my surprise, I saw an overgrown backyard full of weeds and a fence around what resembled a black pool. At that point I had heard my 1st cry from my all-day companion. I closed the curtains and held him.

Hours later the Mother finally arrived and I was just thankful that the youngster was still alive and well in my hands all day.

The mother thanked me and paid me for the day. I asked her why if she had a beautiful pool outside, the curtains were closed and the pool not in use?

She immediately closed the curtains and said her boy was not always like this. He was born very healthy (the pictures I'd seen were him.) He had an accident in that pool 3 years ago for about ½ hour and went into a coma. He awoke as in the condition that I met him w/ Cerebral Palsy.

I was so frightened by my whole day and my experience with a handicapped youngster. I realized I couldn't go on w/ this kind of job again until I was emotionally ready. I cried a lot, what if he choked, and the fact that I carried a mute and physically disfunctional boy around all day.

When the shock of my experience wore off, I called the Reynolds Center and discharged myself from further work explaining that I wasn't ready for it yet.

I left with a wonderful understanding of the handicap population which started by an interest in the word "Autism" that I read in an article in the Times. (*sic*)

* * *

The poignancy, pathos, and poetic word choice of Nora's essay touched me deeply and revealed her true potential for the narrative storytelling she had previously expressed interest in, all the while showing a marked improvement in her sentence structure. She had painted such a vivid portrait of her day and the emotions it evoked that I could completely support her decision not to continue. Fortunately, she did not seem to feel guilty about that decision. Indeed, from now on, we would take each work situation as a new learning opportunity and analyze all the lessons learned. Our list from this one experience was impressive:

1. She had *read the article* on autism, pursued her interest, *made the appointment* at the Center.
2. She *took the training* and *accepted the job.*
3. She *showed up* for the job on time, *followed the mother's instructions, cared for the child* as instructed, and both of them *survived the day.*
4. She had the *courage to inquire* about the cause of the child's condition.
5. She *discovered* the horrifying consequences of a near-drowning accident.
6. She *handled her decision to quit* with maturity, calling the Reynolds Center immediately and explaining her *honest reason for termination*—"I wasn't ready for it yet."

In reviewing the list, I remembered my prior warning to her that this was a first step in her explorations of work. Together, we concluded that this was a remarkable growth experience—even if it proved to be an unlikely career direction at that time.

*　*　*

Learning about this unfortunate child's history set new wheels in motion in Nora's mind. She decided to ask her mother about the circumstances of her own birth, something it had never occurred to her to ask, either of me or of her mother, before hearing this story. I had presumed she had been told.

[Another lesson for me: never presume that information from a young adult client's history has been shared, although many older clients come to us without any family or source of information. It is critical that all known historical information be shared at an opportune time, either by the parents or by the educational therapist with parental permission.]

Nora was profoundly interested to hear about her birth, which she knew was "bad" but she never found out why. She reported her mother's descriptions: her late birth—almost 10 months of pregnancy for her mother to endure; her coming out crying after the long, painful birth; and her continued crying for about two months straight. She learned that she never crawled, walked too early, and was an uncontrollable baby for months afterward, which her mother believed was caused by the long, emotional birth and may have to do with the reason she has learning disabilities.

I could tell that Nora felt very relieved to learn this story directly from her mother. She said, "I've always known that Mom wanted me to get help, and she was the one who almost experienced all the pain I did in school, because she was so upset when my teacher and tutors would say things that weren't true. She knew all along I'd been trying so hard. But I never knew about my birth." She had never before thought about putting together the puzzle pieces in her life story by just asking questions of those who could give her the answers.

14

DECEMBER

Social Challenges of the Holiday Season;
Reviewing a Year's Growth

This final month of our first year finds Nora on the college track, succeeding in her first courses while also dealing with holiday challenges—parties, movies, gift-giving and receiving. A threatening notice from the bank leads to lessons on the real meaning of "form letters" and when to worry. In retrospect, we consider what has been accomplished in Nora's first year of educational therapy—and what is yet to come.

This was the second December for Nora and me, another shortened month owing to the Christmas break. After a whole year since our first meeting, Nora was now on the full-time college path, as unbelievable as that had seemed 12 months ago. This week she reported getting a B on her first psychology exam but minimized the success by declaring the test "too easy," a sign that it was still hard for her to believe she could succeed in the academic world. Meanwhile, in the basic English course, so resented at first, she admitted that she was improving her proficiency at proofreading to eliminate her sentence fragments, apply the comma rules, and check for those homonyms. Her progress with that troublesome triplicate of skills earned a well-deserved drum roll from me.

The holiday season was coming, and, with it, the dreaded party scene where Nora still felt "like I've just come from Mars because I'm so different." She dreaded all the holiday movies, too. Her friends were planning to go see the new movie, *Yentl*, which, from the trailers, she was sure she wouldn't understand. Attending movies with friends encompassed her with the relentless input of dialogue both from the film and their discussions afterward.

Since movies would play a big part in Nora's life this month, I gave her some strategies for a different way to view them. "Nora, it isn't important for you to know every word from the dialogue. Just try to just get a *feeling* for the movie. Where is it taking place, and what is the time in history? What's the message of it—the whole point of the story? How did it change your mind or make you think differently? Try to watch for the attitudes of the people by reading their body language and facial expressions—you know, the way we practiced by studying people in the soap operas. Try to see what your overall feeling is about the film—what mood it puts you in."

She took notes of my suggestions, and *Yentl* would be her first chance to try them out. If this helped, we would add movies to our curriculum and fine-tune her new movie-watching skills by discussing plot lines in advance to give her a frame of reference before viewing each one. It would be a little like having Cliffs Notes before reading literature. She could relate to that idea. [**Today, of course, every movie could be Googled to learn about the plot in advance.**]

It was not only holiday time but the end of the fall semester, and Nora had to make plans for the spring. We studied the catalog looking for possible required course offerings to fulfill her coveted AA degree, but this goal was sidetracked by a worry she couldn't put out of her mind. She had just received a notice from the bank regarding her overdrawn account. The intimidating notice, written in legal-speak, accused her of "negligence," a word she understood well enough for it to induce some panic. I explained that banks automatically send out these "form letters" to anyone who overdraws on his or her account. Their wording is deliberately threatening, no matter how small the amount of money, because the same one goes to everyone (hence the expression "form letter"), whether they owe $10 or $10,000.

Nora's amount overdrawn was $32.16—hardly evidence for high crimes and misdemeanors. No need to panic, but she couldn't ignore it either, because, as the letter stated, every check that bounces will cost her $10 (*the fee at that time*), even if the check itself was for only $4.50. She got the message, but she hated it because she still hadn't mastered balancing her checkbook and was never sure of the balance in her account. We talked about two possible solutions: calling the bank near the end of each month to find out her balance, or possibly keeping a "buffer" of $100 or $200 extra in it but never recording them in her checkbook. [**From her look of semi-understanding and confusion with the buffer concept, my instinct told me that bank books and Nora could be in conflict for some time. Until a solution came from Nora herself, most likely there would not be a change in habits, and she'd be in for more financial anguish, but now she'd know why. This was one more situation where awareness was the root of learning.**]

* * *

Just before the Christmas break, Nora surprised me with a glass coffee mug, etched with the words "#1 TUTOR." I thanked her sincerely for such a touching gift and responded with my gift for her—a jar of my homemade fudge sauce complete with its personalized "From the kitchen of . . . " label, the annual gift for my clients to sweeten their holidays.

[**Gift-giving and receiving is somewhat controversial for educational therapists, and some have a policy of neither giving nor receiving gifts because some clients go to uncomfortable extremes or feel an expectation. I believe that gifts are a part of life and can influence one's values regarding giving and receiving, so they deserve some thought. My practice is to keep the gift simple, inexpensive, homemade if possible, and for birthdays, relevant to the client, such as a page holder for copying at the computer, a pencil holder that improves handwriting, or an inexpensive necklace with some symbol that represents their progress. For Nora, I used to tell her I wanted her to grow to be a rose, which took a lot of work and care to become so special, and not a weed that just grew wild without any attention. So for one of her birthdays I gave her a little enameled rose on a chain with a certificate stating she'd achieved "rose-dom."**]

Nora's other gift to me was her report about the movie, *Yentl*. She saw it, trying to keep in mind the guidelines we'd discussed, and by concentrating on the visual cues of the storytelling the fog of verbiage lifted a bit. She actually came away with some sense of the setting, historical period, and message of the film—religion's prescribed role for a woman's place in society—in spite of all the dialogue. With all the holiday movies opening that month, I hoped this approach to movie viewing might make the season more fun and a little less stressful for Nora. With luck, it might even give her new meaning for those words coming up on December 31—"Happy New Year!"

* * *

The passage of one whole year in Nora's educational therapy called for a circumspect review of what we had accomplished. Our limited weekly hours had been apportioned, not always equally, between the academic demands and the life demands as each arose. As I looked back on those 12 months, I had to ask myself some tough questions about the choices made and priorities given to each intervention.

What about English grammar? If we had addressed only the rules of grammar in her writing efforts, would she ever have been free enough to let her thoughts flow and allow her journal notes to be our curriculum guides? Probably not. What about the amount of time given to curriculum content? If we had addressed only the textbooks and curriculum demands, would she have performed with higher test scores? Probably so. But what would she have retained of that information? What would really be integrated as knowledge that she could use as she neared the end of her teens? Would she simply have "answered the questions right but not understood what anything meant," as she had described about her past performance with academics?

These are just samples of the multiple questions educational therapists must ask as we re-evaluate our goals and the effectiveness of our interventions with each client, and as we tailor the sessions to each one's individual and constantly evolving needs. Our Organic Curriculum had given Nora and me the flexibility to customize what worked for her during the vital formation of a trusting relationship in this first year of interaction. She had truly mastered academic content through contextual patterns of vocabulary applied experientially. Now the test would be how she could fine-tune those strategies to function well in college and enter adulthood with the ability to acquire knowledge, ask questions when she needed answers, and advocate for herself when situations didn't fit with her type of neurological "wiring."

Since Nora's auditory processing disorder was first identified for her so late in her life—age 17—and was so all-encompassing in affecting her academic and social/emotional life, our work together extended for a much longer time than is usual for educational therapy (typically one to two years). Her weekly course of educational therapy went on for four years, with the number of sessions steadily decreasing from 93 in the first year to 40 in Year Four. After that there were sporadic sessions, which we jokingly called her "oil and lube" visits for very specific needs, the kinds of "will-call" sessions alluded to earlier.

Read on in Part Three for particular "magical moments of change" in subsequent years of our journey together—through the lessons in life and the quest for resolution of some of its unexpected challenges.

PART THREE

Continuing Change

Short Vignettes from Subsequent Years in Educational Therapy

The chapters of Part One and Part Two provided a chronological journey through the first year of Nora's educational therapy, defining her history, needs, academic interventions, and struggles in multiple life situations.

Part Three is a selection of vignettes capturing some critical changes following the first year, as Nora emerged from self-consciousness to self-confidence. The vignettes explore: two different employment situations; lessons in personal appearance and style; health issues and development of assertiveness; "fitting in" vs. rejection in different settings; a new awareness of her learning style from the study of one word; new ways to address an old fear, and obstacles in college and work on the road to respect.

There was one difference after Year 1. Now Nora understood the reasons for all those breakdowns in her acquisition of language and knowledge. Consequently, she finally became her own advocate and, even more, a champion for justice.

Year 2

WORKING FOR DAD'S OFFICE

From Doubt to Confidence

Up until this time, Nora's exposure to employment, other than the disastrous time at McDonald's, began with two volunteer positions—first, at the Dinosaur Museum where she apprenticed to classify and restore fossil fragments; and second, as a sitter-respite worker for mothers of autistic children. This vignette describes her first real work in a paid position during the second summer of our work together. A whole different set of needs surfaced in this new setting, illustrating a few of the kinds of educational therapy interventions that are relevant to the world of work.

Walter Tarlow wanted Nora to have some work experience, so he arranged a "go-fer" job for her at his office, which was involved with the entertainment industry. She was reluctant, since she was still attending summer school, but she didn't want to disappoint her father, so she accepted the job.

Unfortunately, her young boss in the office was highly strung and abrasive. He screamed rather than talked, shouting out fast instructions to Nora and leaving her afraid to ask him to slow down. As she described her first work week to me, she said that, so far, she had done everything wrong! Somehow she managed to "mess up" the typing, the following of directions, and even the photocopying. Then he gave her a new assignment that terrified her—to get into her car and deliver papers to different addresses all over the city.

Nora called me the very day that she got her "driving papers" to schedule an emergency session on map reading. It was the first time I knew that she had difficulty orienting herself in geographic space, because she had been driving for years, and this issue had never come up. Then I realized that she was always going to familiar places and had time to figure out the ones that were unfamiliar. Now, with this demanding boss and her hours of work being limited, she had to add speed, and therefore anxiety, to the mix of her driving demands. Given Nora's history of frequent speeding tickets and minor auto accidents, I understood why this situation was such a stressor.

We spent our hour together with a huge map of the city spread out on my office floor in order, first, to orient her about north, south, east, and west as they appeared on the map.

I had her locate her home street, my office street, her school, the Pacific Ocean, her favorite beach, and her best friend's home across the valley. She practiced visualizing which ways to turn her body if she was heading for the ocean, then the mountains, and then the downtown portion of the city. With each turn of her body, I had her call out the north/south/east/ or west direction that she thought she was facing. Next, she had to try it with her eyes closed. By revisualizing the map internally, she surprised herself as she began to "feel" the directions. [**Since Nora's strength was visual memory, I felt that this exercise, combined with her visual point of reference—the map on the floor—would allow her to internalize the picture of the map and its different points of orientation.**]

Then, we studied the various freeways that were familiar to her and determined which were the north/south freeways and which ones went from east to west. She knew which way the ocean was, saw it on the floor map, and connected it to her own home, reciting which way she would have to turn to go west. She knew how to get from her home to my office by going over the mountains, which meant, she discovered then, that she was heading north. By studying the paper map, she could instantly connect the directional opposites—that the opposite of north was south (which is the way the freeway went to get her back home) and the opposite of east was west (which is the way she would travel from downtown to the ocean).

Since Nora already knew some of the main boulevards near her father's office, she focused on the most frequently used one to orient her, announcing her discovery that she would be going from east to west. Then we marked all these familiar locations and destination on the paper map and practiced using a highlighter to mark the routes from Dad's office to a couple of the addresses she had been given by the boss. [**Remember: these were the days before MapQuest, so planning for city travel became a much more tedious strategy "BC" (before computer-assist).**]

Once Nora had built some practiced comfort with directions and routes to her new destinations, I raised the topic of her distress over the new boss. We talked about how she might assert herself, politely but confidently, trying not to be intimidated when talking to him. As she thought about the tension this man instilled in her, she kept saying, over and over, that she just wanted to quit.

But then something quite unexpected happened. On hearing the word "quit" come out of her mouth a third time, a smile broke out, and she confessed she was suddenly hearing my voice saying, "Nora, you can't quit until you've mastered the problem!" I kidded her that I might be accused of "brainwashing" her, and we ended the hour with my explanation of such a totally confusing expression.

That evening, Nora went home, took out the city map and practiced finding every address she had been given for the following day's deliveries. However, the boss himself had failed to complete a document on time that day and get it delivered by a deadline, so he screamed at Nora and sent her on a last-minute wild goose chase to a wrong address—but, amazingly, she found the office that needed the papers and delivered them under the final deadline. On her own!

Her report of this latest success against great odds earned her my vigorous drum-roll-on-the-desk for taking our rehearsed strategies and applying them to this most challenging assignment. But there was another obstacle. Just when she had figured out the deliveries, her boss decided to put her on a whole *different* assignment—at the switchboard. Nora had never worked a switchboard before (and neither had I). She started to panic, but I knew there could be no running from this. We worked out a plan: to write down the procedure, step by step, and to read and reread and practice until she had mastered it. And master it she did, demonstrating to me exactly how, two days later. Something worked—and Nora was now a switchboard operator.

Since she still had to deal with The Screamer, I used this opportunity to review the lessons from Dr. Beltran and her autism explorations. Rather than believe *she* was failing, we would discuss what might be wrong with *her boss*. Nora had never considered that the boss's behavior indicated his own insecurity and inadequacy in *his* job. We separated her problem (hearing rapid orders correctly) from her boss's problem (rage and loss of control). She understood. This was the same lesson she had learned before—that there were *two* people involved in this interaction, each bringing his and her own issues to the table, and this time the problem was really not hers.

A week later The Screamer was fired. It seems that others in the office had observed the same erratic behavior and no one wanted any part of it. In addition, one week later, Nora was offered a permanent job at her Dad's office, and the offer did *not* come because she was the daughter of Walter Tarlow. It came because she had earned it for exemplary work—a job well done. She reported the offer to me with pride. Then, reflecting her new confidence, she said she had turned it down!

Her reason: this was just a job. She was on her way to a career—and one day, to an occupation.

Year 2

ROLE MODELING

The Pressure of Personal Appearance

An educational therapist's role includes many different kinds of modeling and guiding in domains beyond the academic. Even in our second year together, our Organic Curriculum still diverged unpredictably. Nora was now becoming aware of her personal appearance—an unfamiliar realm requiring new thinking and decision-making vital to the next phase of her life. After high school graduation she would be dealing with college, considering independent living, seeking new friends, and interviewing for jobs. She was beginning to be—and needed to be—aware of how she presented herself.

As she came through the door one day, Nora uncharacteristically commented on my nice outfit, a particularly colorful combination of my usual sweater and slacks, but this time I had added a long, brightly printed neck scarf tied with an experimental new flair. She was in her favored pre-bleached jeans and white tailored shirt. I thanked her for noticing my outfit, and since she lives in a different part of the city than I do, we joked about the fact that even the styles are different in these two locales separated by more than just a range of mountains. Our discussion of the different styles led to some agreement that, wherever you live, there are always some kinds of standards, the "unspoken social rules" about how to dress for different occasions—something with which all of us struggle as we grow up.

"But how do you know? I don't have any idea about any rules." She sounded frustrated. "I just sort of watch my friends, and sometimes I go shopping with them, so that helps me."

"You don't know it, Nora, but that's exactly the way it works. We all look at each other to see what our peers are wearing, and then, without realizing it, we also notice how people dress on TV and in the movies and wherever we go in the city. You noticed my outfit today. You were aware of it. Awareness is the first lesson in learning those 'unspoken rules.' Of course, how you dress depends on the occasion and where you're going. What you wear to school will most likely be the same kinds of clothes that everyone else is wearing. But when you get dressed up a bit on the weekends or to go out for special occasions, that's when the choices begin. I think the key is finding out what looks good on *you*. Once you know that, then the hard part is knowing where to go to find what you like. One of the tricks I use is to study the store catalogs. Would you like to see how to study them?"

Nora was definitely interested in that idea.

[I save clothing catalogs from the large department stores for various uses with different clients—sometimes to make math problems, or just for page-turning to look at the different styles and ways of making complete outfits. The world of fashion is so complex, ever-changing, and financially taxing that it requires a strong sense of self-confidence for clients to own their own "look."]

I pulled out three different catalogs, but before we studied them, I asked Nora if she knew what styles she likes. She didn't. She had never thought about it. She just put on clothes from her closet that felt comfortable, since comfort was important to her. Without realizing it, she had provided that first criterion: comfort. I explained how I made my decisions for determining what styles were "my own"—the ones that I thought looked best on me when I tried on different outfits in front of a mirror.

We started with her thinking about necklines—did she like turtle necks, crew necks, open collars, scoop necks? She wasn't sure. She didn't even know that each one had a name.

What about skirts vs. pants? She was sure of that one—"Definitely pants."

What kinds of pants? Straight legs, flared legs, high waists or low waists, denim or corduroy, heavy or light fabric? She had no idea there were that many choices, and she wasn't sure about any of them, so we compared the fabrics and styles we were both wearing at that moment.

That day, I found another advantage to having a home office. I knew that a picture from a catalog and a conversation about choices weren't enough for Nora. There wasn't time to go out to a department store, but I could go to my closet and bring a few different styles of shirts and sweaters and pants of different weights and fabrics into the office. There, in privacy, Nora could select what appealed to her. Then we would head to the room with the full-length mirror where she could hold them up against her to see what she thought would look good and what felt good to the touch. I could tell what she favored by which items brought a smile when she saw her reflection in the mirror. Clearly, the open-collared shirts and straight-leg, waist-high pants were Nora!

Then we could peruse the catalogs for clothing that fit her new idea about her choices. We looked through the ones from three types of department stores in town: high-end Magnin's, the more moderate Robinson's, and the bargain Sears, so that she got exposure to the differences in styles, prices, and accessories. A few of the Magnin outfits, especially the jewelry, were particularly flashy, and I explained that those were for people who enjoyed being "conspicuous"—being noticed and calling attention to themselves. I followed that word with the expression "conspicuous consumption," and Nora was fascinated to hear about the whole idea that people would wear gaudy clothes in order to stand out.

Although Nora had not given much thought to her clothing outfits, she had thought even less about accessories. We concluded that her style was "modest but classic" (she loved having a label for "her style") and, with that in mind, she could go through the catalogs and mark the styles that fit her, thinking about variations in color to change her look from time to time. She realized then that her modest-but-classic could be embellished with jewelry, scarves, sweaters, jackets, or even hats.

Her homework that night was to start looking through her mom's catalogs to begin thinking about what accessories would fit her.

* * *

One week later, Nora arrived wearing bright red sunglasses with red-tinted lenses! I showed my delight at such an original choice and asked how she came to select them. Grinning, she explained, "I bought them because they were conspicuous! I wanted to practice being a conspicuous consumer!" No question that she understood *that* lesson.

Now she had new questions—about make-up. She wanted a lesson in eye make-up "to look more sophisticated." I knew Nora would still be too shy to have such a lesson in a department store or beauty salon, but I could give her the basics in the office of some very simple tools that she could buy and experiment with at home. I showed her the eyeliner, mascara, and eye shadow products, explained the different ways each was used, and made sure she knew I was *not* an expert on eye make-up. But with these beginning basics, she could do what all young women do when they first discover the world of make-up. She could go to a drug store, buy inexpensive products in one or two different colors, and see what worked for her. Then, some day in the future, she might try those free make-up consultations that the department stores frequently offered.

After our lesson on clothing and styles, Nora had begun, on her own, to look at catalogs and newspaper ads with clothes on sale. The ads triggered a new question: What was the real meaning of "20 percent off?"

[**Despite years of math throughout her schooling, Nora continued to regard math as her nemesis, and she had never really understood that the amount of the "percent" was how many cents they would take off "per dollar" in the original price. By the later years in math studies, percentages were no longer being reviewed, and in true "use it or lose it" fashion, without review and use, Nora had lost it. Because of the massive numbers of concepts we had to address, we had never dealt with this application of it together until it came up in our Organic Curriculum.**]

Taking her question to the most concrete level for just a few minutes, we started with that 20 percent figure, using my box of real coins and fake dollars. I handed her a dollar bill and had her give me back 20 cents. Then we'd try two dollars, and she'd give me back two sets of 20 cents each. It didn't take many dollars for her to grasp the idea that "discount" meant how much less you'd have to pay for each dollar of the price.

[**It's really helpful to keep a box with several dollars' worth of real coins in different denominations, to be used for multiple purposes. Real ones have the authentic feel and can be used to practice making change, sort and count by different denominations, and any number of creative applications. The fake dollar bills are fine because you can use those in single dollars, fives, tens, twenties, and hundreds with minimal investment.**]

Then we checked the ads. Calvin Klein jeans were on sale at 20 percent off the regular price of $60. How could she find out *20 percent* of the price? Nora needed reminding (old facts gather dust in the brain) about how to write percentages as decimals, and also that the fickle word "of" in mathematics means you have to multiply. Twenty percent means that 20 cents *of* each dollar will not have to be paid. Now if you have 60 dollars and you get 20 cents *of* each dollar off the price, how many times will you get those 20 cent coins?

Smiling, she took the pencil and wrote "$60 × .20."

A drum-roll moment.

Fantasizing that our names were Bill Gates or Barbra Streisand, we pretended that we could afford everything, from the $80,000 Mercedes which, said one ad, would be 10 percent off that Tuesday, to the $179 Liz Claiborn pants suit at "half off," computing actual costs after the discounts. That led to a brief lesson in conversions of fractional terms like "half off" or "a third off" to their decimal forms. With satisfying insight, Nora observed that fractions and decimals were like nicknames for people—just different ways of saying the same thing.

[Having diverged from style to make-up to discounts, the learning was real for Nora, and she could hold and apply it. As for conspicuous consumption, her experiment was very short-lived. She decided it just wasn't "her look."]

Year 2

KNEE SURGERY, PAIN, AND FACE-OFFS WITH PROFESSIONALS

The following intervention involved Nora's medical issues, some unusual communication breakdowns, and the beginning empowerment of self-advocacy. Adult clients sometimes want an outsider to intervene briefly when the possible benefit seems greater than the risk of being identified as "different." The risks vs. rewards must always be weighed with the client.

During the spring of our second year of educational therapy, Nora finally had surgery on that troublesome left knee. With a mixture of satisfaction and confusion, she brought me Dr. Sheen's explanation, written in full medical-speak: "Nora Tarlow had arthroscopy of left knee with chondroplasty of the medial femoral condyle, removal of loose articular cartilage flakes and subcutaneous lateral release utilizing operative arthroscopy technique." Neither one of us knew exactly what it meant, but we knew it was real, a physical malfunction that had caused enough pain to require real surgery. Now came the rehabilitation process. Nora's pain had become more acute than ever, bringing a different set of conflicts, as I learned from her journal. Margo is her physical therapist:

> I'm so confused right now. Yesterday I got back from Doctor Sheens. He says it's quite normal for me to be in pain. But 2 weeks ago, Margo insisted that I was an unusual case, being in so much pain, that she insisted that I go for psychiatric help because its Phantom Pain. I didn't understand her, and I got worried. So I read up on Phantom Pain, the past few days. I don't know whether my pain is Phantom or real, I don't know whether Sheen is right or Margo. I wanted so badly to invent someone who could come into every situation with me and be an interpreter so I wouldn't look so foolish.

Besides the journal entry, she said that she was also having trouble falling asleep because of the pain and her turmoil over the disagreement between Dr. Sheen and Margo. She feels that Margo is tough with her, teasing her for her complaints. Margo told Nora that she'd get a raise if Nora could raise her leg higher, and Nora believed it! Clearly, Margo's style of using jokes or sarcasm were lost on Nora, and Nora's misunderstandings were lost on Margo—a lose-lose situation.

Respecting Nora's anguish, I speculated that perhaps Margo believes her approach is a way to get people to cope better with their pain and not feel sorry for themselves. Nora had never thought of that, but then she rejected it. She made it clear that she was *not* feeling sorry for herself—that she *was not* a person who enjoys pain or wants it in order to get sympathy, so we discussed ways she might respond if she feels unfairly abused by Margo's comments.

At that point I asked, "Nora, do either Margo or Dr. Sheen have any idea about your auditory processing difficulties? Do they realize that you may not always understand what they're explaining to you?"

As I expected, her reply was, "No . . . I didn't think about telling that to a doctor or a PT. They wouldn't understand anything like that, and they'd only think I'm stupid."

"But you see, Nora, they *need* to understand, and you have to learn how to help them understand. This is just like talking with friends, or understanding TV news, or any other conversation. They need to know why you need *time* to understand what people say, and it doesn't matter whether it's a friend or a doctor or a PT. It's all the same—it's all talk, all words—coming at you in a rush. And you're the same *you*, wherever you go, so the way you deal with each situation will depend on other people understanding you so you can understand them! If they know the problem they may speak slower and even use more everyday words."

This information was painful for Nora to hear. Here was another problem in another setting—when would it end? This time, her posture indicated feelings of defeat.

Hesitating for a moment to be sure I wasn't overstepping her autonomy, but recalling her journal wish for an "interpreter," I made an offer. Perhaps in this situation, my input could help everyone understand what they had mistaken as Nora's "stubbornness."

"Nora, would it help if I called Dr. Sheen, professional to professional, to explain your particular difficulty? Perhaps, if I hear his words directly, I can see if what he is saying is really different advice from what you're getting from Margo. Then I can explain it to you more clearly."

Nora not only accepted the offer but seemed greatly relieved by it and promptly signed a written release giving me permission to make the call.

[A major function of an educational therapist is consultation and collaboration with other professionals involved with our client's well-being. In the early years, such communication is directed to family, teachers, and various professionals. As clients mature, they are often reluctant to ask for such help, but instances arise that sometimes require input from us. This is necessary if clients have not yet learned to adequately explain their processing difficulties, are uncomfortable calling attention to their differences, or are dealing with people at school, work, or other settings who regard "disabilities" as excuses for irresponsibility.]

* * *

On the phone, Dr. Sheen was surgeon-brusque but willing to answer my questions. He may or may not have understood my thumbnail explanation of Nora's auditory processing struggles that led to language confusions, although he made an effort to listen and ask questions. I told him of her confusion when Margo mentioned "Phantom pain" implying that Nora's pain was not real but imagined. Then I asked for his explanation of the questions about pain and procedures that had caused such conflict for Nora.

Dr. Sheen explained: "Some people are great in three days after arthroscopy. It's important not to let them get stiff or limp. The PT knows I want her to do whatever doesn't hurt Nora. Margo has to wean her off crutches—how fast is up to the patient. Each one is different. If the knee swells up and there's more pain, then we try for another day. Try 'em and watch their limp—that's how we proceed. Most patients are nervous, you know, reluctant to bend their knee and put full weight on it. But we have to be sure the kneecap stays loose. The surgery was on the underside of the kneecap, and it should be healed by now. In this procedure, the work *after* the surgery is just as important as the surgery. I have no idea why Margo was talking about Phantom pain—that only occurs after an amputation. That has nothing to do with Nora's case."

I shared this news, phrase by phrase with Nora, to be sure she understood it

* * *

Nora's pain continued, and Margo continued to believe it was all psychological. In preparation to see Dr. Sheen and convince him of the reality of her pain, she independently conducted a library search of real pain and "Phantom pain," preparing charts with pain pathways and copying text that defended her argument.

Unbeknownst to Nora, Dr. Sheen had asked Margo to be at their meeting, which Nora later reported to me. She came in, ignoring Margo's presence, and presented her charts and references in evidence of her research about pain to Dr. Sheen. He was impressed and told her so. Then, in front of Margo, speaking slowly and clearly [**was this because he understood my explanation?**], the doctor told Nora that he had done much more repair on her knee than he had told her about in the past. He explained that bone chips were continually being created in her knee joint from the misalignment there, and if he went in every few months he would be able to extract handfuls of bone chips. He went on to say that all of her pains were real and explainable, and they *should* be taking much longer to heal than he originally thought. In short, he was verifying the reasons for her real pain.

Margo said nothing.

Nora thanked the doctor for giving her time and answering her questions so helpfully. She said nothing to Margo.

At our next session, a vindicated Nora told of her plans to "take on" Margo—to confront her, right up front, and ask why she confused Nora with her comments. Empowered by the doctor's verification, she made a list of questions to ask Margo, starting by asking if she agreed with Dr. Sheen at that meeting.

And that was what she did. She asked the questions, even took notes (*another first*) of Margo's response and almost flew into my office a day later to give her report. The essence of her interview: Margo actually apologized, said that she learned something from Dr. Sheen which she hadn't understood before, and that she didn't really think Nora had Phantom pain "but that expression was just an analogy."

I grinned with pleasure at Nora's report of Margo "eating crow."

You can guess what our next session was about—"eating crow" and analogies!

Year 2

OVERCOMING A FEAR

Becoming a Flyer

Because educational therapy is often done in a private setting, we are able to explore unconventional ways to make learning real, even if the issue is sometimes based on a fear, whether real or irrational. Nora's fear of flying was something that often came up because of the family's desire to take frequent trips together. The following vignette relates a very unusual "field trip" that led to a dramatic outcome from this unconventional intervention.

Summer always brought talk of family vacations, and family vacations brought talk of flying. Nora was terrified of flying, and that fear made her consider missing the family trips. Even the temptation of a summer in Maine or Europe was not enough to overcome her anxiety about flying. In one essay for school where her topic was "Danger," she chose to write about what seemed most dangerous to her:

> Danger is flying in an airplane—Real high in the sky, past all the clouds, with a pilot you never even get to meet. Feeling too much closeness with all the other passengers, you tend to get closterfobic. Then when you get real sweaty and dying for just a fresh breath of air, you can't open a window. (*sic*)

Reading between lines like "a pilot you never even get to meet" and the reference to claustrophobia, I decided to consider finding an opportunity to seek out the specific sources of her alarm. This was a situation that we couldn't role play in the office.

"Nora, what exactly makes you worry when you get on a plane?"

"I hate when they close the doors, and I hear all those sounds, but I don't understand what anything means. I hate being in crowded, small spaces."

"Well, I don't know what those sounds mean either, and I think it's natural for all people to feel some anxiety when a plane is about to take off, but what would you think about our going to the airport and trying to find out, for both of us, what all those sounds mean?"

Nora laughed, probably thinking that the idea sounded ridiculous. What would people think about us wandering around the airport asking "stupid questions?" However, when

I explained my idea further to her, she began to get excited about such a field trip. Then and there, while the idea was fresh, we set our plans to drive together the following week to Los Angeles International Airport. We brainstormed the kinds of questions she might want to ask the pilots or stewardesses, since we had no idea who we would meet on our upcoming adventure. Her major questions concerned the noises on take-off and landing, and of course the bumps that occurred in mid-flight.

[At that time, airports were open, friendly places. People who were not planning to fly could accompany their family and friends right to the gate to kiss and wave goodbye. There were no checkpoints or security cameras, no magnetic gates or guards to check through your belongings and wand you if something on your body set off a screeching buzz. Pilots and crew left the planes after the passengers had disembarked, and both flyers and non-flyers had opportunities to talk to them as they walked through the airports. Such an open system allowed Nora and me to do something that would be unheard of today.]

On our drive to the airport, we discussed how much her language misunderstandings played a part in her fears when she only partially understood the situations that caused those fears. The topic of therapy came up again because of the many different causes of the origins of fears. I explained that the purpose of our trip to the airport was to answer some factual questions, the stuff of engines and aeronautics and mechanical truths about airplane workings. Maybe, once those questions were answered, the facts might allay some fears. If not, there would be another reason for her to consider psychotherapy. She liked that explanation.

[Educational therapists must always be cognizant of the boundaries between our work and the domain of psychotherapy. My purpose in taking this unusual field trip was to explore the language factors that might be a rational source of Nora's fears, in contrast to some more deep-seated emotional basis.]

We arrived at the airport, parked the car, and rode the escalator to the second floor where the gates were lined up for arrivals and departures. All around us were folks of every size, shape, age, and ethnicity—coming and going, dragging, rolling and lifting bags, babies and bottles. We studied the scene for a while to decide the best place to encounter some pilots or crew that might just be coming off duty.

Within minutes, we spotted our target: two smiling United Airlines pilots walking briskly through the door of their arrival gate, chatting with each other and clueless about our plans for them. I approached them first and briefly explained our mission regarding Nora's fear of flying, asking whether they would be willing to give her a few moments of their time to answer some questions.

Cordially, they said of course they would talk to her, and with that, Nora came forward, shyly at first, but then she spoke up about her fears—her feeling of suffocation on take-off when the doors closed and all the noises began. As the older of the two pilots began explaining, walking as he talked, I took notes of the terminology he was using, knowing we would need to interpret it back at the office. He connected the different noises to *retracting landing gear*, the *flaps* on the wings, the *turbulence caused by air pockets*, the *vacuum caused by changes in air pressure*. As we trotted to keep up with their escalating pace through the terminal, the second pilot added to their answers with tangents of information about *altitude, oxygen, molecules,* and *pressurized cabins,* and the meaning of *"thin air."* With that, I noticed Nora looking like *she* was in thin air, all of this information coming at her within less than five minutes. She saw, through her side vision, that I had been taking notes, so some of the pressure was off. The information wouldn't be lost in space.

We thanked both gentlemen, wished them safe journeys on all of their flights, and said goodbye, feeling our mission had been accomplished. Nora would now know, factually, the cause of the previously unfamiliar sounds on airplanes once we got a chance to dissect my notes that were taken on the run.

We returned to the office that very day and tackled the challenge of making the new terminology comprehensible. We combined dictionary, encyclopedia, and experimental work to demystify words like retracting, flaps, turbulence, vacuum, pressurized. We made sketches of mountains rising from sea level, discussing that in relation to altitude. Nora had seen planes take off and watched the wheels slowly go up into the plane's belly, so the word "retracting" was easy to connect to the process of "taking back or drawing in," as the dictionary defined it. For flaps, we looked at pictures of airplanes from a book that showed the wing flaps in different positions, and talked about how the position in which they were turned would affect the wind hitting them.

The pictures were just a start. "How do you think the wind hitting the flaps would change the plane's directions, Nora?" I wanted her to try to imagine how flaps were like sails on a sailboat or like a bird's wings, directing them which way to go—up or down, left or right turns. With that, we went out to look at some birds as they took off from my yard, to see if that would help with the concept. It did (thanks to that Mourning Dove that hangs out there).

Next, we turned our attention to the words *vacuum* and *air pressure*. Nora knew the word *vacuum* from vacuum cleaners, but had no idea what made them suction in the dirt. We then tried the simple but dramatic and fun experiment of creating a vacuum in a bottle by dropping in a lighted match, using up the oxygen, and immediately blocking the opening with a peeled, hardboiled egg. The drama of that egg being sucked through the opening which was narrower than the egg's dimensions always delighted students of any age. After some simple talk about the why, she began to understand the remarkable force of air pressure, so we related it to the vacuum, or loss of air, that might be created in a plane as it goes up to high altitudes where air pressure changes. We concluded that this was why the plane cabin had to be "pressurized"; that is, kept with the air pressure balanced to near the same as it was at ground level so that passengers could breathe (and not be sucked out of the plane, as she had once seen in a comic movie that must have added to her terror). All those blowing sounds she heard were related to the pressurization.

After that, "*turbulence creating air pockets*" was relatively easy for Nora to understand once she learned the definition of turbulence. She could visualize huge "pockets" in the air, pockets that the plane could slip into and out of just like putting your hands in and out of a pocket. The difference in pocket types, however, was that air pockets shook everyone up quite badly and caused fright for some but not for others—those few daredevils on board who seemed to be oblivious to everything that caused terror in some.

The day had been exhausting and fulfilling, making the known from the unknown, but the outcome of that day was even more fulfilling. Nora did, indeed, begin to take plane trips with her family, perhaps feeling some pride in explaining to them what had been explained to her. Over the following years, she started with small flights from California to Nevada, working up to New York, then over the small ocean to Europe, and finally to the ultimate extended flight over the big Pacific—to Australia, where, I later learned, she flew in 10 different planes, both big and small, even including open-sided helicopters.

As for me, I got the postcards to prove it!

[It was not until some months later, after she had finally entered therapy with a psychologist, that Nora shared what may have been the emotional root of her fear when those airplane doors closed. She had remembered being locked in a closet at age 10 by her cousin who was baby-sitting while her parents were away. She had been terrified, not knowing how long she would be in this skimpy, dark space unable to open the door. That was apparently the origin of her fear of crowded, small spaces—and her unusual response to my comment about "opening a door for her to learn." But this real-time project to investigate real airplane sounds from real pilots somehow helped alleviate the surface fears enough to enable her to board airplanes to increasingly distant destinations.]

Year 3

THE WHOLE DAM THING

This exchange happened early in our third year of work. I include it to give an example of Nora's continuing need for clarification of some words in a more concrete manner, when the dictionary definitions or contextual formats in which the words were used still left her confused. This particular example was chosen because what we did made such a lasting impression that it was quoted by her years later as her example to others of how she learns most effectively.

"What's a dam?" Nora asked as she walked through the door on that autumn afternoon. The question was intensely delivered, something clearly on her mind and bothering her.

"Where did you hear the word?"

"I keep hearing it in different places. My folks used the word when they were talking about Las Vegas, and I didn't understand it the way they explained it! Then, this week, it came up in my social studies class. The teacher was saying something about energy and power, and I got completely confused about what 'dam' would have to do with THAT."

It occurred to me then that the only time Nora might have heard "dam" in conversations was probably the other damn—the one in "damn fool" or "I don't give a damn" or the "Damn it!" so often expletive-d when any of us hurt ourselves or bump into something or drop something. We had studied the homophones before—those words that sound alike but have totally different meanings. This was a perfect word for us to use to review that concept.

"Nora, what may be confusing you is the fact that there are two different words pronounced 'dam,' and the one you've probably heard all your life is the swear-word 'damn.' "

"Yeah! That's what's so confusing about that word. I know the swear word, and I know it has nothing to do with energy. So what is she talking about?"

I reached for a book that had pictures of Hoover Dam and other famous dams and showed her that this kind of a dam could stop a river and control the way the water moved from one level of height to another. I explained that the huge dams they built for this would have all kinds of engines inside with giant wheels that would be turned by the water, and that turning of the wheels could make a kind of electric power.

Nora looked at the pictures for a full minute with that familiar furrowed brow, trying to have my words make some sense to her, but this time she just couldn't connect the pictures with any kind of action that suggested potential for power.

When I saw no understanding from the photographs, I got an idea that might make it real for her. We went out to the garden, where we picked up two large bricks and a board. Then we carried them out to the curb in front of my house. I knew that there would always be a steady stream of water running by the curb on my street because our house was half-way down a steep hill, and all the run-off from people's sprinklers provided a little river. I had Nora place the two bricks one on top of the other to form a small wall perpendicular to the curb so that it would block the water's flow. Next, we used the board to close up the side of the brick that faced the street, forming a kind of three-sided container of the curb, the bricks, and the board to hold the water. The result was a perfect little pond formed above the bricks—our dam—and as the "pond" filled up, the water flowed over the top of the bricks. Nora understood it immediately. In fact, the experience impressed her so completely that for several weeks she would refer to our little experiment and how much it made the word real for her.

Interestingly, during one of those dreaded parent conferences, Nora used this story for her parents when they began asking about the new computers that were just coming out and whether they might be a quicker way for her to learn vocabulary instead of coming to my office. Nora, always fearful that her parents would decide to end our educational therapy just as they had done with her tutors in the past, used the story of the dam as an example of why a computer couldn't do what our experiences together were doing to help her learn and remember language.

Nora never forgot that project with the dam. A full year after our lesson, I received a postcard from her with a picture of the Hoover Dam. On the back, she wrote that she had just flown over it and knew exactly what it was and why it had formed Lake Mead (the Hoover Dam's version of our homemade "pond"). She didn't sign her name to the card; she knew I would need no signature. Instead, she just drew a Happy Face, which looked just like the happy face I was wearing when I read the card. Indeed, together we were still discovering ways to teach Nora knowledge that she would own forever.

Years 3 and 4

JOB AT COZY CLOZ

No Longer a Victim

Nora's job in the retail store, COZY CLOZ, described here, was truly a milestone on many different fronts and deserves its own chapter for her growth there. This chapter also discloses my changing role as more of a cheerleader and sounding board than a teacher in educational therapy as she becomes her own decision-maker and problem-solver. She remained at COZY CLOZ for two years, taking some time off from school.

Christine Tarlow saw the "NOW HIRING" sign in the window of the young women's retail clothing store. It was within walking distance from their home, and she rushed to tell Nora about it. The store was near the Christmas break, and Nora was no longer working at her dad's office, so this might be wonderful for her to try over the holidays. She was guarded in her response but filled out the application. The store called three days later to request an interview, and Nora got the job.

She reported the outcome to me with mixed feelings, calling it a "no-brainer." Why? Because she was hired to be a gift wrapper.

Nora had never done gift wrapping. Ever.

So that day, for the umpteenth chapter of our Organic Curriculum, we practiced wrapping—cutting paper to size, folding and taping the ends, estimating the ribbon needed, and practicing various styles of tying and bow making. Nora learned quickly and reported her mastery on the job at our next meeting. Then she told the story of an older woman who came in to buy a sweater for her granddaughter and asked Nora's opinion about a particular sweater. Nora, with a tone of authority, told the grandmother, "Men's sweaters look better on the girls. Oversize is in—I wear them all the time." The woman thanked her for her advice and purchased the men's sweater Nora had recommended.

It was a little moment of power. When complimented for such boldness, Nora said, almost as if she were learning this for herself, "I don't want to tell them I don't know, so I'll tell them what I do know." When asked if she would like to try sales, she rejected the idea immediately. Making change was a responsibility that terrified her.

I assured her that we could practice making change in my office, too, but there was another reason she wasn't interested. She had heard that sales girls get paid on *commission* (she knew about that) and she didn't like that uncertainty regarding take-home pay, preferring the wrapping job and receiving a salary by the hourly, minimum wage.

By January, Nora had received a raise over someone who had been at COZY CLOZ longer than she. Another moment of power.

"They don't give raises easily, you know, and by the way, I've saved $400! The boss seems to trust me, because when she goes to lunch, she leaves me in charge," she reported with the pride of an acknowledged employee.

As the weeks passed, Nora advanced steadily in her job. She had become an expert at mail-outs and was even asked to supervise a one-week sale. Then she was transferred to stock, which involved organization of all the clothing shipments and inventory as goods came and went. [**Throughout her high school years, one of Nora's strengths was in organizing. Everything had its place—her notebooks, her study space at home, her backpack, and even her closet. She was the one at home who helped the family organize the household messes. This kind of skill is unusual in individuals with learning disabilities, so when a client has such a strength, much can be made of its potential for employment options.**]

Nora blossomed in the stock-room, feeling safe in applying her splendid organizing skills and enjoying being busy. Her supportive stock manager, Yoshiko, made her feel secure in her position, especially since Nora had learned that the people in sales were being fired. She knew that stock management was very necessary to the workings of the company, and she was good at it. She had never seemed happier.

We talked about all the new learning that was going on for her in the working world. I commented that she even looked different these days—losing weight, sporting a great new haircut, wearing eye make-up and stylish-looking clothes. I had her stand in front of a mirror to study herself. Even Nora noticed the difference, acknowledging my remark that the look of a young teen had been replaced by the look of a young adult.

We decided to make one of her favorite things—a list—of all that has been happening in her world of work. The list impressed both of us. She had learned:

1. How to coordinate clothes into outfits.
2. How to express herself to her boss in the stock-room.
3. How work is unlike school: "You have to be much more responsible at work. Even when you don't want to go, you *have* to."
4. About people. She's noticing the problems all people have regarding first impressions and realizing that others may be judging her just as she was judging them.
5. About money—how easy it is to spend it quickly and how hard to save.

In response to this last item, I suggested that we compute her salary by the hours per day times the dollars per hour times the days per week.

"This is a trick. This is a word problem," Nora accused with a sparkle.

I grinned back. "Life is a word problem, Nora. This is just the beginning."

The next word problem was for her to figure out her "gross" salary compared to the "net." After she had learned the difference, she understood better the notion of "take-home pay" and how much the taxes and deductions cut the total. She was horrified until I told her that if she hadn't earned a certain minimum amount of income at the end of the year, the government would actually refund the deductions for her to keep. That led to a whole discussion of fairness for those with low incomes. She was pleased with all this new information.

We decided to make up a mock budget with a list of costs for rent, utilities, food, gas, insurance, and entertainment so that she could have a better understanding of the reasons her friends, most of whom were already self-supporting, may be resentful of her still being cared for by her parents. When she compared the total of expenses to her current earnings, she became silent. Reality bit hard.

In the first week of February, Nora was made assistant manager of the stock department. *Assistant manager*—she loved the important ring of it. Her responsibilities were considerable. She had to oversee transfers of merchandise to other stores, re-mark prices, and prepare new merchandise for display in the store. Her new status was a rather mixed blessing, because she was not really accepted by the employees in sales, while conversely she suffered from *too much* respect from her peers in stock.

When I questioned how respect could ever be "too much," she explained that, in this new job, she couldn't just be buddies with her co-workers any more. She had crossed the line. Now she's a "boss," and because she was so conscientious about her duties, she sensed that others resented it. This was a new dilemma: wanting to be liked by her peers and respected by her bosses but seeing that these two wants may be very difficult to achieve.

By April, one of the employees whom she had trained in stock got a raise that put his salary ahead of hers by 50 cents an hour. She was very offended and complained to Yoshiko, who spoke to the manager, and Nora was then given the same raise as the newcomer. In fact, they even decided to send her out of town to the home office for further training, acknowledging once more how happy they were with her work.

Her report to me was summed up in one self-respecting sentence: "I think I'm awesome at that job!"

By June, Nora's pride in her job at COZY CLOZ got another boost when she was introduced separately at the staffing as "the assistant manager of stock" and asked to train four new workers. She was also helping Yoshiko, who is Japanese, to write letters in English. This time, Nora was the expert in letter writing! Her dream of respect was coming from unexpected places.

In spite of all her successes in stock, Nora didn't get the raise she expected by July, but the store manager didn't know that Nora had been reading *Pulling Your Own Strings*, the popular self-help book by Wayne Dyer (1994). She felt ready to deal with her own issues, announcing to me with newfound strength, "Dorothy, I can't be manipulated any more. I'm no longer a victim!"

That moment was, indeed, the beginning of a significant shift away from victimhood toward assertiveness.

* * *

After Nora's second anniversary at COZY CLOZ, Yoshiko had to leave, and Nora was promoted to the position of manager of stock. Her joy was diminished, however, by the salary—only $6.25 an hour—but she took a break from school that semester and gave all her effort to the job, always making clear her long-term plans: to return to school, get her AA degree, "no matter how long it takes," and become a physical therapist.

Another significant sign of growth surfaced when Nora said she would have to miss our session during the coming week in order to work full time during the January inventory.

The comment, so casually delivered, was a milestone—she could see me less and still get along. [**This was a major acknowledgment of internal strength. During Year 3, I had learned that gradual detachment had to come from Nora. I could plant the seeds, but outright suggestions by me that we cut down the number of sessions were still seen as rejection by her. Educational therapists are always aware of the need for goals that include the lessening of sessions and the increase of independence.**]

After alerting her boss to her need to give up the manager's job, Nora began training someone to take over and hiring other stock boys. She had other milestones as well: her first firing of an employee after a week of warnings; and her presentation of a 15-minute speech to the whole staff about problems in the stock department (for which she made an outline and prepared a handout). In less than two years, Nora had indeed become an expert in her domain, earning a portrait labeled "Stock Manager" on the wall of management hierarchy at COZY CLOZ.

A few months later, a new dilemma arose. Upon return from an unpaid three-week vacation, she learned that the new worker she had trained to cover for her while she was away was getting almost the same wage as she after her two years in the job. To add insult to injury, she found the stock bunker filled with untended paperwork everywhere and merchandise orders unfilled. The main office was expecting her to put everything in order after three weeks of chaos. Tempering her fury at the neglect in the stock-room, she decided to see her boss to discuss this and to go ahead with her plan to argue for a raise.

She spent the whole weekend preparing her case. A self-confident, almost brazen Nora emerged, ready to defend her right to a higher salary. However, with very little thought, the boss denied her request, giving the reason that she "wasn't working full time." But Nora was not to be denied.

[**The following excerpts are taken from a session I taped to record the language Nora used to describe this confrontational exchange with her boss. She wrote out her thoughts five times the night before and "memorized it so I wouldn't have to look at the paper—that would look kind of funny." She was so matter-of-fact about memorizing the speech, and I flashed back to all of her former terror at having to present speeches in front of her class. Now, verbal rehearsal for memorization was an automatic skill that she expected of herself.**]

Here is Nora's recall of the exchange:

> I said to him, "I've worked part-time here for a year and a half, and last night I took all my check stubs and it equaled to five months of full-time. I quit school for the job to be full-time. And since last October, I was acting manager. Even when I was working part-time, I was still maintaining the full-time responsibility of stock manager. And I always stayed until I got everything done.
>
> "You told me yesterday that each department has a budget and within that budget, there should be more than a 50-cents-an-hour difference between somebody who has two years of experience and somebody who has none. But, the worker I trained was making only 50 cents less than me, with no experience. He came in at that price. I came in at $3.50 two years ago and worked myself up to $6.25.
>
> "If the company is so frivolous with money that they can start somebody at that, then they can give me a raise also. I don't want you to think that I'm leaving on bad terms, but that I'm giving you an alternative about what you pay someone with experience."

And then I said, "So I'll be finishing up today. I feel that I cannot stay any longer under the circumstances."

The boss, stunned, told her that she had to give him at least two weeks' notice. But Nora had done her homework.

> "According to the rules, a full-time employee needs to give two weeks' notice, but since I haven't been considered a full-time employee, I'm not going to bother to give you two weeks. If I stay for two more weeks, I'm going to be responsible for all the work that hasn't been done while I was away, and its going to be put on me from the home office, all for 25 cents' difference."
> And he said, "Well, let me see what I can do. I didn't think you were going to walk out. Besides, I can only give you 25 cents more."
> And I said, "Well, 25 cents is charity, and I don't work for charity. I spent three weeks before I left on vacation, training five guys who all could have replaced me, but you decided to fire them, and I'm not going to take the responsibility for this . . . I'm not walking out on *you*. I don't have that little self-respect that I can stay. I'm standing up for something, and I don't think its right to go back on my word."

And she didn't quit there. She actually asked him for a letter of recommendation, since "we've worked together pretty closely for two years." I was sure he would refuse such a request after what she had just said, but Nora, the expert now, educated *me* about business law. She knew her rights on this issue as well.

> "I read up on that, too, in a book at the library, and I found out that only if you're fired from a company, you can't have a letter of recommendation. But if you leave on your own, whether you give two weeks' notice or not, you're guaranteed a letter of recommendation. In the past, he promised me if I ever decide to leave the company, he'd always write me the most excellent recommendation. He said, 'Even if you leave on bad terms.' He told me this, and I remembered it."

When I asked her what her parents thought about this whole exchange, she described their pride and support. Her father even told her, 'Y'know, *you just stand up for your rights*, and if you do that, I'll pay you!'"

I joined in with that enthusiasm, summarizing the dramatic changes in her, but then, lapsing into an old habit from our early years together, I said, "It's so terrific, Nora . . . So, now, what are your plans?"

Laughing out loud then, Nora said, "I knew that was going to be your question! What's my next goal, right? Well, my parents don't want me to get situated with a job just yet until I get squared away with school. But I'll decide."

* * *

And she, alone, did decide. That September, to meet her expenses for her return to school, Nora found and took a job with a silk-screen T-shirt company, earning $400 in one week and getting a raise to $8 per hour. Her new boss was so impressed with her competence that he entrusted her to seek contacts for big orders from clubs, restaurants, and local businesses, often leaving her alone in the office with full responsibility.

In October, Nora got a surprise—a call from a new supervisor at COZY CLOZ, begging her to come back, on *her* terms, as manager. The power she felt in that moment was indescribable. On that day, she realized that having a PhD was not the only way to earn respect.

Year 5 and On

BUMPS AND POTHOLES ON THE ROAD TO RESPECT

This narrative explores the two sides of Nora's self-concept that surfaced during the same semester—first, her budding self-confidence in the "twenty-something" bar scene; and second, the devastating blow of a second major rejection from school. Her tenacity in solving this obstacle led to unexpected decisions, creative solutions, and an outcome that was her ultimate reward for years of effort. The following are some highlights on this bumpy road.

Through her relationship with some new friends, Nora had learned the art of "bar banter" between strangers at the bar scene in town. She reported going into taverns now with new people and having conversations that lasted one or two hours! Formerly invisible Nora never used to acknowledge that she was even there, but she'd learned to study her friends' flirting body language and observe what they talked about. On her own, she'd rehearsed certain topics she felt comfortable discussing, such as her job, or asking the standard "Where are you from?' or (the new skill she seemed proud of) "adlibbing," which she defined as "rambling off about dumb things." She had begun to feel accepted—a part of the crowd.

During this same period of social exploration, Nora was given an assignment in her English class at college to write a paper on an extended definition of a word that had significant meaning for her. She picked the word "rejection." In the lengthy paper, Nora described her lifelong torment of a memory she couldn't erase: her expulsion from Kingsley Hall when her knee injury prevented her from starring in their sports teams. Her essay detailed the whole experience and precursors before this terrible moment of her meeting —alone—with her teachers:

> I would turn in assignments that were the result of hours of hard work and effort, but the highest grades I received were Cs and below. No one knew how hard I was trying.
>
> After my second year there, all of my teachers met with me. They explained in a rather cold but professional way that they would not be able to renew my contract for the fall. I just wasn't smart enough. I was shocked. They had never told me I was

failing out. Losing total respect for myself, I pleaded with these teachers to let me stay. I couldn't go back home to tell my parents that I was kicked out because of being too stupid.

The teachers turned their backs on me because they thought I was stupid and lazy. They rejected a student who was evidently trying her hardest. They didn't and wouldn't believe that there was anything wrong with me because I could read and write; so obviously I wasn't trying enough or I'd understand as well. This feeling of rejection and worthlessness came from both the teachers and the other students.

[The painful scars from this encounter, occurring without the presence or even notification of her parents, continue to resurface to this day, and the writing of the essay years later was further testimony to its continuing significance. Nora felt completely unprepared for such an abrupt, unexplained, and sudden rejection.]

A year after this paper was written, Nora received another rejection just as devastating as the Kingsley Hall expulsion. The source of this new blow was a consequence of her survival strategies at Santa Lucia. Nora had adopted the pattern of course repetitions that I had proposed; i.e., take each course with high vocabulary demands twice—first to master the unfamiliar vocabulary, and second to achieve passing grades. This became her essential blueprint for survival, but it created a very weird-looking transcript. More importantly, this strategy was never officially authorized, and I had failed to suggest that she clear the plan with her counselor.

Consequently, a letter came from the Admissions Office one day informing her that she was no longer qualified to attend Santa Lucia Community College. The rules stated that only two semesters were allowed on academic probation. Nora had three. Even more cutting was the proclamation that she was "no longer eligible for enrollment at *any of the other community colleges.*" That pronouncement shattered her sustaining creed: "Do your best and try your hardest." Now she knew an awful truth—"that others *will decide what hard looks like and what your best looks like.*"

With assertiveness, she decided to plead her case eloquently, in writing, to the Dean of Admissions:

Dear Dean _____,

I am a student at Santa Lucia who has been disqualified. I was not notified until the first week classes began, after I had already registered. I was sent a notification stating that I was to withdraw from all of my classes, *at which point I was no longer eligible for enrollment at any of the other community colleges.* I then made an appointment with you to get reinstated in the current semester, but I was given an appointment that was *too late* for the semester.

Since the spring semester a year ago, I have had to fight for permission to continue at the school, being on academic probation. I feel I work too hard in school to have to try to convince a school that I am trying . . .

It usually takes me two semesters to complete a course because of my learning disability. I am only capable of absorbing half the material each semester. I am not like other students who may not know *why* they are in school. I *know* I need to be in school, and I feel I should not be discriminated against because it takes me longer than the average student.

As quoted in the school catalog, *"Santa Lucia College is a community oriented, open-door, educational institution dedicated to the principle that society benefits when all its members have the opportunity to develop to their fullest potential."*

What does this mean when this educational institution closes the door on a student who learns in a unique fashion at a slower pace? Does this mean that this educational institution is designed only for those students who do not require the extra help as I do, who already perform well?

Sincerely,

Nora Tarlow

Nora never received a reply to her letter. Consequently, she went to that "too late" appointment to meet this man who stood in her way—to see how he would respond in person.

The Dean's response to her plea that day was, "Nora, you have to accept your limitations just as I, myself, did when I couldn't get into medical school."

Blessedly, Nora completely rejected this comparison. Instead, his insensitive comment, made without any knowledge of her history, led her to take action. Defying the Dean's warning about other colleges being unable to accept her, consulting neither her parents nor me, Nora changed colleges! The very next day, she enrolled at Alabaster Community College, using her social security number rather than the student ID number on file at Santa Lucia—giving herself a completely fresh start.

When she came to my office after the fact and announced what she had done, completely on her own, my applause was immediate. This was another "magical moment of change"— Nora taking charge of her fate. Then, with equal satisfaction, she declared a career decision—to become a PTA, a physical therapy assistant. She was moving beyond job to career.

The angels were on her side to improve her chances for success in that goal, too, because I referred her to an extraordinary counselor at Alabaster—Maggie O'Brian, in Special Services, whose heart was larger than her head and for whom "the glass was always half full." Maggie became Nora's champion for the rest of her academic life. From that meeting forward, it was Maggie who handpicked Nora's teachers to best fit her learning style, advised her when to withdraw instead of taking Fails, found her subject-matter tutors on campus, and warned her not to negotiate with the teachers but to come to the counselors instead, "so they can fight for your rights." Maggie's contagiously positive attitude worked to assure Nora that "it's *not* crazy for you to stay in your major. The PTA certificate program is definitely possible for you."

[Every now and then a Maggie O'Brian comes into one's life and makes us all believe that systems really can work when such tender, knowledgable humans are in decision-making positions.]

In addition—thanks to the inefficiencies of bureaucracy and Nora's new enrollment number—Alabaster College never connected *this* Nora Tarlow to the Nora who had been declared "no longer eligible for enrollment at any other community college." Sometimes, justice and determination triumph.

* * *

Throughout the ensuing years at Alabaster, Nora balanced the obstacles creatively with measured successes. She survived the mass of science courses by taping the lectures, drawing pictures to translate the concepts into a graphic mode, and meeting with the professors, using a script that we had practiced for such situations: "I'm really interested in what you're telling me. Could you please say that again slower so I can write it down correctly? I want to be sure I've got it right."

To become fully self-supporting for one three-year period, while taking college classes at night, she worked simultaneously in three orthopedic facilities.

With humor, Nora described the way she fielded the questions during each of the hiring procedures.

"They asked about my grades in school, so I told them I got a B in anatomy and an A in physiology. I didn't mention that I took the anatomy four times," she laughed, "and when the interviewer asked me how people would describe me, you'd be proud because I said 'Reliable, loyal, and dependable.' How about that for selling myself?!" Indeed, I was proud.

Still, Nora was growing discouraged by the interminable length of time the school courses were taking and the strain of the dual school/work schedule. Then, quite coincidentally, she learned that there was another way to obtain a physical therapy assistant's license—by taking an exam. If she passed it, she would be entitled to practice without getting her degree from the college. Here was a way out of the classroom.

She bought all the prep books, borrowed notes, and began a relentless regimen of study while picking the brains of her licensed colleagues and planning out study strategies with me. Months passed while she waited for the results, only to learn then that she had missed the qualification to pass by five points.

But Nora, racquet ball champion, was not a quitter. She tried again six months later. The second time, her score was four points *above* passing! That November, she received her notification: *"CONGRATULATIONS! You have passed the national Physical Therapy Assistant's examination."*

On that momentous day, Nora Tarlow became a person with a real *license*, a state-regulated, legal document with an official title—PTA—that commanded *respect*. She was 30 years old, and it had been a grueling, bumpy road, but she had made it to her destination.

Nora Now

LIFE LESSONS AND UNCOMMON COURAGE

> I started thinking that all your students have a very important bond—that we so much need a place to succeed. We need someone to go first, tell us that we *can* when we cannot even imagine that could be possible. Then, miraculously we can have the confidence to try. You went first for me. My therapist says that we cannot *do* what we cannot *imagine*.
>
> (Nora Tarlow, 2009)

Over all these years, Nora and I have stayed in touch either by phone, mail, or in person, to share exciting breakthroughs or brainstorm strategies to resolve new challenges. Major changes began to happen for Nora, especially in her twenties and thirties, through her remarkable employment history as a PTA, moving up as job opportunities or new trainings arose. The scope of her employment history is impressive, ranging from private rehab offices, hospitals, and clinics to private home healthcare cases. She cross-trained, on the job, in three disciplines—physical therapy, occupational therapy, and recreational therapy—experiences that kept building her skills and knowledge more than any four-year college could have provided, especially for such an experiential learner.

In her different places of employment, as her skills grew, Nora also made some sobering observations about the field in which she worked. She saw neglect of patients, lack of ethics, and even insurance fraud at some nursing facilities. In one facility, when she refused to sign her name to authorize services to patients she had never seen, she learned later that they had actually forged her name to the documents. To protect herself and her license, she quit immediately. The following day, the State Medical Fraud Department shut down the site. Fortunately, she had photocopied every document they had forged and kept it for evidence, which became vital to the subsequent fraud investigation. The formerly insecure Nora had become part of the solution with an uncommon courage that came from her solid moral compass.

[I was especially proud of this because we had studied the importance of always keeping files of any incident that could become a problem. "Evidence" is concrete and is a concept that she really understands.]

She continues to have a gift for written expression, having mastered many of the technical skills in her college English courses so that the power of the pen will always be a power she owns. How she chooses to use it will be her decision.

* * *

After all those years of my urging Nora to seek psychological counseling, she finally connected to and remains in therapy with a psychologist, "Sarah," whom she trusts and respects completely. Besides helping Nora gain insights into the reasons behind her own behavior, Sarah encouraged her to fight for what she needs without being fearful. Thanks to this competent, empathic woman, perhaps Nora finally understands the difference between the goals and outcomes of psychotherapy and educational therapy, seeing how one could enhance the other once she learned to apply the insights of both.

Now in her early forties, Nora is completely self-supporting, a very rare trait among my adult clients. Describing herself as "someone who never gives up," she pays her own rent, utilities, car expenses, insurance, food and entertainment costs, although not without some of the money struggles common to all young adults working to balance a budget. She even finds ways to deal with the most daunting demands of adulthood, such as taxes, medical insurance forms, and record-keeping.

Her personal worth has risen with her steadily increasing salary in excess of $83,000 last year, an unimaginable feat when she first began working at $3.50 an hour (with no benefits) and fighting for every 50-cent-per-hour increase.

Socially, she has developed new friendships, renewed old ones, and enjoyed crowning achievements in patient relationships in the workplace. She has earned an almost mystical appreciation by her patients because of her great empathy for their plights and circumstances. I have been told that parents and spouses of patients come to request "only Nora" when they need a PTA. Even physicians refer their family members to her because of her reputation for the kind of compassion rapidly vanishing in healthcare today.

In spite of all of her impressive successes, life for Nora could never be called easy. She still has trouble explaining her auditory processing problems, usually skirting the topic because others have their own theories about learning disabilities, usually lumping them all into one box—dyslexia.

In fact, we had one session just to address this question—how to explain an auditory processing disorder to average folks who haven't a clue. Although we had dealt with this many times before when she needed to advocate for herself in school to receive necessary accommodations, nothing seemed to come naturally to her, so I offered one more suggestion for modifying people's beliefs about "dyslexia" to fit her situation.

I suggested she might agree that she has a kind of dyslexia, but it's a listening dyslexia—that her brain needs time to think and give meaning to what she hears. She might even say, "It's hard for me to hold on to spoken information, but once I get it, I own it."

She listened, saying she'd try it and report back.

And that's how it works for her. Always asking, trying, refining, changing.

During one of our recent meetings, Nora gifted me with a story she wrote—a most remarkable metaphor for her lifelong reality—the continuing struggle to process new, incoming language as yet unconnected to her own previous life experiences. The story illustrates so clearly how her concrete thinking affects her expectations of reality. I could never have said it this well.

My trip to Muir Woods

I went up to San Francisco because I've been fascinated and terrified of the Golden Gate Bridge, and I wanted to TOUCH it and walk across it (I'm afraid of heights, cliffs, and bridges.) Sarah *[her therapist]* suggested that, while up there, I should visit Muir Woods. She said the tree trunks there are so massive, they are as wide as her office.

So I got up the courage first to drive across the bridge—8 miles an hour—at 8:30 a.m. when there weren't so many other cars taking up weight and causing possible car accidents. Sarah had said, "As soon as you cross the bridge, to the left is Muir Woods and to the right is Sausalito with its beautiful waterfront." When I asked, "What's a waterfront?" she explained that there were no beaches or sand, and the water comes right up to the land.

When I finally got across the bridge, I saw nothing but a large tunnel. I kept driving, and miles later, I finally saw the signs for these two places, so I decided to see the woods first. I saw signs about narrow roads, and I realized of course, narrow roads would be because the tree trunks are so wide, like Sarah said. All of a sudden, I'm driving on the side of a mountain and there are cliffs and guard rails. Never did it dawn on me that I would need to drive alongside mountains to get there.

I had envisioned a large lot of redwood trees right after I crossed the bridge. Just as plain as Sarah described it was as plain as my brain saw it—on the right, water, and on the left a massive lot of redwood trees the width of Sarah's office.

I went on a 2-mile hike in these woods, but I never saw a tree trunk as wide as Sarah's office, but they were beautiful and massive.

After the woods, I drove back to Sausalito, and water really did come right up to the land without a beach or sand! I got my DAM memory back then—remembering that when I learn something and see it in real life, it's so exciting to me that it really sticks.

However my most powerful moment had to be the disillusioning experience that once again my concrete mind develops much different pictures than abstract life. But the real life experience then puts the abstract part back into a concrete memory and experience. Then I'm back on track!

Epilogue

AUTHOR'S REFLECTIONS

We have come to the end of our journey into the world of educational therapy. This book told two stories—the first about Nora, her difficulties living with an undiagnosed disorder, and the second about the interventions of educational therapy; what we *do* to undo the years of hurt and failure. You were invited to walk in Nora's shoes—to feel the deep insecurities formed by her imperfect understanding of spoken language; to experience her dependence on others for decision-making, and the torment from past experiences that caused such anxiety and pain.

You had a chance to wander through the brain of one educational therapist in search of answers, strategies, or unusual experiences that might lift the fog through which Nora wandered. More than just academic needs, Nora needed demystification of the *causes* behind her learning failure—a clear understanding of auditory processing and its impact every day and everywhere. She also needed help in understanding the impact of learning struggles on emotions—how they were linked, each one affecting the other.

You became a witness to the changes and how they came about. Nora's excitement was clear with each victory over a new piece of knowledge that she could own and apply. You learned, perhaps before she did, of the remarkable *strengths* inborn in her, hidden gifts waiting to be released—her exceptional sense of responsibility and capacity to organize, a strong work ethic, fine visual and rote memory, a desire for knowledge at any cost in time and energy, and tenacity. As she says, "I never quit."

With such inherent strengths, why had her learning struggles not been defined or alleviated in all those early years? Nora blames her "ignorance" as the cause. It was "ignorance," but not hers and not what she meant by that word. It was the ignorance of the teachers and tutors who just didn't know what was wrong with her. Her family persisted in seeking help and then giving up on the help that didn't work. She had outsmarted many of the testers in school by using her superior rote memory to fill in answers without ever taking in the knowledge. She had no clue of how to succeed in that constant fog of words, and those who cared about her just didn't know how to help her.

Although this is only *one* educational therapist's journey with *one* client, do you now have some answers to my seminal question, *"What is educational therapy, and what do you DO in that job?* Just as Nora learns by experience, I wanted you to *experience* educational therapy and its many facets of intervention—to *experience* the "blend of educational and therapeutic techniques applied to evaluation, remediation, case management, and advocacy on behalf of clients with assorted breakdowns in learning."

But that is only a group of words in a definition. I wanted you to *feel* the constant impact of each academic demand upon Nora and the glitches in her neural wiring that got in the way of her thinking and performing. I also wanted you:

- to hear my thoughts—my quest for answers, my strategies, my reasons for each intervention, my mistakes, my search for corrections—and how all of that impacted upon Nora;
- to *experience* the workings of the Organic Curriculum as each lesson grew from the unknowns of the previous one—all made possible by a trusting relationship in a safe place;
- to *experience* those "magical moments of change"—real change and insights into the causes of that improved performance.

Some of Nora's changes, of course, are from life lessons and the influences of maturity, but the stories here describe different kinds of changes—those that came from a self-understanding of her disorder and the discovery that she *could* learn, like others, but she had to do so by following a different path.

In addition, do you now have some better sense of APD—this phenomenon called "auditory processing disorder" and its destructive potential to a child's ego? Can you see how easily it can be missed in the diagnostic world? You may hope that Nora is "cured" of her APD, but APD doesn't get cured. It gets understood. It demands awareness of its existence and adaptation to its constant trials and torments.

Nora's own mother told Nora that she didn't really understand what was wrong until she read this book. After that, she looked at Nora differently, knowing for the first time what a torment each day in Nora's life had really been for her. This comment from Christine Tarlow and the response from Nora about her self-discovery made my years of work on this manuscript worth the whole effort.

Finally, let me say that this book was worth the risk of my inviting you behind and beyond my office door. I use the word "risk" because such detailed disclosure of a clinical practice invites challenge and criticism. Perhaps that is why this book is the first of its kind in educational therapy, but hopefully others will take courage and disclose their own styles of intervention. Indeed, none of us is perfect but our goals are all the same—to do the best that we are able in the most ethical way for the good of our clients. The efficacy of our work can only be revealed by our clients' outcomes.

What Nora has become is my reward!

NORA'S RESPONSE TO THE BOOK

I am in my forties now, and I'm so grateful for the work I did with Dorothy because I no longer have to think about my learning disability on a daily basis. I have a life today because of her expertise, patience, encouragement, and refusal to give up on me when many other teachers did. Because of Dorothy's example, I have much respect for teachers. I may not be able to describe my learning disability to others but I understand that my brain works differently than most others, something I didn't believe before I met Dorothy.

I have empathy and compassion for students like myself. The struggles can be so isolating and lonely. I was devastated when I sat at a table opposite from the 8th grade teachers who had supported me when I was a star athlete. After a debilitating injury that left me unable to compete and win awards for the school, they essentially told me I was not smart enough to remain in their school. After graduating from a different high school and attending junior college, I received another devastating rejection. I was told by the Dean of Admissions that my goal to become a physical therapist was impossible. He advised that college wasn't for students with learning disabilities and that I was no longer welcome.

Struggling through school was a huge challenge—having teachers insist that I was lying about work done outside the classroom (because I needed extra time), that it was not mine, or that I wasn't doing my best. I was ridiculed, called stupid, lazy, and retarded. My teachers couldn't find the reason for my lack of achievement. Even though I could read and write, I couldn't make sense of much of what I read despite spending hours with the dictionary, the encyclopedia and Mom's endless explanations. I often felt exhausted and confused by words that had no meaning to me.

My response to this book is twofold. First, reliving those humiliating experiences was eye-opening and painful. In fact, the shame still impacts upon me today. Second, I realized that Dorothy had not recognized or understood the full emotional impact of this treatment, even though it was life-defining for me. In fact, those experiences were initially omitted from this book. That was almost as painful to me as the experiences themselves, because I felt invisible again. It was no surprise that it was difficult and embarrassing to read about myself at 17. Many of the memories were painful and, initially it was impossible for me to be objective. Nonetheless, I was still comforted by the recollection of the safe walls that comprised Dorothy's office. I remember vividly the black Formica desk that brought me so much strength and comfort. It was a significant part of my safe haven. It was sad to realize that teachers in my new school also perceived me as a student who was essentially incompetent. There seemed to be no understanding or curiosity about my behavior, only judgment. I felt broken, invisible and withdrawn. I felt ashamed about being so dependent on Dorothy and afraid she might terminate our work together. Fortunately, in Dorothy, I finally found a teacher who was on my side and willing not to give up on me. I was terrified that I could not change, yet came to believe I could.

Professionals who read this book should understand the struggle and trauma that can result from an invisible learning disability. My brain remembers the humiliation. Yet I have overcome and recovered from much of my school experience. I earned my physical therapist assistant license and have a good career. Today I still sometimes have difficulty believing that people really *see* me and take me seriously; that I'm not invisible. I hope that the teaching professionals will have the desire to understand real reasons for lack of academic achievement.

Thanks to Dorothy and my own determination, I am creating a life for myself. I appreciate and thank my parents for their ability to seek Dorothy's help. Finally, I thank my therapist for helping me to deal with the residue of my school experiences and have pride in my accomplishments.

Heather K. (The real "Nora Tarlow")

Appendix A
RULES FOR THE USE OF COMMAS

1. Words, phrases, or clauses that are used in *a list or series* should be separated by commas. However, if these words in a series are joined by *or*, *nor*, or *and*, they do not require a comma.

   Examples:
   A worthwhile philosophy includes *honesty, industry, and kindness*.
   He was *strong and brave and good* [no commas needed].
   Ham and eggs, waffles and syrup, and cereal were served for breakfast.

2. Words called *appositives* should usually be separated from the remainder of the sentence by commas. Appositives explain who or what the noun is or does.

   Examples:
   Mr. Jay, *our coach*, taught at Wilbur Street, *a boy's school*.
   He voted for Antonio Villaraigosa, *our new Hispanic mayor*.

3. Words of *direct address* and of *direct quotations* should be set off by commas. "Direct address" means you are talking directly *to* the person, not *about* the person.

   Examples:
   "I am depending on you, *Lois*, to prepare the luncheon," said Lupita.
   Ken, put your shoes in the closet [comma because we're talking *to* Ken].
   Ken put his shoes in the closet [no comma because we're talking *about* Ken].

4. Commas are used to separate the *street address* from the name of the *city*, the name of the city from the name of the *state*, and the name of the state from the name of the *country*.

   Example:
   Henry lives at *213 Main Street, Philadelphia, Pennsylvania, U.S.A.*

5. An *introductory dependent clause* or a *long introductory phrase* should be separated from the remainder of the sentence by one or more commas.

   Examples:
   After the storm was over, we went home.
   Having rung the bell loudly, the guard fled.
   In 1516, soldiers were hired mercenaries [comma needed to clarify meaning].
   In the room we found no signs of life [comma not needed].

6. Commas set off a special clause called a *non-restrictive clause*. This group of words does not change the meaning of the sentence but gives more interesting information.

   Example:
   Franklin D. Roosevelt, *who was crippled*, built a hospital for crippled children.

7. A *compound sentence* is made up of two *independent clauses* joined by connecting words (conjunctions) such as *and, or, but*. These two clauses should be separated by a comma before the connecting words. No comma is necessary for a sentence with a *compound predicate*—two verbs that modify the same subject.

   Examples:
   The whistle blew, *but* Carol did not stop [compound sentence].
   My brother came home, *and* my mother opened the door for him [compound sentence].
   Carol *paused* at our house and then *went* on to town [compound predicate—*paused* and *went* are both actions of one subject, *Carol*].

8. Commas should be used to *separate the parts of the date* (the name of the month and the number of the day form a single part).

   Example:
   Today is *June 29, 2005*.

9. A comma should be used after the *salutation of a friendly letter* and after the *complementary close* in all letters.

   Examples:
   Dear Susan,
   Yours truly,

10. Commas should be used to set off *parenthetical expressions* and to set off such expressions as *yes, no, well, of course*, and *however*, from the remainder of the sentence. *Parenthetical expressions* are like thoughts or comments that break from the meaning of the sentence. You can almost imagine the speaker whispering them to him or herself.

Examples:
She will, *I think*, make an excellent doctor [parenthetical expression].
Yes, he will accept the nomination.
Of course, I love to go on cruises.

11. A *mild interjection* should be followed by a comma if the entire sentence is exclamatory, i.e., if it ends with an exclamation mark.

Example:
Oh, that was an excellent play!

12. Use a comma between *adjectives of equal importance*.

Examples:
His *kind, sympathetic* words calmed the child.
This is a *sturdy, strong, dependable* ladder.

From *English Mastery*, by Jewel Varnado. Copyright © 1976 by Steck-Vaughn Company. All rights reserved. Adapted and reprinted by permission of the publisher. Houghton Mifflin Harcourt Publishing Company.

Appendix B

PLACE VALUE CARDS

How to Play with Your Place Value Cards

1. Lay out the cards in vertical lines by ones, tens, hundreds, thousands, ten thousands, etc. Look at all the zeros and notice how there are more and more of them.

    Can you guess why this is true?

    These are the *place-holders*, just like putting *plates on the dinner table* to save a place for a guest. Even if the guest doesn't come, the plate will stay there, holding his or her place.

2. Pick one number card from each group, placing the largest number of all those you picked on the table. This card will be at the bottom of the pile. *Start playing with the biggest number that you understand* (once you get the idea, you can work up to millions).

    Notice the bold line running down the right side of the diagram of each number strip. When you prepare your cards, color those lines red. Then, when you place one number card on top of the other, *be sure each red line is on top of the red line* of the number below it. Those red lines will guide you to keep the numerals in their proper places.

	2	0	0	0	0	0
		4	0	0	0	0
			8	0	0	0
				6	0	0
					5	0
						3

Example:
200,000 + 40,000 + 8,000 + 600 + 50+ 3 will look like 248,653.

3. Next, take turns having one person close their eyes while the other carefully slides out one of the number cards (such as the 100s or the 1s).

   Example from numbers above: 208,053 or 240,050.

4. Then the person who closed their eyes will open them and try to read the new number, talking about which card was removed and how much it represented.

   Example: the 4 that was removed was from the 10,000s place and the 6 was from the 100s.

5. Take turns making numbers for each other and closing your eyes while some place cards are removed.
6. Next, practice reading all kinds of increasingly large numbers on paper. Finally, when you really understand the system, take turns writing numbers that you dictate to each other.

You will learn to read numbers that used to seem very weird.

   Example: 3,010,235,004 or 10,003,030,303.

Template: Place Value Cards

ones

1
2
3
4
5
6
7
8
9

tens

1	0
2	0
3	0
4	0
5	0
6	0
7	0
8	0
9	0

hundreds

1	0	0
2	0	0
3	0	0
4	0	0
5	0	0
6	0	0
7	0	0
8	0	0
9	0	0

thousands

1,	0	0	0
2,	0	0	0
3,	0	0	0
4,	0	0	0
5,	0	0	0
6,	0	0	0
7,	0	0	0
8,	0	0	0
9,	0	0	0

ten thousands

1	0,	0	0	0
2	0,	0	0	0
3	0,	0	0	0
4	0,	0	0	0
5	0,	0	0	0
6	0,	0	0	0
7	0,	0	0	0
8	0,	0	0	0
9	0,	0	0	0

hundred thousands

1	0	0,	0	0	0
2	0	0,	0	0	0
3	0	0,	0	0	0
4	0	0,	0	0	0
5	0	0,	0	0	0
6	0	0,	0	0	0
7	0	0,	0	0	0
8	0	0,	0	0	0
9	0	0,	0	0	0

millions

1,	0	0	0,	0	0	0
2,	0	0	0,	0	0	0
3,	0	0	0,	0	0	0
4,	0	0	0,	0	0	0
5,	0	0	0,	0	0	0
6,	0	0	0,	0	0	0
7,	0	0	0,	0	0	0
8,	0	0	0,	0	0	0
9,	0	0	0,	0	0	0

ten millions

1	0,	0	0	0,	0	0	0

hundred millions

1	0	0,	0	0	0,	0	0	0

trillions

1,	0	0	0,	0	0	0,	0	0	0

Appendix C

BARSCH LEARNING STYLE INVENTORY AND SCORING PROCEDURES

A Summary

By Jeffrey R. Barsch, EdD

© 1996 ACADEMIC THERAPY PUBLICATIONS, NOVATO, CA 94949

There are two parts of the inventory: a checklist of statements that reflect the various types of learning styles, and a collection of study tips geared specifically to each learning style.

How to use the inventory:
The *Barsch Learning Style Inventory* consists of 32 statements; for each, the learner checks one category—"often", "sometimes", or "seldom"—depending on how accurately the statement describes their preferences. The inventory looks like this:

	Often	*Sometimes*	*Seldom*
1. I remember more about a subject through listening than reading	————	————	————

When all 32 statements have been rated, scores are determined. Each of the three categories is given a different number of points. The statements are grouped according to the four types of learning styles and scores are determined for each; the highest score reflects the preferred learning style: Visual, Auditory, Tactile, or Kinesthetic.

The scoring page looks like this

Visual		*Auditory*		*Tactile*		*Kinesthetic*	
Item	Points	Item	Points	Item	Points	Item	Points
2	———	1	———	4	———	3	———
•	•	•	•	•	•	•	•
•	•	•	•	•	•	•	•
•	•	•	•	•	•	•	•
•	•	•	•	•	•	•	•
VPS=	———	APS=	———	TPS=	———	KPS=	———

Once the learning style has been identified, the learner can refer to the Study Tips brochure to obtain specific recommendations to improve their study habits.

The *Barsch Learning Style Inventory* (order # 905-2) can be obtained from Academic Therapy Publications, 800-422-7249, www.AcademicTherapy.com.

Appendix D

TEST SCORES AND EXCERPTS FROM PSYCHOEDUCATIONAL TESTING

By "Dr. Dixon"

For Nora Tarlow at Age 18 years 9 months

Wechsler Adult Intelligence Scale-Revised (WAIS-R):

Verbal IQ = 84		Performance IQ = 89	Full Scale IQ = 85	
Verbal Tests			*Performance Tests*	
Information	5		Picture Completion	8
Digit Span	6		Picture Arrangement	6
Vocabulary	7		Block Design	10
Arithmetic	6		Object Assembly	9
Comprehension	6		Digit Symbol	8
Similarities	8			

Ms. Tarlow's subtest scores ranged upward from dull normal (2nd standard deviation below the mean) to low average (1st standard deviation below the mean). Fifty-five percent of her scores were in the low average range (i.e., scaled scores of 7–10). Verbally she attained the 14th percentile, non-verbally (performance), the 23rd percentile and her overall intellectual function is at the 16th percentile. There was an absence of significant inter- and intra-subtest scatter which adds a measure of evidence suggesting that her "true" intellectual capacity is not significantly higher than the functioning level she attained.

SAS-R. The Sklar Aphasia Scale-Revised. Ms. Tarlow showed no indication of either Broca's or Wernicke's aphasia. Basic language functions were within nominal tolerances. Her weakest area was memory in both encoding and decoding tasks.

Test Scores from Testing by Dorothy Ungerleider

Name: Nora Tarlow
Age: 17 years 5 months
Grade placement: 12.4

I. WOODCOCK-JOHNSON PSYCHOEDUCATIONAL BATTERY

BROAD COGNITIVE ABILITY

	Percentile Score
Verbal Ability	31
Reasoning	35
Perceptual Speed	20
Memory	7
Reading Aptitude	30
Math Aptitude	28
Knowledge Aptitude	22

SUBTESTS	*Grade Equivalents*
Visual Matching	7.0
Spatial Relationships	6.2
Blending	8.1
Memory for Sentences	2.2
Numbers Reversed	5.8
Analysis/Synthesis	7.0
Concept Formation	11.3
Picture Vocabulary	6.3
Quantitative Concepts	8.8
Analysis/Synthesis	10.0
Analogies	8.2

ACHIEVEMENT	*Grade Equivalent*	*Percentile*
READING Overall	8.5	24%
Word Attack	12.0	
Letter/Word Identification	11.2	
Passage Comprehension	5.0	
*Teaching Resources, 1977		
MATH Overall	8.3	23%
Calculation	10.8	
Applied Problems	6.6	15%
KNOWLEDGE Overall	7.4	16%
Science	7.0	
Social Studies	7.1	
Humanities	10.0	

II. PEABODY INDIVIDUAL ACHIEVEMENT TEST

Reading Comprehension	6.2	46%

Source: American Guidance Service (AGS), 1970

Rey-Osterreith Complex Figure: Copied

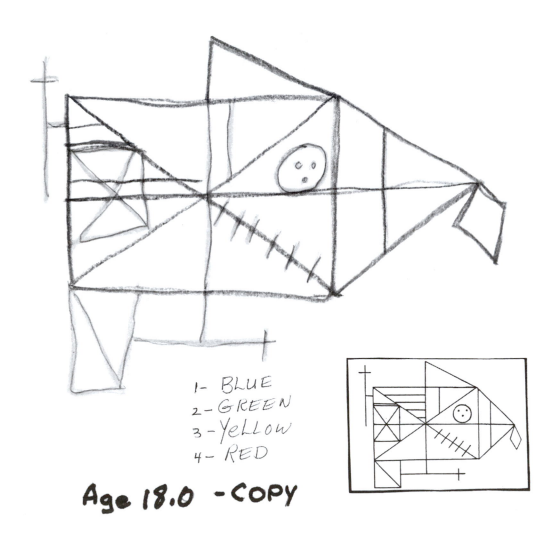

1- BLUE
2- GREEN
3- YeLLOW
4- RED

Age 18.0 - COPY

Rey-Osterreith Complex Figure: Immediate Recall

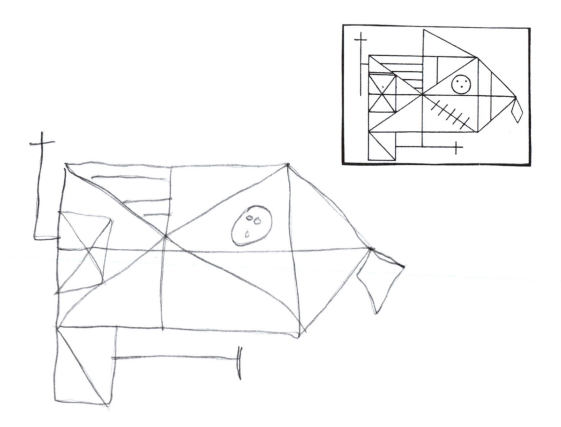

Immediate Recall

Age 18

BIBLIOGRAPHY

Barsch, J. (1991). *Learning Style Inventory*. Novato, CA: Academic Therapy Publications.

Barsch Learning Style Inventory: www.sinclair.edu/support/.../Barsch-%20learning%Style%20 inventory.doc.

Bellis, T.J. (2002). *When the Brain Can't Hear: Unraveling the Mystery of Auditory Processing Disorder*. New York: Pocket Books.

Bender, L. (1958). *Bender Visual Motor Gestalt Test*. San Antonio, TX: Pearson.

Dunn, L. & Marquardt, T. (1970). *Peabody Individual Achievement Test*. Circle Pines, MN: American Guidance Service.

Dyer, W. (1994). *Pulling Your own Strings: Dynamic Techniques for Dealing with Other People and Living Your Life as You Choose*. New York: HarperTorch.

Ficksman, M. & Adelizzi, J. (2010). *The Clinical Practice of Educational Therapy: A Teaching Model*. New York: Routledge.

Gwynne, F. (1970). *The King Who Rained*. New York: Young Readers Press.

Holmes, J. & Waber, D. (1994). Rey-Osterreith complex figure test. In *Developmental Scoring System for the Rey-Osterreith Complex Figure*. Odessa, FL: Psychological Assessment Resources, Inc.

Lipkin, M. (1990). *The Schoolsearch Guide to Colleges with Programs or Services for Students with Learning Disabilities*. Belmont, MA: Schoolsearch.

Mangrum, C. & Strichart, S. (eds) (1989). *Colleges with Programs for Learning-disabled Students*. Belmont, MA: Schoolsearch.

Mangrum, C. & Strichart, S. (eds) (1994). *Peterson's Guide to Colleges with Programs for Students with Learning Disabilities*. Lawrenceville, NJ: Peterson's.

Margalit, M. (2010). *Lonely Children and Adolescents: Self-perceptions, Social Exclusion, and Hope*. New York: Springer.

Phoenix, D. (1985). *RX4LD*. Novato, CA: Academic Therapy Publications.

Scholastic Aptitude Test. New York: College Board Publications.

Sperling, A. (1957). *Psychology Made Simple*. New York: Doubleday/Made Simple Books.

Terr, L. (2008). *Magical Moments of Change: How Psychotherapy Turns Kids Around*. New York: W.W. Norton.

The World Book Encyclopedia (1986). Chicago, IL: World Book, Inc.

Ungerleider, D. (1986). History of educational therapy: The profession, the association. *The Educational Therapist*, 16(3), 3–11.

Ungerleider, D. (1991). The Organic Curriculum. *Psychoeducational Perspectives*, 23–27. Los Angeles, CA: Association of Educational Therapists.

Ungerleider, J.H. (1983). Poem. Personal communication.

Varnado, J. (1976). Commas: usage. In *English Mastery*, Book 1 (pp. 12–13). Austin, TX: Steck-Vaughn Company.

Warriner, J.E. (1988). *English Composition and Grammar: Fourth Course*. Orlando, FL: Harcourt Brace Jovanovich.

Wechsler, D. (1974). *Wechsler Intelligence Scales for Children*. Rev. edn. New York: Psychological Corporation.

Werbach, G. (1998). Special education therapy. In S. Eth & S. Harrison (eds), J. Noshpitz (Editor-in-chief) *Handbook of Child and Adolescent Psychiatry* (pp. 581–588). New York: Wiley.

Westman, J. (1990). *Handbook of Learning Disabilities: A Multisystem Approach*. Boston, MA: Allyn & Bacon.

Woodcock, R. & Johnson, M. (1989). *Woodcock-Johnson Psychoeducational Battery—Revised*. Allen, TX: DLM/Teaching Resources.